D0897686

BEHIND
THE HEADLINES

BEHIND
THE
HEADLINES

by

Harold M. Slater
and
George Sherman

The Westphalia Press
The Dohman-Boessen House
Loose Creek, Missouri 65054
1989

Published by The Westphalia Press

Loose Creek, Missouri 65054

Printed and bound in the United States of America

Copyright © 1989 by Harold Slater and George Sherman

All rights reserved. No part of this book may be
reproduced or transmitted in any form or by any means,
electronic or mechanical, including photocopying,
recording, or by any information storage and retrieval
system, without the written permission of the publisher,
except where permitted by law.

ISBN 0-915637-09-X

*News photos courtesy of St. Joseph News-Press and Gazette.
Photos of President Truman from Harold Slater's personal collection.*

**Behind
the Headlines**

is dedicated to all newsmen
who have always intended
to write this book.

Contents

FOREWORD

From Memories that "Bless and Burn"

From its turbulent origins as the trading post of French fur trapper, Joseph Robidoux, the city of St. Joseph, Missouri, has had a colorful and often bizarre history far in excess of cities of similar size.

Outsiders, if they've heard of the city at all, associate it with two historical events. It's where the Pony Express started and where the six-gun career of the infamous bank robber, train robber and killer Jesse James ended.

Library shelves are filled with the exploits of the Pony Express riders and their remarkable mail delivery achievement, as well as of the rapacious roamings of the James gang up and down and across the muddy Missouri River. There will be no attempt here to add significantly to those already thoroughly documented subjects.

Rather, the purpose of this book is to record for posterity some of the less legendary, but sufficiently weird, wicked or wonderful events which have become a part of the tapestry of this now comfortable city of 80,000 in Northwest Missouri.

Like Halley's comet spinning across the heavens, some of these happenings flared spectacularly into world headlines, then evaporated as the sensationalism fizzled out. In others, the story behind the headlines never reached print.

No single individual has been in a better position to chronicle these events than Harold Slater, who for fifty-two years faithfully recorded history in the making for the St. Joseph *News-Press*, initially as a reporter pounding a beat and a typewriter, and later as a city editor pounding some sense into the hard heads of a host of young cubs eager to use the *News-Press* as a springboard to the New York *Times* or the Washington *Post*.

Slater covered politics for the paper and almost all of its runs—police, fire, Courthouse, jail, City Hall, state capital, business, movies. And he was church editor once for three weeks when he was laid up with a badly sprained ankle.

Using personal and newspaper files, but mostly drawing on a prodigious memory, this seasoned journalist, now retired, tells of the tragic and the comic, the pathos and the perfection of human beings. They are all here, the good and the bad. Some perhaps escaped justice, but none escaped his typewriter.

Harold was the *News-Press*, the afternoon paper, and I was the *Gazette*, the morning stepchild.

Although *News-Press* and *Gazette* newsmen shared an office, teletypes, telephones, typewriters and desks, we operated as arch rivals, using every trick in the book and a few of our own invention to "scoop" the other paper.

Those were the pre-television days of evening paper supremacy. To make matters worse, the *Gazette* had been acquired by the *News-Press*. Those of us who staffed the *Gazette* always felt like the poor relation, unwanted interlopers on the more affluent members of the family.

Actually, the powers that governed the two newspapers were wiser than we gave them credit for by fostering this rivalry. The competition made better journalists of us all, even though the good citizens and news sources, trapped between these competing elements, couldn't understand why we were not just one big happy family.

Years later after returning to St. Joseph, having followed a more lucrative but less exhilarating career than journalism, I realized that Harold wasn't the enemy, indeed never had been. He was just a first class newspaperman doing his job.

This is the kind of a book that could be written by thousands of journalists who have covered the news in midsize and small United States cities.

Those could-be book authors have reported on news events from the platitudes of high school graduation to the lurid facts of a murder, from speeches at a Rotary Club luncheon to a legal execution. Like Harold Slater, they have done such things as interview the leading madam of the town and a future president of the United States on the same day (although at different places).

They have seen life and society uncensored, and they are knee deep in memories that both bless and burn.

GEORGE SHERMAN

A "Who's Who" Notebook

The People
A Newsman
Runs Into

To my good friend Harold Slater, with warm appreciation for many years of friendship – Very best wishes – True Davis
Asst. Secy. of Treasury

Along with his daily news grind, Harold Slater met (and usually interviewed) a passing parade of celebrities. Some are listed here, not as name dropping but to show the extent of experiences in a career in journalism in a midsize Missouri city.

President Harry S Truman.

Vice-President Charles Curtis.

Vice-President Lyndon Johnson.

Alex Kerensky, first Premier of Russia

Postmaster General James A. Farley.

Missouri Governors Henry Caulfield, Guy B. Park, Lloyd Stark, Forrest Donnell, James T. Blair, John M. Dalton, Warren Hearnes, Joseph Teasdale.

Senators James A. Reed, Bennett Champ Clark, Thomas C. Hennings, Edward V. Long, Stuart Symington, John Danforth, Thomas Eagleton.

Speaker John McCormack and Speaker Sam Rayburn.

Kansas Governor Alfred M. Landon.

President Richard Nixon, twice briefly at national conventions.

Senator Barry Goldwater.

Sally Rand, truly a close friend.

Michael Kinney, dean of Missouri Senate where he served 52 years.

Ralph "Bottles" Capone, brother of Al (he told me to drop dead).

Jack Dempsey, Joe Louis, Max Baer.

Stan Musial (at his farewell party).

Dizzy Dean.

President Herbert Hoover, Mrs. Hoover and Secretary of Agriculture Arthur M. Hyde.

Vice-President Henry Wallace while in St. Joseph.

Thomas Dewey, interviewed here on crime.

Supreme Court Chief Justice Earl Warren.

Homer Croy, author.

Fred "Killer" Burke, Chicago gang machine gunner.

Supreme Court Justice Hugo Black when he was a United States senator.

True Davis, Ambassador to Switzerland and Assistant Secretary of the Treasury.

INTRODUCTION

This Was St. Joseph

It was a riverfront town. It was a great meat production center. It was endowed with a galaxy of wholesale houses of merchandise ranging from exotic imports to shoes, dry goods to hardware, saddles to an ice cream manufacturing plant.

It was a lusty, vibrant city, probably with more than its share of bootlegging places, gambling establishments and houses of ill repute.

But it had another side. It was a city with a heavy religious element, a lot of old families, many quiet and demure establishments and neighborhoods.

In St. Joseph, it depended on where you landed or, more correctly, just where you wanted to go.

That was St. Joseph when I first became a reporter for the *News-Press* in 1927. Today it is still a most interesting city, although vastly changed in some respects. It has grown sedate with the years. The gambling is almost entirely gone; the need for illegal liquor doings vanished with repeal fifty-six years ago, and prostitution, as far as the general public is concerned, has gone the way of the dodo bird.

Industry and business are in a new and far different sphere than what the city knew sixty-two years ago. Wide diversification has taken place to absorb the loss of packing houses with their excess of five thousand employees, combined with the general demise of the wholesale houses as they operated back in those distant 1920's.

St. Joseph is a changed city but it still retains the worthwhile values it knew when to some it was a wide-open river town. Today St. Joseph is a city of progress, of good will and of the friendly spirit that made it great during all of its yesterdays.

HAROLD M. SLATER

PROHIBITION

Bootleggers, Madams and Other Colorful Characters of the Bad Ol' Days

This building with its classic turret at Seventh and Messanie Streets was the Central Police Station from 1891 to 1939. It was from here, shortly after the turn of the century, that Bill LaTrasse, legendary "Last of the Train Robbers," made the first of his escapes.

Chester Fee teamed up with Charley Morris to form St. Joseph's topnotch liquor raiding team of the Prohibition era. Fee later served as chief of police.

2

PART ONE

Assorted Sins and Pastor Tripp

Residents of St. Joseph today generally view their city as a quiet, comfortable place, near enough to Kansas City to share in the cultural, athletic and entertainment advantages of the big city, but far enough removed to be free of the traffic, crime and general hubbub of a metropolitan area.

Probably the most common response when outsiders ask a native about St. Joseph is that ". . . It's a good place to raise a family." It wasn't always so, although little evidence remains of the lusty, colorful, brawling, wide open river town of the 1920's when bootlegging, prostitution and gambling flourished.

In the late 1920's, St. Joseph was beginning to acquire a reputation as a city of churches. There were more than seventy places of worship here along about 1928, but an enterprising journalist discovered that by actual count, there were more bawdy houses and places of assignation than houses of worship. Admittedly, some of these were single rooms out of which lowly street walkers operated, but these along with the more celebrated houses of ill repute actually out-numbered the churches in the community.

Bootlegging establishments (places where alcohol and homebrewed beer were sold illegally by the drink and by the bottle) were even more numerous. There were at least one hundred twenty known illegal drinking locations, but these were not flourishing at the same time. As soon as raids by local police, county and federal officers would close one down, two or three others would spring up around the city. For many, the "get rich quick" opportunities in homemade booze and brew were worth the risk of being arrested and prosecuted.

Gambling also was big business and the click of dice emanated from at least four separate locations on downtown Edmond Street

3

and a craps game could be found almost any hour of the day or night. At one time, as many as twelve policy wheels were operating downtown and there was little effort toward secrecy. In fact, several policy wheel operators listed their business addresses in the city phone directory. (Policy is more widely known today as the "numbers" racket, a gambling game in which the bettor pre-selects a combination of numbers and receives a payoff based on how many of his numbers are drawn from a container or show up on the spin of a wheel.) The numbers draw or spin usually was held twice daily and players could wager anything from five cents on up to really big money.

Policy or the numbers, however, was primarily a game for the poor and the average citizen. True gamblers didn't like the odds or the slow turnover. They concentrated on craps, roulette and blackjack along with vintage poker and a fast-moving card game called "Pan", short for Panguingue.

St. Joseph actually became something of a "training ground" for croupiers, crap and blackjack dealers and specialists in other games of chance. Many eventually gravitated to Las Vegas where their illegally acquired skills earned them substantial salaries in Nevada's legally operated casinos and drinking establishments. Many had Damon Runyon-type nicknames like "Fuzzy" Bolts, Friday White, Pistol Pete and Burk Eye or Pig Eye.

Payoffs to law enforcement officials reportedly were not uncommon and a relationship of sorts often developed between those who were expected to enforce the law and those profiteering from breaking it.

One proprietor of a gin mill out on Saxton Road had worked out a very practical arrangement with sheriff's deputies. Whenever they raided him, he told them which bottles of whiskey and gin on the back bar they should take as evidence. That way he was able to make sure he still had the quality stuff for his own and preferred customers' consumption.

There were several loopholes in the anti-liquor laws of the Prohibition Era; one was the prescriptions doctors were allowed to issue. Each doctor was allowed to issue two hundred prescriptions a month to patients who needed whiskey for medicinal reasons. Quite a few fellows, some with red noses, suddenly learned they needed whiskey for their physical well-being. They found some doctors would accommodate them.

Druggists charged three dollars a pint for prescription whiskey. Some of the doctors, a very few, and some of the druggists, also a very few, worked in collusion. A doctor would issue a patient two prescriptions. If you gave both prescriptions to some druggists, you got your pint of whiskey free, the second prescription going to freeing a pint of whiskey to some "needy" friend of the druggist, a fellow willing to pay $6 to cover the cost of both pints.

The law required that physicians file their liquor prescriptions with the county clerk. One way to kill time in that Prohibition Era was to go over those prescription lists in the vault of the county clerk's office.

A lot of jokesters got their liquor prescriptions in the names of the town's most militant drys. Also, some other very sober citizens found friends had used their names. One of the names that showed up most regularly on the liquor prescription lists was that of Dr. Frank Tripp, pastor of the First Baptist Church, and the outstanding dry leader in St. Joseph. Of course, he didn't touch a drop but seemingly, as a good sport, never complained about those who used his name in vain.

Boozing It Up at the "Bathhouse"

The Volstead Dry Act that spawned the Prohibition Era provided St. Joseph with a number of unusual speakeasies and bootlegging joints. But "The Bath House" was unique.

That institution which actually had no formal name was in the basement of 521 Edmond Street, reachable only from Edmond Street by a set of stairs with an iron railing. It had no connection or association whatever with Burson and Dearden's restaurant, an excellent and popular eatery on the first floor of that address.

No one ever bothered to work out the exact statistics, but it is conservative to say that for every person who entered the Bath House for a bath one hundred came there to get a drink of hard liquor.

Riley White ran the drink operation there during the latter part of the Prohibition Era. He was a former cab driver who knew everyone and he had a vocabulary that would make the leads in "Tobacco Road" blush.

5

The "wine list" there was not extensive. It contained only straight alcohol at twenty-five cents a jigger. Water and sweet soda was available as a chaser or mixer for sissies.

One patron used to come in regularly for a pint of alcohol, which he had Riley pour into a quart bottle. That was then filled with what was purported to be distilled water, but which cynics believed was from the same tap that provided the water for the bathing facilities. The fellow used to explain that he drank his quart of refreshments while watching the movies at a nearby Edmond Street theater. The quart lasted him just two hours.

Mr. White had his own bookkeeping system for credit customers. A white asbestos-covered pipe of the St. Joseph Light and Power Company steam system ran through the upper reaches of the bath house and directly over the skimpy little bar where Riley dispensed his beverages. Riley used a lead pencil to write the customer's name on the asbestos. He placed a plain mark after it for each drink charged. When the bill was paid, Riley just smudged out the marks, then refreshened the surface with a wet rag.

As far as we know, he never had a credit complaint.

In St. Joseph in the Prohibition Era there were numerous homebrew flats and private homes where the brew was offered. Some tasted pretty terrible, and not in the least like real beer, but the price was cheap, with patrons usually being charged fifty cents a quart. Some of the flats also had ladies present and available for other entertainment.

Bootleg whiskey here sold from one dollar a pint up, with the higher tariff for stuff that was supposed to be imported but probably came from nearby Kansas.

During the waning days of Prohibition, one of the major raids resulted in the heavily-publicized collodion case. The collodion, which also figures in fingernail polish, was used in a whiskey-making operation in a garage near Seventh and Patee Streets. Among items seized were about two thousand whiskey labels for pint bottles. Half were labeled Scotch and half Bourbon.

One of the men in on the enterprise confided to a reporter they had no complaints from purchasers. He said, in effect, the buyers just wanted to get something that said whiskey on the bottle.

Repeal eventually ended the interest in the collodion case. Nobody went to jail.

St. Joseph's "Untouchables"

All was not to remain rosy for the booze brokers, however. A pair of St. Joseph detectives emerged who were to strike terror into the hearts of liquor peddlers all over town. Their names were Charlie Morris and Chester Fee and they operated with a zealous efficiency that rivaled anything the famed federal agent, Elliott Ness, ever achieved.

Although they resembled the Mutt and Jeff comic strip characters of that era, there was nothing comic about the way Fee and Morris operated. Without a doubt the towering Chester Fee and the dumpy, stocky little Charlie Morris comprised the top raiding team in the history of the St Joseph police department and probably the most efficient duo anywhere in the United States.

They were feared, respected and incorruptible, and bootleggers cringed at the very mention of the team. Fee and Morris were sharp and efficient and knew all the tricks. They had courage and were masters of the raiding art, to the great sorrow of law violators who wound up behind bars, and to the chagrin of building owners who found their places padlocked for one year by federal order when liquor sale violations were discovered in their buildings.

Fee and Morris bore the rank of detective but operated fairly independently of the detective department. Inexplicably, they were not even allowed the use of a squad car for their work. Usually, they used public transit to reach the raiding site and quite often they walked. Always, or so it seemed to the bootleggers, they got results.

The devastating duo developed a set pattern. They would stroll leisurely along the sidewalk, always with Fee on the outside and Morris on the inside. Suddenly, they would dart into some place where they believed liquor was being sold. Typically, it would be an establishment ostensibly selling soft drinks, a pool hall, a card room or even a grocery store.

If the place had a bar, the athletic Fee would place one hand on the bar and vault over it while Morris would stand in the doorway waving a revolver that looked to the law violators like a small cannon, just in case anyone might have the silly idea of offering resistance. Fee's leap over the bar was not just a dramatic gesture. It was intended, and usually succeeded, in preventing the barkeeper from destroying the liquid evidence.

7

Those who dispensed liquor illegally developed ingenious methods of concealing their stock but Fee and Morris had an uncanny knack of ferreting out the hiding place. It was necessary for Fee to get over the bar in a hurry as some establishments kept their beverages in glass jugs adjacent to a hole in the floor with rocks directly beneath. The idea was to kick the jug into the hole where it would smash on the rocks, thus destroying the evidence. It was Fee's goal to leap the bar and prevent that happening.

There is no record of Morris ever shooting anyone, yet his appearance was that of a fellow with an itchy trigger finger and put an effective damper on any thoughts of resistance on the part of an irate owner or tipsy patron.

On occasion, Fee and Morris would be accompanied by Dorus Roderick, a federal alcohol agent, and that was bad news indeed for the law breakers. Roderick's presence meant that federal charges would be filed and these culminated in much heavier penalties and even prison terms as opposed to the penalties handed out to those convicted of only state or city violations.

Many of those engaged in the business of illegal liquor sales demonstrated amazing ingenuity and creativity in concealing their supplies. For instance, Fee and Morris once arrested a small supplier who carried his stock with him at all times. He kept three pints of whiskey concealed in his wooden leg. On other occasions they found liquor hidden in such places as chandeliers, stove pipes, the hollow center leg of a dining table, in wall safes behind pictures, behind false partitions and even under the seat of a wheelchair.

Fee and Morris were publicity conscious. They were a joy to newspaper reporters, making no effort to clothe their activities with secrecy.

One of the highlights of their career—although they probably didn't regard it as such—came one day in the early 1930's when the Women's Christian Temperance Union held its state convention at the First Methodist Church in St. Joseph.

The woman presiding at the afternoon session asked that Fee and Morris attend. She led them into the pulpit with her, told of their raiding activities, and then said dramatically:

"Here are nature's noblemen."

No one at the police station ever forgot that, nor did they allow Fee and Morris to forget it.

Fee and Morris probably felt like punching some fellow officers who taunted them with the nobleman tag, but it didn't hurt politically. In 1945, Fee was named chief of police.

A Variety of Concoctions

Illegal liquor here in the Prohibition Era took in a wide field, ranging from strawberry wine imported from Kansas to "genuine" Scotch turned out in a tire shop at the edge of South Sixth Street.

Undoubtedly the most unique of all beverages offered was a concoction sold under the name of Pekok. There were two schools of thought about that name. One was that the two brothers who invented the concoction didn't know how to spell peacock. The other was that a company here had printed thousands of Pekok labels in the hope they could produce a soft drink that would rival Coca-Cola, Pepsi-Cola or Dr. Pepper in popularity. It didn't.

Pekok was marketed out of only one place, a small "soft drink" establishment on North Second Street, long since swallowed up and covered over by the sprawling Wire Rope plant.

The drink was grayish in color and the two brothers guarded its formula as closely as the late Colonel Sanders protected his fried chicken recipe. It was sold in bottles of various sizes and origin. Everything from medical prescription bottles, catsup bottles, Mason jars and discarded whiskey and gin bottles was used in marketing the product.

The brothers who sold it grew wealthy and the police became very annoyed. That was when chemical tests revealed there actually was nothing alcoholic in Pekok, even though the officers encountered many hale fellows who seemed to be on a jag after imbibing it. The operations never drew anything heavier than a fine as a result of their sales, so the brothers didn't worry too much when police regularly raided their humble establishment.

The rank and file drinkers in St. Joseph during Prohibition weren't too discerning. One fellow who did an excellent bootlegging business for years operated his own still and turned out thousands of gallons of whiskey. He once confided that he put Bourbon labels on half the bottles and Scotch labels on the other half. He said he got no complaints.

On one occasion during Prohibition in St. Joseph the floor of a house on Holman Street caved in from the weight of too many barrels of whiskey mash. A nosey neighbor called police. Officials were puzzled at first about what to do with the mash but finally turned it over to the garbage company, which fed it to its hogs out in French Bottoms. That must have been a happy bunch of hogs.

On another occasion, a husband was secretly brewing and bottling homebrew beer in his attic, all unbeknownst to his wife. The jig was up one late afternoon, however, when a series of machine-gun like explosions in the attic disrupted the family dinner. It had been an uncommonly hot day and the explosions were the caps popping off the beer bottles as the excessive heat caused the gases in the brew to expand.

During the Prohibition Era many of those who appeared on liquor law violation charges before Federal Judge Merrill E. Otis were sentenced to a year and a day in Leavenworth prison.

By adding that extra day the judge actually was doing them a favor. Federal prison regulations then provided that if the sentence was for more than a year the prisoner could earn considerable more good behavior time off his sentence than he could if sentenced to only one year.

Doing Time the Easy Way

In those Volstead Act days some of those convicted on federal liquor charges were sent to the Buchanan County jail and certain other neighboring jails to serve their time.

The Buchanan County jail was rated as one where it was easy to do time, but the Andrew County jail was preferred. That was because the wife of the Andrew County jailer not only served delicious meals but sent a dishpan of delicious popcorn up to the prisoners' cells each night. Also, some outsiders were known on occasion to sneak wine into the jail to the prisoners' delight.

Down in the Buchanan County jail three bootleggers in about 1930 were living a jail life comparable to Riley's. They included the most popular illegal dealer in St. Joseph, a gentleman known as Izzie, and two Kansas City citizens, one of whom became proprietor of one of the best known restaurants there.

They shared a large cell originally intended for juveniles. They didn't like its decor, so an obliging sheriff let them change it at their own expense. They had the steel bars painted silver, the ceiling blue, and the floor red. They did not care for jail fare, so they arranged to have most of their meals brought in from the town's top delicatessen.

One of them on completion of his jail term came out with a sun tan. He had convinced friendly jailers that he had numerous days that it was absolutely necessary that he spend the greater part of the day in his place of worship. No one ever served an easier sentence in that jail than he did.

Pity the Poor Landlords

The bootleggers themselves weren't the only ones who suffered as a result of the raids. Their landlords also were losers.

That was because the federal government on obtaining speakeasy convictions would go into court to secure injunctions to padlock the places of business under United States regulations for a full year. That meant those buildings could not be used at all, not even for some new legitimate business, until the year was up. Large public notices were placed on the doors of those buildings along with genuine heavy-duty padlocks.

Quite a few protesting landlords went to court with grinding teeth and other signs of anguish to ask if the injunctions couldn't be lifted so the place could be rented again.

But Uncle Sam just didn't relent in those cases. The padlocks stayed and often were still in place when the chap who had operated the establishment was back home after serving his sentence in Leavenworth.

The Night the Thirsts Were Quenched

Legalized beer came back on April 7, 1933. Long lines of keg-loaded trucks lined up in the area of the M. K. Goetz Brewery at Sixth and Albemarle waiting for the midnight signal when they could be started on their way to taverns where many patrons were waiting to quench their thirteen-year Prohibition thirst. That first legalized beer was actually just 3.2 alcohol by volume.

Some speakeasies were not certain just how the legal beer would taste or how it would sell. They played it safe by having their usual supplies of homebrew on hand for those not entirely sold on the switch to the legal beverage.

There was a lot of celebrating by beer drinkers that night, but practically no disturbances. In fact, the only man arrested for drunkenness was a police officer who had been on duty!

The reign of bootleggers and gamblers and the exploits of Detectives Fee and Morris provide a colorful, albeit somewhat gaudy, tapestry of life in St. Joseph in the 1920's and 1930's, but the tapestry would not be complete without reporting on the proliferation of prostitution during this period.

A Colorful Collection of Madams

Several colorful madams flourished in St. Joseph during the heyday of drinking, gambling and sex, well-known brothel operators such as Ma Dougherty and Minnie Himmelberg, for example. But the two most flamboyant were Lizzie King and Diamond Tooth Nell Williams.

Contrary to Hollywood versions and popular fiction, St. Joseph's "madams" by and large were not glamourous, sophisticated beauties and they were notably lacking in Dolly Parton type natural attributes. With rare exceptions, they were dour individuals, not inclined toward light repartee or fun-loving qualities.

They were strictly business and did not engage personally in sexual activities at their establishments. Harold Slater uses a baseball analogy, describing them as ". . . . . non-playing managers". The one exception was Diamond Tooth Nell, who limited her personal bedroom talents to a few very special patrons.

Although not in the same class as Lizzie King or Nell Williams, Ma Dougherty was noted for running something of a traveling bawdy house. When she first came to the attention of journalists of the times, her business was located on North Fourth Street, across the street from what at that time was the City Auditorium. She had a brother who was a musician and who spent considerable time at her establishment, but somehow the place never quite caught on as a "classical music salon".

Slater's first contact with Ma Dougherty found her in anything but a "motherly" mood. Slater was in the office of Prosecuting Attorney Homer C. King one afternoon when a worried and somewhat sheepish citizen dropped by and displayed a bill for seven hundred dollars that Ma Dougherty had mailed him.

It seems that while "painting the town" one evening he had gotten carried away with the spirit of things at Ma's place and ended up pouring several bottles of homebrew beer into the innards of Mrs. Dougherty's cherished piano.

Since beer wasn't the recommended lubricant for pianos, the action caused Mrs. Dougherty considerable irritation. However, she elected to forget if not forgive the incident when Prosecutor King pointed out that in her business she hardly was in a position to take the man to court to collect damages.

From North Fourth Street, Ma Dougherty moved to a succession of locations—North Thirteenth Street south of Frederick Avenue, 518½ South Sixth Street, Seventh and Mary Streets (both just a stone's throw from the old police station at Seventh and Messanie Streets). Police finally concluded she was carrying her nomadic tendencies too far when she moved her "palace of pleasure" to a house near Fourteenth and Frederick which several years before had been the home of one of the most prominent families in St. Joseph society. She didn't quarrel when police suggested she find a less controversial location.

Minnie Himmelberg, a short, dumpy rather frowzy woman, wore a perpetual snarl. She wouldn't have scored very high in a popularity contest but what she lacked in pulchritude and personality, she compensated for with her entrepreneurial skills. Minnie operated as many as five or six small, shotgun type houses of prostitution on Fifth Street, just south of Messanie, even nearer the police station than Ma Dougherty.

Minnie had another edge on her competitors other than just more locations. She had a relative who was a cab driver, in a unique position to steer considerable business her way.

Her Smile Was Brilliant—but Expensive

Diamond Tooth Nell, on the other hand, went in more for "quality" rather than quantity. Nell operated only one house, a very small place in the 600 block on Corby Street, and she kept only two girls on the premises.

Nell also was an innovator, having the distinction of being the first to introduce an electric, standing reducing machine with a vibrating belt for the convenience of her patrons. It was left to the imagination of the customer and his companion of the evening to figure out the best way to utilize the device. Like today's more successful professional wrestlers, Nell recognized that some sort of "gimmick" was necessary to distinguish her from others in the business.

Actually, Nell's beauty and glamour compared to other madams in St. Joseph would have been sufficient, but Nell came up with the idea of having a real diamond imbedded in the center of a false upper front tooth that was part of a bridge. Consequently, periodically she was able to take it to Benny Gordon's jewelry store to be tightened so as not to risk swallowing it while chomping on an ear of corn or perhaps while being vibrated in her fancy reducing machine.

Reporter Slater once had a personal contact with Diamond Tooth Nell—in connection with *his* profession, *not hers*.

Slater had written a news story about a court case in which Nell Williams was seeking title to a motor car concerning a situation in which she thought she had been cheated. Nell and her attorney, elderly Judge Amick, were in court to clear up the matter once and for all.

In his story, Slater referred to a smile from the witness stand that was "different", a beautiful diamond smile.

Slater's first thought when the flamboyant madam came to

the news office the next day was that she had somehow taken exception to the reference and was in the newspaper office to register a complaint. As it turned out, she liked the article so well she had come to buy six extra copies of the paper to send to friends.

Veteran police officers claimed that on only one occasion did they ever see Nell "lose her cool". That was when she was being placed under arrest during a raid on her bordello. It wasn't the raid or the arrest that bothered her, however. It was one of her patrons who took advantage of the situation to go to her kitchen and raid the icebox, fixing himself a sandwich.

Diamond Tooth Nell was a professional to the end. She died at a relatively early age and knowing approximately when she was going to die, she made all necessary arrangements ahead of time. Her will specified that her pallbearers would be six bellhops from the St. Francis Hotel. Her reasoning was to avoid embarrassment to any of her men friends who otherwise might have felt guilty about it all.

Also, as one of her last requests, she was buried in a flaming scarlet dress in one of the most ornate caskets ever seen in St. Joseph.

In death as in life, Diamond Tooth Nell dared to be different.

The Legendary Lizzie King

Although Nell Williams was the most colorful and certainly the most physically attractive of the St. Joseph madams, the most enduring and the best known was Lizzie King.

Perhaps her name wasn't exactly a household word in St. Joseph, but suffice it to say that almost every man and boy over the age of twelve in St. Joseph knew who she was and the kind of business she was in.

Her fame had spread far and wide. Once during an American Legion parade in Cleveland, Ohio, when the St. Joseph delegation came marching down the street hoisting high a banner carrying the name of the city, from high up in one of the skyscrapers towering over the parade route, someone shouted, "Hi, St. Joe, how's old Lizzie King?"

Lizzie King has become something of a legend in St. Joseph, perhaps not a legend that the Chamber of Commerce includes in any brochures along with the Pony Express and even Jesse James, but still a legend. As is the case with many legends, there are many misconceptions about Lizzie and several of these can be put to rest here and now.

Some have tried to perpetuate the notion that she was a beautiful woman. Quite the contrary. Physically Lizzie King was one of the homeliest women in reporter Slater's memory. She suffered from dropsy. Her figure was disproportionate. The upper trunk of her body was not very large but from the waist down she was quite large. She wore big skirts that flared out and came to the ground, concealing the disparity in size between her lower and upper anatomy. The skirts also helped to hide her enormous drooping ankles.

In her later years Lizzie was almost bald, with just little wisps of hair here and there and she used, of all things, rouge to fill in the bald areas. One St. Joseph tavern which is almost a museum with memorabilia and historic artifacts scattered around the premises, has a photograph on one wall purporting to be a picture of Lizzie King. It isn't. Newsman Slater recalls the photo is a picture that once was used in a cigarette advertisement around town. There is no record of Lizzie ever having had her picture taken, unless very early in her career there may have been a police "mug" shot. Lizzie herself would have been one of the first to laugh and scorn anyone who claimed she was a beauty.

Not as widely known is that Lizzie in her own fashion was a generous and charitable woman. For a number of years she had a standing arrangement with police officials for any poor soul who came to the police station and who needed an overcoat, a hat or a pair of shoes. That person was to be taken care of at Lizzie's expense. She had established a charge account at a clothing store on Felix Street and police were advised to get whatever the poor soul needed and then charge it to Lizzie's account. Veteran police officials said there were at least a half dozen such instances a month, and even more derelicts benefitted from Lizzie's generosity toward the downtrodden in the winter months.

There were rumors from time to time that certain police officers occasionally sent a proxy to get themselves an overcoat or pair of shoes of the right size, but Lizzie accepted this philosophically as an ongoing business expense.

There is no record of Lizzie ever having been a prostitute herself, although that may have been the case when she was very young. During the thirty-eight years that she operated in St. Joseph, she was purely and simply a business woman. Lizzie sold sex the way some people sell Buicks or others sell bon bons.

Another bit of revisionist history that has emerged over the years is that Lizzie's King's place was glamorously and extravagantly furnished. Some have left the impression her place was like plush palaces of pleasure you read about in fiction magazines or see depicted in the movies. It wasn't. If anything, Lizzie's place resembled nothing so much as a very cheap boarding house.

There were no chandeliers with glittering glass, no velvet draperies, no cushiony carpets and no ornate furnishings. St. Joseph bordellos provided only the "bare" necessities.

Lizzie's original establishment in St. Joseph was located at 124½ South Second Street. It was upstairs over a hide and fur company and Lizzie's bordello was referred to by the sporting gentry as ". . . the hide house." Oldtimers who admitted to having visited the place were emphatic that the odor was quite different from roses. Downstairs workers sweated all day long on processing muskrat hides, wool and various and sundry other animal skins, and the smell permeated Lizzie's establishment along with a considerable area of the immediate vicinity.

Otherwise, the location had certain advantages. At the time, the St. Joseph City Hall was located in Market Square. The entrance faced south on Edmond Street and was no farther away from the entrance to Lizzie's place than the distance from third base to home plate. There were cynics who commented how convenient it all was for City Hall patrons, but newsman Slater professes to be too young to know if that was true.

The location over the hide processing business was opened about 1901 and was Lizzie's first in St. Joseph. She remained in business there for thirteen years, moving in 1914 to a more circumspect and certainly less odoriferous location at 415 Messanie Street.

The Messanie Street house was a squat, two-story red brick, and as mentioned earlier, the furnishings were anything but fancy. There were two parlors, one on either side of the entrance, which was located squarely in the middle of the structure. There were bars on the downstairs window, but these were not designed to keep patrons in. They were protection against vandalism and especially against "peeping Toms," even though all business was conducted on the upper floors for reasons which most readers can appreciate.

In one parlor, there was a twenty-five cent coin-operated player piano and in the other parlor (obviously for the less elite patrons) there was a ten-cent operated player piano. Lizzie didn't cater to music lovers and the selections were not in the symphonic class.

Each parlor was furnished much the same. There were overstuffed chairs, a divan or two and a plethora of pillows scattered around. They were the type pillows you might win if you were lucky (or perhaps unlucky would be more the case) at a cheap carnival. Many were covered with gaudy sequins and bold lettering, carrying such nostalgic phrases as "Niagara Falls by Moonlight", "St. Louis World's Fair 1904", "Home Sweet Home" and even "God Bless Our Happy Home".

Slater insists that his first-hand knowledge of Lizzie's place was acquired in the line of duty.

"There always will be some who won't believe me," Slater acknowledges, "but as a reporter from 1927 until Lizzie's death in 1939, I had occasion to go there with the police at various times and also on a specific assignment from my editor."

Behind Lizzie's place at 415 Messanie, she shared a common backyard with a house located at 523 South Fourth Street. It also was a bordello, operated by a younger madam by the name of Laura Burjo, whom many claimed was Lizzie's daughter.

The arrangement offered some convenience for skittish patrons who didn't want to take a chance of being followed and a record kept of how long they stayed at Lizzie's. After completing whatever business they transacted at Lizzie's, those who so desired could depart through the back door and emerge from the front door of Laura's place on South Fourth Street. Of course, the arrangement also worked in reverse for Laura's patrons.

Incidentally, one City Hall jokester at one time posted a thirty-minute parking deadline in front of Lizzie's place.

Lizzie above all was a business woman and she ran her place in a business-like fashion. Just as a plant has a foreman or an office has a supervisor, Lizzie employed a "floor lady", a craggy, stone-faced, no-nonsense woman known only as Claudia.

Claudia took care of protocol, price and whatever else was necessary when Lizzie was away. If necessary, she could even serve as a bouncer. A patron had to be very drunk or very foolish to get crosswise with Claudia.

Lizzie handled the recruiting, kept the books and records, did the banking and the "customer service" arrangement and details. Lizzie also handled the liaison with the police department and took care of all fines as well as "mutually beneficial" arrangements with the authorities. It also was Lizzie's responsibiltiy to see that her "employees" received periodic medical checkups so that their health cards were up to date when police came by on an inspection tour.

They Were "Eyes and Ears," Too

Police tolerance of prostitution in those days was not primarily because of bribery and corruption, although that undoubtedly was part of it at fairly high levels. Even officers who were never linked to the payoff system favored preserving the so-called "red light district" for purely practical reasons.

Chief of Detectives Verne Starmer once told *Gazette* reporter George Sherman that he ". . . hated to see the do-gooders get into power and start campaigning to clean up the town and close down the whorehouses.

"The way it is now," Starmer explained, "we have them all in one area. We can control the situation, we check them regularly for disease and if they try to roll some poor drunk, we usually can go down and recover his money."

Closing the red light district, Starmer maintained, ". . . would scatter the prostitutes all over town where they would work the bars and hotels and where the police would not be in control of things."

There was an even more legitimate reason from a police standpoint to keep the places operating under close police scrutiny. For the most part, the prostitutes worked closely with the police in catching criminals. They served as the "eyes and ears" of several detectives in the St. Joseph police department.

A tip from a prostitute known simply by the inelegant name of "Dirty Legs" led Detectives Glenn Thomas and Pat Nash to the capture of a murderer. Thomas rose to chief of police before he died and Nash went on to serve as Buchanan County treasurer. Subsequently, Thomas also was elected Buchanan County sheriff.

The murder case in which the prostitute "Dirty Legs" played a major, though behind the scenes, role was that of a woman whose body was found on the city dump at Elwood, Kansas. One of the lurid detective magazines of the times called it the case of the "Girl With Flaming Red Hair Found on Dump". It was a particularly distasteful case in which the victim had been raped, strangled and her body ravaged again after she was already dead. The murderer then hauled her body to the Elwood dump.

The killer, subsequently arrested by Detectives Nash and Thomas based on the tip from "Dirty Legs", was a St. Joseph man by the name of John McCord, who drove a delivery truck for a local tobacco company. Thanks to "Dirty Legs", McCord was brought to justice. McCord entered a guilty plea and was sentenced to life imprisonment. In this case, life imprisonment meant just that and McCord died in prison.

The prostitutes gave many tips to local police. More often than not, when a prisoner was released from the state penitentiary, one of his first visits would be to a bordello. The girl who accommodated him saw to it that the police were alerted immediately that he was in town as he would be a likely suspect for any burglary or other criminal act.

Often, also, strangers would blow into town, wind up in one of the local bawdy houses flashing a bankroll and in some instances even bragging about the jobs they had pulled. Here again, the cooperation between prostitutes and police led to the solution of crimes not only committed here, but in other communities as well.

St. Joseph police came close to pulling off the coup of the century when a local prostitute advised them that a man who had been with her the night before had bragged that he was a big-time criminal, wanted all over the United States. She said all the time he was with her he kept a belt close at hand with two holstered pistols. The man advised his bedroom companion he would be back again in a night or two and at her first opportunity she reported the incident to St. Joseph police officers.

Police brought her to the station to go through their active file of photographs of wanted criminals. She picked out a photo of John Dillinger, noted bankrobber and Number 1 on the FBI's "Most Wanted" list. "That's the man," she exclaimed, "that definitely was the man."

Police kept a close watch for several days on that particular bordello, but Dillinger, if it was Dillinger, never returned.

Not all the prostitutes and madams cooperated with law enforcement officials, but those who didn't had cause to regret it. For example, a young man was positively identified by the victim as the one who had held him up and robbed him at a local lumberyard office. When the case came to trial, however, a local madam (not one of the better known operators) testified that the young man had been with her and her girls at the time and couldn't possibly have committed the robbery.

The jury failed to bring in a conviction, but Chief of Detectives Starmer and Glenn Thomas, assistant chief, had no doubts about the young man's guilt and that the madam and her girls had provided a phony alibi.

Starmer had the madam brought in and said to her, "We're not going to close you up. I'm just going to arrest you for investigation."

Explaining that she would be held for twenty hours and then released, Starmer advised her that "When you get released, after you've been free for an hour, you will be arrested again for investigation and held for another twenty hours."

The madam saw the handwriting on the police station wall. She left town. She opened a place in another northwest Missouri community and never returned to St. Joseph.

On another occasion, a well-known local prostitute came to the *News-Press* newsroom to ask reporter Slater about an execution.

"I saw in the paper that you covered the execution of my husband the other day," she said to Slater. It turned out the man's name was Hershon and he had been hanged at the Jackson County Jail in Kansas City for the murder of a policeman.

Slater acknowledged he had covered Hershon's execution and added, ". . .but I didn't know he was your husband."

"I loved him," she told Slater, "We had been married a long time. I never took his name." Then she told Slater why she had come to see him.

"I want to ask you one thing for my peace of mind," she said. "Did Joe die like a man or did he squeal?"

"You can rest in peace," Slater consoled her. "Joe died like a man. He said nothing as he went to the gallows to forfeit his life for his crime."

The Real Reason for the Red Lights

Those "red lights" in the windows eventually became known as a sort of advertising for the kinds of services available within the houses. But, according to Slater, their original purpose was considerably different.

"Originally, they were to let the police know that business was being conducted inside and it wasn't a good time for one of the routine raids that was part of the informal licensing system that went on," Slater explained.

Although police staunchly denied the concept of a "licensing system" for prostitution and the idea would have been sharply chastised from the pulpit, the reality was that a subrosa system of legalized prostitution did emerge—one of mutual benefit to the police, the city and the prostitutes.

In the late Twenties and early Thirties there were as many as eighty bordellos actively operating in St. Joseph. On one block on South Fifth Street, bordering Messanie, there were fourteen houses. There were houses on the west side, downtown, the south side and in the area of Seventh and Mary Streets and Seventh and Patee Streets. Although they were fairly well scattered throughout the community, police had them all pinpointed and subject to the informal albeit unofficial "licensing" system.

Here is how the system worked. On a Friday afternoon or a Saturday morning, a woman would come to the booking desk at Central Police Station and say, "Miss Lizzie sent me over and she said to tell you she has eight girls working now."

The desk sergeant would say, "Okay, we will need four names and the bond will be $15 each."

Sometimes Lizzie would send four girls over to give their names and identification but, more often than not, police simplified matters by just writing down four names of prostitutes they knew had been associated with Lizzie in the past.

They posted the fifteen dollars bond in each of the names of the prostitutes and then in police court the following Monday none would appear to contest the charges and the bonds would be forfeited. Lizzie always put up cash for these fines, never any checks. What worked for Lizzie worked for all the other bordellos in St. Joseph. The police knew where all the places were located and exactly how many prostitutes were working at any one time.

The madams paid approximately one fine every two weeks for every two girls working in her establishment. The money went into the city revenue fund and the police didn't overlook putting a share into the police pension fund.

An important aspect of the arrangement was that each bawdy house was required to have in the back of its front door health cards identifying each woman employed at the establishment and stating that she had been examined by a medical doctor within the past two weeks.

The health card certified that the woman identified did not have gonorrhea. A flaw in the system was that while the health card guaranteed protection against contracting gonorrhea, there was no provision for identifying syphilis or any other social disease. Police maintained a card file on the working prostitutes and at one time the file contained the names of more than a hundred prostitutes all operating within the city limits.

The system had another benefit to the authorities. It circumvented the necessity of making constant raids on all the houses. They would make periodic raids, but rarely did they raid the better known establishments such as Lizzie King's. They knew that Lizzie and certain of the others were playing absolutely fair with them, and were not trying to chisel on the system and pay fewer fines by claiming they had fewer girls working than actually was the case.

One detective was assigned to make the rounds of the bordellos and cheap hotels where the prostitutes operated. He made afternoon rounds three or four days a week, making certain that all in a given location had up to date health cards. If he turned up a girl with no health card, the madam was ordered to "Flag her out. She can't work until she gets cleared away." Even the common streetwalkers were required to show their health cards. There were no exceptions.

Lizzie Aids Good Government

Albeit somewhat reluctantly, Lizzie King helped bring better government to St. Joseph.

At one time, vote fraud registration was rampant in St. Joseph. When a preliminary investigation revealed that the fourteen-room Saxton Hotel at 215 Francis Street was listed as the voting residence for 110 citizens, *News-Press* and *Gazette* Editor Arthur Burrowes decided it was time to do something about it.

Harold Slater was assigned the job: Check out every cheap hotel, every bordello and certain specified "rooming houses" as to whether they were spawning grounds for vote fraud. Slater was armed with registration records listing each address in the third, fourth and fifth wards, specifying how many citizens supposedly lived at each address and how many had voted from those addresses.

Lizzie King's establishment was on the list. Approximately twenty-five registered voters were shown at Lizzie's address. But there were only three or four upstairs bedrooms in the place, and these were not used primarily for sleeping purposes.

Lizzie cooperated and went over Slater's list with him name by name. At each name, Lizzie would make appropriate comments, such as "She worked here about two years ago and I don't know what happened to her," or, "I never heard of her." In other instances, she would recognize the name of a girl from another house and say, "She used to work over on Fifth Street," or "Why, that woman has been dead for three years." At other names, Lizzie would identify the girl in question as one who " . . . works here occasionally," and when one name cropped up as being domiciled at her establishment, Lizzie bridled and remarked waspishly, "I wouldn't let that girl put a foot in my door. I don't trust her."

The list for Lizzie's place was long and helped provide additional ammunition for the newspaper to succeed in eliminating the vote fraud practice which had influenced local elections for several years. Lizzie could have refused to cooperate but didn't and the information she provided did help in bringing about reform in the system.

Lizzie had been married several times but never changed her name. Slater believes she had an established "brand name" for her business and wasn't about to sacrifice all the advertising value built up over the years. Swift or Armour wouldn't give up their brand name just because they had acquired new stockholders or managers, reasons Slater, and Lizzie wouldn't either.

Even in death, Lizzie presented something of a dilemma to the St. Joseph community. She died November 5, 1939 when the mores were considerably more strict than today. Lizzie's obituary presented something of a "hot potato" for them and the staffs of the two local newspapers reacted quite differently.

The *Gazette* editor, who had first crack at the story, played if safe, glossing over Lizzie's true identity and saying nothing of her notorious reputation or her business activity.

Floyd Evans, assistant city editor of the *News-Press*, was more adventurous and won himself national recognition and publication of his story in a journalistic annual featuring the best stories of the year. Evans correctly decided that Lizzie was too much of a town character and her life too colorful not to do an honest reporting job on her demise. The problem, of course, was to make the article interesting and remain within the bounds of the rather strict propriety that prevailed at the time.

The story was handled as straight news on the front page, and public reaction was immediate. There were numerous telephone calls and letters of complaint to the news room. Many women readers were especially outraged. Even the Catholic community was divided. Some Catholic laymen objected to Lizzie's identification with the religion, but other Catholic religious voted approval of her choosing their faith in the final days of her life.

This is the front page account of Lizzie's death as published in the *News-Press* edition of November 6, 1939:

LIZZIE KING IS DEAD
by Floyd Evans

Lizzie King, who for more than 40 years operated a notorious bagnio here, died last night at a local hospital. She was 82 years old, and long had been a subrosa legend, not only in St. Joseph but in many other cities where her notoriety spread.

Lizzie King was a forceful character who belonged to the "old school" of vice which combined predatory aims and business-like conduct with a view to obtaining the utmost profit and the utmost toleration of the community. As a member of what Rudyard Kipling called "the oldest profession in the world," she accumulated and spent several sizable fortunes.

Charity took a great deal of her money, for despite the sharpness of her business methods, she had an extremely soft spot in her heart for the needy and the down-and-out. Too, she was extravagantly generous toward persons she especially liked. She is said to have purchased many expensive horseshoe diamond stickpins for men who won her favor. She had been married several times.

Police knew her as something of a paradox—a brothel keeper whose word could be trusted. It was said she would never voluntarily inform on wanted criminals who came to her place, but would not cover up for them if police asked direct questions about them. Police had raided her place many times, sometimes because of disturbances, but usually in accordance with routine. Few of her cases were tried in court. Usually she put up the necessary cash and entered a plea of guitly.

Her first place, veteran police officers recalled, was over a Felix Street store near Second Street. From there she moved to a location at Second and Edmond Streets. Some 30 years ago she moved to 415 Messanie Street.

None of the places was ever elaborately furnished, as some old-time brothels were. Beer at 50 cents per bottle and dime-in-the-slot pianos added to her profits.

Lizzie King was born in Breathitt County, Ky, and had lived in St. Joseph 45 years. That was not her real name, but what's in a name? Her real name was Ritz! Her last marriage made her Mrs. Elizabeth Ritz.

She died a Catholic, affiliating with that faith in her recent illness.

Newsman Evans wrote what probably will serve as the final epitaph for Lizzie in response to some of the calls and letters of complaint:

"Let God be the judge of poor old Lizzie King, who even in death was identified by a name that was entirely strange to almost all those who knew her."

Slater says that he had one cardinal rule when his police reporter duties required him to call on Lizzie or any of the prostitutes or madams.

"My rule was to always schedule my call in the afternoon," Slater explained, adding, "The reason is clear. You wouldn't call on a night watchman and ask for an interview at 8 a.m. and you had to extend the same courtesy to other night workers.

"Lizzie and her crowd qualified as night workers."

Ima Payne Really Was

Probably one of the most appropriately named prostitutes in St. Joseph was one whose actual name was Ima Payne. Police said the name, spelled "Pain," was especially accurate when she had been drinking.

Many of the inmates in some of the bordellos were almost captives under the madams, recalls Slater. They were restricted from leaving the premises or if they were permitted to go shopping, they were allowed only a limited amount of cash to discourage skipping town in search of greener pastures.

In numerous instances, arrangements were made by the madams with local clothing stores to have clerks bring samples of garments to the houses so the prostitutes could make their purchases without going to town.

When permitted to leave the house, the prostitutes were under the strictest of orders, never to display even the faintest sign of recognition for any of their male patrons they might happen to meet on the street.

Life for the inmates of the bawdy houses was neither glamorous nor exciting. Nor was it even pleasant. Slater's personal evaluation of the prostitutes he came to know (in line of duty, of course) was that they were grateful to anyone who treated them like human beings.

27

"They were accustomed to being battered around and given ill treatment, and scorned in the community," Slater recalls, "and they were well aware that they were overcharged for many things, including clothing and medical supplies.

"They refrained from talking about their patrons and they showed a loyalty to others of their profession, well knowing the problems that they all faced."

Editor's Note: For the record, Harold Slater wants to make it "perfectly clear" that his contact with the prostitutes always was at a discreet distance. When he was police reporter at the impressionable age of twenty, Harold says Chief of Detectives John T. Duncan gave him the following piece of advice: "It would be very foolish to ever get intimately involved with any of the prostitutes. You'll be around them a lot but if you ever get mixed up with one of them, all of them will soon know about it and from then on you wouldn't be worth a damm as a reporter."

It was excellent advice and Slater is happy that he followed it to the letter.

Gambler Polly Loses to Human Nature

One of the better-known gamblers along Edmond Street more than sixty years ago was a gentleman known as Polly Wurst. He actually was a big-time gambler and he went about it in a very scientific way.

Early in 1928 there was some talk that Texas might turn down Al Smith. Texas had never failed to give its vote to a Democratic nominee for president, but there were rumors that this time the situation was different. For one thing, there was considerable anti-Catholic sentiment in Texas.

There were stories that because Al Smith, the Democratic nominee, was a Catholic, many Texas voters would opt for a Republican for the first time. Polly didn't listen to the gossip alone; he subscribed to several Texas newspapers (including some from small towns) and he got a good picture of the situation.

He came back to Edmond Street where the cigar stores along that thoroughfare used to post the bets that were offered. Polly posted odds of one to three that Herbert Hoover would carry Texas. The rest is history. Polly cleaned up when Al Smith was beaten. Herbert Hoover carried Texas, and enough other states to become the president of the United States.

One of the stories, by the way, during that hectic political time, was that the day after election Al Smith was supposed to have sent the Pope the shortest telegram on record. The propaganda had spread over Texas was that if Al Smith became president he was going to request the Pope come to the United States to live in the White House.

The telegram, according to the bigots of that era, was one word, "Unpack."

There is an aftermath to the story. Polly was getting along in years, and he decided that he ought to do something charitable to help ease his way through the Golden Gates. The winter of 1929 was extraordinarily cold, so Polly, still counting all his winnings on the Texas vote, put an ad in the paper stating, "Anyone who wants coal, call John Bruce Coal Yard and charge it to Polly Wurst."

The idea was, of course, for the poor people to be taken care of, the people who really needed it. You can guess what happened . . . All the gamblers along Edmond Street responded to the ad. In those days, coal was a more popular heating fuel than gas, and many of the gamblers along Edmond Street had their basements full of coal by the time Polly realized his blunder.

He took it philosophically, in typical gambler fashion. He did say it wouldn't happen again!

Chili, Poker and Andy Pappas

Perhaps the greatest example of psychology ever used in a poker game here happened one night in an Edmond Street restaurant. The victim was Andy Pappas.

Andy, with Tom Athens, owned and operated the Sanitary Lunch at Eighth and Edmond Street, which was the headquarters for many of the sporting gentry as well as many business people and office workers.

Andy loved to play poker and he was good at it. One night, in a game where the stakes were high, a fellow looked at Andy's cards and said, "Pappas, I'll raise you one thousand bowls of chili."

At that time Andy was getting ten cents a bowl for his chili. He started thinking about how long it would take to cook and sell a thousand bowls of chili, so he turned his cards over.

Had his opponent simply said, "I will raise you a hundred dollars," Pappas would have called him on the spot, However, the psychology of translating the hundred dollars into one thousand bowls of chili was just too much for Andy's business sensibilities to absorb.

Andy had the better hand, but lost the pot—the bowls of chili.

The WCTU Bride and Her Wine-ful Wrath

Making people angry sometimes goes with a newsman's work. And some very angry people on occasions came to the *News-Press* office to vent their spleen.

One of those was a middle-aged woman who was a leader in the Women's Christian Temperance Union, that flagship of the forces against liquor. She had been married a week or two before she sailed into the office in full fighting trim.

The society editor had written that this lady had worn a wine-colored dress at her wedding. The lady was incensed, to think that anyone could possibly associate her with anything like wine. The society editor informed her that the information had come in that way—written by the woman who had made the dress and who had prepared the wedding announcement.

Another time a man walked into the office, on crutches and dragging one foot. His head was bandaged and one arm was wrapped for apparently severe cuts on his hand.

With his good hand, he waved a news clipping and demanded, "I want to see the guy who wrote this."

The clipping was a news story reporting that the fellow had been in a motor car accident the night before, had been taken to the hospital and that his condition was satisfactory.

"I want to see the idiot who wrote that my condition is satisfactory," he said.

"Satisfactory" did indeed appear to be an unsatisfactory term for the poor man's condition. But the "idiot" reporter had used the word from the standard release from the hospital. Unfortunately, hospitals are inclined to call anybody's condition "satisfactory" unless the patient is in an Intensive Care Unit. But also, unfortunately for reporters, it's the newspaper that "said it."

The WCTU Backs "Big Whiskey"

One day in 1932 when Prohibition was still the law of the land a very embarrassed woman came into the office. She said she represented a number of other women who had similar red faces for what they had done the day before.

They were members of the Women's Christian Temperance Union and on the previous day they had held a meeting to which they had invited all candidates for public office to appear, state their backgrounds and tell of their aims and goals in the offices they sought.

One of the candidates they had endorsed, and whose endorsement had appeared in the morning paper, was a fellow who told the group that if elected he would rigorously enforce all the laws—especially the Prohibition laws.

They discovered too late that the man they had endorsed was well known around town by the nickname of "Big Whiskey."

Mr. Truman shows Slater the Bible on which he took the oath of office as president. The picture was taken in the basement of the Truman Library in Independence.

POLITICIANS

Mostly Good Ones, from Harry S Truman to Mike Costello

The completion of General Eisenhower's first year as president was the occasion for this press conference with Mr. Truman in his Kansas City office. Newsmen in the picture include Randall Jessee, Walt Bodine, Johnny Johnson, Seth King, George Wallace and Harold Slater. Edward C. Burke, at the far right, was there as an observer. His Secret Service duty years before had included assignment to President Truman. Burke later became chief of police at St. Joseph.

PART TWO

The "Fine Little Fellow" Wanted Publicity

Every reporter usually can quickly recall the best break he ever got while on newspaper duty. I still have sharp and vivid memories of mine, although it occurred fifty-five years ago.

I was courthouse reporter and a political writer for the *News-Press* in early May, 1934, when I stopped to visit with Chief of Police Charles A. Enos.

"I was down at the St. Francis Hotel this morning and met a fine little fellow," the chief said. "He's running for United States senator and I think he would like some publicity."

I went down to the lobby of the St. Francis and introduced myself to Presiding Judge Harry S Truman of Jackson County. It was the start of a newspaper and personal friendship without flaw until thirty-eight years later when I attended his funeral at Independence, Missouri.

The dapper little man stood out in the drab lobby of the hotel. He wore a gray, double-breasted suit and a bow tie. His hair was perfectly combed and parted neatly to both sides. He was fifty years old. Mr. Truman was friendly and open in his answers. I talked frankly to him that morning about his support for the Democratic nomination from the Pendergast organization.

I mentioned the four killings in the Kansas City election just a little more than a month before and the many allegations of crookedness aimed at the Pendergast machine. I told him that I knew he was not to blame but wondered what effect the machine reputation would have on his candidacy.

"Tom Pendergast or no other member of his organization has ever asked me to do a dishonest thing. They knew I wouldn't," said Mr. Truman.

"I have just finished spending $40 million in bond money in Jackson County and I have patches on my pants. No one can ever say I ever took a dishonest penny and they never will be able to say that in truth."

We talked about a variety of other things that morning including his vision problems. He said he had an ailment that amounted to flat eyeballs. He showed me how the problem was being corrected by his glasses which had half-peanut size protrusions on the lenses.

"My vision was what kept me out of West Point," said the man who later was to be commander-in-chief of the greatest armed fighting force in history.

He chuckled and said, "I wasn't able to play baseball on account of my eyes so they made me umpire!"

He was courteous and delightful that distant May morning and he never changed. As president he was just the same as he had been when he was out seeking votes in his first campaign for national office. A friend once commented to me "Harry Truman grew; he didn't swell."

Fortunately for me, I was to be present at many important events in his life. I was there the afternoon of the opening day of the 1944 Democratic National Convention in Chicago when the Missouri delegation at a luncheon session at the Hotel Sherman drafted him as a candidate for the nomination for vice-president. Mr. Truman was unwilling but stood by while they replaced him as head of the Missouri delegation so that he could be presented as a candidate.

I was in the convention hall three days later when he defeated Vice-President Henry Wallace for that nomination.

I was on hand that hot summer night in 1948 in Philadelphia when he was nominated for president at a convention when so many were doing so much to bring about his defeat. And I was at Washington to cover his inauguration as President in his own right on January 20, 1949.

I also visited with him a number of times in his office in Kansas City, his library and home in Independence, in St. Joseph and at the dedication of the armory in Maryville, Missouri.

Always he was the same—a man who never forgot a friend and who always tried to be helpful.

Truman Didn't Want to be VP

Senator Truman was put on the spot at that luncheon in 1944 when the Missouri delegation announced, "We are going to plunk down all our votes for Franklin D. Roosevelt for president and Harry S Truman for vice-president."

Senator Truman earlier had been advocating others for the vice-presidential nomination, including Speaker Sam Rayburn and Secretary of State James Byrnes.

Early the morning of the day Senator Truman was to be nominated for vice-president, Arthur V. Burrowes, editor of the *News-Press* and *Gazette*, and I were in the lobby of the Hotel Sherman in Chicago when we met Senator Truman and Jim Pendergast, the head of the Kansas City machine. We mentioned that he probably would be nominated that night.

Truman said that might happen and it might not, adding, "I'm serious about not wanting the nomination. I've already got the best job in the world, a senator of the United States."

That night when photographers swarmed about him in his convention floor box they asked him to pose kissing his daughter, Margaret. Senator Truman brusquely declined. "In our family," he said with dignity, "we don't make public displays of our affection."

Senator Truman carried the brunt of that 1944 presidential campaign, his running mate, FDR being busy with the war and having little time to spare for political machinations.

FDR Needed Him

The Democrats won in 1944, but due to the war, the January 20, 1945, inauguration was an extremely austere one. It was conducted on the White House grounds—not at the Capitol as usual—and there was no parade or major social events.

For new Vice-President Truman, there was a White House luncheon with President Roosevelt. So busy was FDR with the war that Mr. Truman was to visit with him only once more before his death seven weeks later. The blunt truth is that Vice-President Truman was fully aware that the administration did not take him on as an insider.

Roosevelt seemed to regard World War II as a one-man war he was conducting, with maybe a little side help from an English fellow known as Winston Churchill.

For example, Roosevelt never did tell Mr. Truman about the atomic bomb that was being developed. Mr. Truman first learned about that bomb the day after he became president on the death of FDR. It was Secretary of War Henry Stimson who then told President Truman of the unbelievable force of that bomb.

Many thought Mr. Truman owed FDR a great debt for tapping him for the vice-presidential nomination. Their theory was that FDR knew his health was such that he probably couldn't live through a fourth term and that the man he tapped for vice-president would be the next president.

President Truman didn't go along with that. He told friends, including some from St. Joseph, "He needed me more than I needed him."

Truman was well aware that the record he made as chairman of the Senate committee that probed war expenditures had given him a national reputation for public service and knew that this fact alone would make him a major asset in achieving a Democratic victory.

"We (the committee) saved the United States at least $15 billion," he said in one interview here.

HST a "Sobering" Influence

The Truman inauguration January 20, 1949, was as fancy and colorful as the 1945 inauguration had been subdued and austere. That was because in 1948 the Republicans were in control of both houses of Congress and generously appropriated luxury amounts for the inauguration in their certainty that Republican Thomas E. Dewey would be the new president. It didn't work out that way and the liberal funds went to enhance the inauguration of Truman.

Typical of President Truman that day was his action in having members of his old World War I Battery D on hand for the gala event. Captain Harry had those veterans at the White House for breakfast that morning.

He told them, "I know you fellows, and I'm telling you this: none of you are going to get drunk until after the parade."

Reports are that they didn't.

The Kind of Man We Need

Truman's passion for honesty and integrity is perhaps best illustrated by a situation during his campaign for the presidency.

He received a phone call from a potential contributor, offering $20,000 for his campaign fund but in return the man wanted a favor. Twenty thousand dollars was a lot of money in those days, but Truman didn't hesitate in rejecting the offer.

"We could put the $20,000 to good use," he told the would-be donor, "but there isn't any amount of money that buys anyone special favors with me."

The happy ending to that incident is that subsequently Truman received a call from another businessman who said he was donating $20,000 to the Truman campaign, no strings attached.

"I heard what you told So-and-So when he offered you $20,000 but wanted a political favor in return, "the caller said to Truman, "and as far as I'm concerned, you're the kind of man we need in the White House."

A Seat for Bishop Cody

About 5,000 persons were present for the dinner given at the Latter Day Saints Church auditorium at Independence, Missouri the day the Truman Library there was dedicated.

Former President Herbert Hoover was at the head table and so was Chief Justice Earl Warren. There were former Cabinet members, United States senators, governors, congressmen and other dignitaries by the scores.

President Truman, sitting at the head table just as the serving of the meal was to start, noticed one Catholic clergyman who seemed to be looking for a place to sit.

Quickly, Mr. Truman rose from the table and took the clergyman to a place of honor. He was Bishop John P. Cody of the St. Joseph-Kansas City diocese, who later was to become a cardinal and head of the giant Catholic archdiocese of Chicago.

A Day in the Oval Office

Certainly one of the biggest days in my news career was January 10, 1949, when President Truman invited Congressman Phil J. Welch and me to visit him in the Oval Office at the White House. Just the three of us were there and he talked freely.

His worries had to be great. The Berlin airlift was a problem at the time, as were the constant threats of the Soviet, and he was busy getting ready for his inauguration in ten days. But President Truman also wanted to talk about Democratic politics in Northwest Missouri.

One of the topics was who might be the next postmaster at Cameron, a small town some thirty miles east of St. Joseph. Congressman Welch had heard a rumor that the man he wanted for that post might not be named.

"Forget about it," said Truman. "You've got the right to select that postmaster and the fellow you want will be named."

He was.

The President autographed cards for my son and daughter and handed me ballpoint pens for them inscribed, "This pen stolen from the desk of President Truman." It was a day never to be forgotten.

That Losing Poker Hand

In St. Joseph there is a legend about a losing poker hand held by Senator Truman in a game here at the Democratic Club rooms over a drug store at 11th and Frederick Avenue.

As a candidate and as a senator, Mr. Truman played poker on a number of occasions at that Democratic Club, the Elks, and American Legion Post 11 clubrooms. I had been in poker games with him at times but was not there the day the legend developed.

It was a fifty-cent limit game, straight draw poker. Truman was dealt four queens, the kind of a hand where you can bet the farm and livestock. Sheriff Stonewall Jackson Shepherd was dealt the three, five, seven of hearts. Someone opened, Truman raised and Sheriff Shepherd stayed.

Shepherd made a miracle draw of two cards, the four and six of hearts, giving him a straight flush, enough to beat any four of a kind. After several raises, Truman showed his four queens and Shepherd proudly laid down his straight flush.

Senator Truman reportedly said, smilingly, what he thought of anyone who could make a draw like that. Those present said he actually seemed to enjoy it—but not many poker players would.

An Autograph Times Ten

In December, 1960, Theo J. Quinn retired as postmaster of St. Joseph, and former President Truman, his close friend, came here to speak at the retirement dinner.

Before the dinner there was a cocktail party at the home of the Quinns' son-in-law and daughter, Mr. and Mrs. William F. Enright, Jr.

One of the young daughters of the Enrights approached the former president with a request. She asked him if he would give her an autograph so her Girl Scout troop could raffle it off to raise funds.

Mr. Truman said he would do better than that. He had the little Enright girl get him a long sheet of paper, then sat on a stair step and wrote his name ten times, carefully spacing each autograph about an inch apart so they could be cut into individual strips.

"Maybe you can make ten times as much now," he said to a very thrilled little girl.

The Day Belonged to the Bride

When our daughter, Rosemary Slater, was marrying Joseph D. Harris in 1957, a wedding invitation was sent to former President and Mrs. Truman. An explanation of why they wouldn't attend was sent by Mr. Truman along with a gift of a silver bowl.

Mr. Truman explained that Eleanor Roosevelt once told him that her wedding to Franklin D. was blighted for her because her uncle, President Theodore Roosevelt, showed up. Eleanor knew she was playing second fiddle that day because some at the event practically ignored her and gave full attention to President Teddy.

Mr. Truman said he thought the Slater-Harris wedding day should belong to the bride and he skipped such events so she could have her special due that day.

President Truman had known our daughter, Rosemary, since her college days. In fact, he had written an introduction on her theme about the Marshall Plan, a plan he had brought into being as president.

He Made a Bad Enemy for Stark

Harry Truman apparently didn't dislike many people but when he did it was with a vengeance.

Several times in interviews he made it clear to me how much he disliked Lloyd C. Stark, governor of Missouri from 1937 to 1941. He had helped Stark in the beginning of his political career and then turned on him when he found Stark wanted to take Truman's place in the United States Senate.

Stark filed against him for the Democratic nomination for senator in 1940 when Truman was seeking a second term and Mr. Truman promptly taught him how to play tough in politics.

Governor Stark tried to get an outstanding political figure to speak in his behalf at the opening rally of his campaign. First, he tried to get the governor of Arkansas. Truman got word to the Arkansas executive that he wouldn't appreciate that at all.

The Arkansas governor backed off. So did a number of others sought by Stark as a keynote speaker when Truman got word to them their speaking for Stark would make him unhappy.

Truman used to chuckle about how he had regularly used his contacts to stop Stark's moves.

"Stark finally got desperate and got a fellow out in Kansas for his speaker," Mr. Truman told friends here. "To have a Kansan tell Missourians how to vote for the United States Senate was like inviting Sitting Bull to be a guest of honor at a reunion of the Seventh Cavalry."

Ike Wasn't a Bad Guy" but . . .

On January 27, 1953, just a week to the day after he had ended his term as chief executive, Mr. Truman sat in his temporary office in the Federal Reserve Bank building in Kansas City with me and my son, Robert, then a college junior. That interview was to produce a full page Sunday story in the *News-Press*.

There had been a rumor that Dwight Eisenhower had been very cool as he rode with President Truman from the White House to the Capitol the morning he was to be given the oath as president.

"That's about right," Mr. Truman said. "General Eisenhower had something to say as soon as we started the ride to the Capitol. He said he wanted to know who arranged for his son, John, an army major, to be brought to Washington from Korea for the inauguration.

"I told him that I had and added I was still president and commander-in-chief of the armed forces of the United States. He didn't have another thing to say during the ride."

In a conversation one day at his library about two years later, Mr. Truman commented to me: "Ike isn't a bad guy but he doesn't know any more about politics than a horse does about Sunday."

His Biggest Thrill

On one occasion I asked Mr. Truman what had been the biggest thrill of his life. Remember, he had twice been elected to the United States Senate, and been elected vice-president and president, had announced the surrender of the Nazi forces and the surrender of Japan among other monumental experiences.

His answer came quickly:

"The biggest thrill I ever had was when we came home to Independence from Washington the day after I had left the White House and there were 5,000 people at the railroad depot to greet Mrs. Truman and me." He was a study in sincerity.

He also mentioned the press conference held during the middle of the 1956 Democratic National Convention at Chicago when he warned the party would err if it again nominated Adlai Stevenson for president, Mr. Truman wanted the nomination for Averell Harriman, former governor of New York and a top trouble-shooter for his administration.

The former president said Stevenson would do no better than he had in 1952. Stevenson again was nominated and Mr. Truman campaigned hard for him. Stevenson carried Missouri, but again lost the nation.

Why He Skipped the 1960 Convention

At a press conference in early July, 1960, at the Truman library, Mr. Truman announced he would not attend the Democratic convention, although selected as a delegate.

He was unhappy, he said, because he thought Joseph Kennedy, former ambassador to Great Britain, was trying to buy the nomination for his son, John. Although he didn't go, Mr. Truman campaigned for Kennedy once he was nominated.

An HST History Lesson

On one visit to Mr. Truman at his home in Independence, I was accompanied by my granddaughter, Susan Harris, who was eleven.

Mr. Truman talked to her like an adult and inquired about what American history she was studying. He suggested she also study Roman history on her own, telling her, "What is happening in the United States today is very much along the pattern that led to the fall of the Roman Empire."

It Wasn't the Men's Room

It was a very simple set of rooms that Mr. Truman had for his offices in the Federal Reserve Bank building in Kansas City when he first came home after ending his service as President.

There was only one picture and one bust on his desk. The picture was of Averell Harriman and the bust was of Simon Bolivar, often called the "savior of South America."

At first there wasn't even any lettering on the glass door of the office. One day the lettering Harry S Truman was placed on the door and Mr. Truman told visitors why.

"I got tired of so many fellows walking in thinking it was the men's room," he explained.

They Didn't Hitch-Hike Back

Mr. Truman's last visit to St. Joseph as president was on October 6, 1952. He came here by train from Shenandoah, Iowa, to speak on behalf of presidential nominee Adlai Stevenson at the yards of the old Union Passenger Station.

He had Congressman Phil J. Welch, City Council President Harry Smith, *News-Press* Reporter Jack Suesens and Harold Slater as his guests in his private car, the Ferdinand Magellan. That car was the famous one in which Mr. Truman had made his whistle-stop tour to win election as president just four years earlier.

On that 1952 trip here he discussed many things with his St. Joseph friends, one of which was that he didn't like the way Stevenson was campaigning. He said the former Illinois governor "should take off the gloves and talk a little rougher." Stevenson was sparing too many personalities for his likes.

Several thousand were on hand here that day to hear the president, among them my son, Robert Slater, and three other students from St. Benedict's College at Atchison, Kansas, who had hitch-hiked here for the event.

When the President learned about their trip, he made the way home easier. He asked a police sergeant to take the four down to the Atchison highway and stop a couple of cars and ask the drivers to take the boys the twenty-five miles to Atchison "for Mr. Truman". The sergeant had no trouble accomplishing the mission.

Claire Booth Luce Not Welcome

All who visited the Truman home were impressed by his deep affection for Mrs. Truman. She was always in his conversation. He called her "The Boss".

If anyone ever offended Mrs. Truman they quickly experienced the wrath of her famous husband. Claire Booth Luce once made an offensive comment about Bess Truman and from that day forward she was never invited to the White House. President Truman on several occasions after that invited her husband, Henry Luce, to White House affairs but Mrs. Luce was persona non grata.

A Rose Without Thorns

As friends visited one day with former President Harry S Truman in his library office at Independence, we noted the efficient manner in which his secretary, Rose Conway, went about her duties.

"What a book she could write!" a newsman commented. He pointed out how she had been Mr. Truman's personal secretary all the time he was president and before that when he was vice-president. She had remained as his personal secretary during his retirement years at the library when the great, the near great and just ordinary folks came to give him homage.

"She has to know countless thousands of secrets about your career. Any publisher would give a few hundred thousand dollars for her memoirs," someone said.

Mr. Truman smiled confidently. "Rose would never tell a secret. Rose will never write a book."

He was one hundred percent correct. She died without ever having written a word about the history she saw in the making or about anything President Truman had ever said or done.

In these days when Reagan, Speakes and others have capitalized on their White House experience by turning out books embarrassing to President Reagan and his family, it is encouraging to know there have been such examples of loyalty to a president as that displayed by Rose Conway.

Notes From Eleven Conventions

I had the good fortune as a newsman to be assigned to cover eleven national political conventions, starting with the the 1940 Democratic event at Chicago where Franklin D. Roosevelt was nominated for a third term as president.

Austerity was the rule at the Democratic National Convention at Chicago in 1944. To show that the party was aiding in the conservation of metal, the convention bosses issued cardboard badges instead of the fancy metal ones associated with most such conventions.

Due to wartime precautions and restrictions, President Roosevelt did not attend the convention, but instead accepted the nomination for a fourth term in a radio address from what was then an undisclosed location. It turned out later to be San Diego. To Missourians, of course, the major happening of that convention was the nomination of our own Harry S Truman for vice president.

One of the memories of that convention was the gathering together of the worst collection of singers in the western world to bellow out the same song almost continuously. It was "Don't change horses in the middle of the stream." The nation bought the idea in spite of the off-key rendition, and Mr. Roosevelt again won easy re-election.

Both the Democrats and Republicans held their national conventions in Philadelphia in 1948. Dewey again was the Republican choice for president and Mr. Truman the Democratic nominee. Dewey captured that nomination only after a hard battle for it with Mr. Republican—United States Senator Robert Taft of Ohio.

I still remember the courageous Taft—he had hoped to win the presidency, an honor once held by his father—telling a press conference that he was a party man and would campaign full force for the man who had defeated him. And he kept his word.

In 1952, both parties held their national conventions in Chicago. United States Senator Estes Kefauver started out with what seemed to be the edge in the Democratic National Convention. His adherents and delegates were everywhere, all wearing the coonskin caps, complete with tails that were the Kefauver theme.

Adlai Stevenson, who won the Democratic nomination that year, wasn't even a candidate as the session opened. He addressed it as the governor of Illinois solely for the purpose of welcoming the delegates and alternates to his state.

When the voting started on the nomination for president there was heavy balloting for Kefauver as the first tallies were taken. But funny things happen at national political conventions and that convention was no exception.

Suddenly some folks in charge decided there was a grave fire hazard. Scrap paper that had been tossed in the aisles on the convention floor was seen as a great danger. The politicos opposing Kefauver asked for and obtained a recess. That recess lasted four hours. We knew that plenty of confabs were going on, that a lot of political trades were being made. So when the convention reconvened it was evident that not only the trash had been cleaned from the aisles, but that also swept out had been the chances of Kefauver for victory. Stevenson won.

At the 1952 Republican convention at Chicago I watched with fascination as the Eisenhower steamroller was put in action. Senator Taft was within ten or twelve delegate votes of clinching the nomination when the Eisenhower juggernaut went into high gear.

I attended the breakfast that Eisenhower gave for the Missouri delegation. The general, still a complete novice in politics, spoke with surprising power as he declared the Republicans will win this year "and we're going to kick the Democrats so hard and so far it will be twenty years or more before they can get back."

As the tide began to shift from Taft to Eisenhower, a novel political device was resorted to. The Ike forces papered the town with cards and buttons reading "Help keep Chicago clean. Don't throw your Taft buttons on the sidewalk."

The 1956 Democratic National Convention at Chicago was a rerun for Adlai Stevenson, once again his party's choice. Former President Harry S Truman was there at his fiery best. He wanted the nomination for his old friend, Averell Harriman, former governor of New York, former ambassador to Russia, and a troubleshooter many times for the Truman administration. Truman told the convention that Stevenson couldn't win.

At a press conference, someone asked Truman if Stevenson could even carry Missouri. "Not unless this old man goes out and works his head off for him," Mr. Truman said. He was right. He did make it possible for Stevenson to carry Missouri but, as Truman had predicted, the Democratic candidate lost badly nationally.

At the 1960 Democratic convention at Los Angeles, Senator Stuart Symington of Missouri at first appeared to have an outside chance for the presidential nomination. Instead the heavy financing for John F. Kennedy and Lyndon B. Johnson took Symington out of the picture.

The convention became essentially a two-man fight and Kennedy convincingly overpowered Johnson. Kennedy did give Johnson the consolation prize, the nomination for vice-president. However, for a time several others were reported to be under consideration for the second place spot. One of those rumored to be in the running was Symingon and TV crews even laid cables to his hotel suite so they could record the story when and if Kennedy tapped him.

The 1964 Democratic convention at Atlantic City was a one-man show. It was LBJ all the way. With one exception, the convention followed the script dictated by President Johnson. No one spoke unless approved by Johnson. No one even got a choice spot in the convention hall unless Johnson so decreed.

But there was one unexpected thing that Johnson couldn't control. A film on the life of martyred President Kennedy was shown and then Robert F. Kennedy, his brother who had been his attorney-general, was introduced. The demonstration that resulted was one of the greatest displays of love and affection ever witnessed at any national convention. The packed hall roared out its feelings for Robert Kennedy and the ghost of his brother. The demonstration was sincere and not manufactured. It was uncontrollable. For a full twenty minutes that tribute continued. It rose and fell like waves. For its ardor it was unbelievable. Its emotion was unforgettable.

All else at the convention had been cut and dried. The Kennedy demonstration was the highlight. Possibly hoping to upstage it, President Johnson delayed the announcement of his choice for vice-president until the last minute when he pinned the garland on Senator Hubert H. Humphrey of Minnesota. The Kennedy deomonstration was still the highlight of what otherwise was an all-LBJ scenario.

In 1964 I also covered the Republican convention at the Cow Palace at San Francisco which nominated Senator Barry Goldwater. It was a runaway for the Arizonian and I remember two side issues as much as the actual nominating mechanism.

One was Walter Winchell creating a scene when Secret Service men would not allow him to go to the floor of a hotel where the Eisenhowers were staying. Winchell was claiming loud and long that "Everyone knows I'm Mamie's favorite columnist." The Secret Service was not impressed. Winchell failed to score.

The other matter of special note was the shameless manner in which those directing the campaign ignored Richard Nixon, who four years before had been the GOP nominee for president. They did everything but hide Nixon in a corner. He had to feel very humiliated and even I felt sorry for him.

One widely circulated report was that Nixon even had trouble getting a few convention spectator tickets for friends. Four years later those who shunned him in 1964 were hovering around him and doing everything possible to curry his favor. Nothing in politics is permanent.

A final convention comment: the most surprising thing about national political conventions is how relatively few pull the strings that produce the action. Many of the so-called leaders actually wind up as little more than window dressing.

Red Meant T.J. Was Serious

Kansas City politician and manipulator Tom "T.J." Pendergast was beseiged by requests from people all over the state for letters of reference to get jobs when Roosevelt came into office. There had been a dearth of Democratic jobs for twelve years during the Republican national and state years.

Pendergast was in solid with Jim Farley and the other powers-that-be under the chief patronage dispenser, FDR. A letter of reference from him would carry weight in getting a job. Pendergast had a system all his own. He readily wrote these letters of reference for anyone who asked, but there was a gimmick. Only when he signed the letters with red crayon did he mean business. The people with whom he dealt, like Farley, knew that otherwise Tom's references were simple courtesy letters. When they were signed with red crayon, T.J. was serious.

Speaking of T.J. brings to mind the 1936 election. Lloyd Stark had been nominated for governor of Missouri on the Democratic ticket and had depended heavily on Pendergast's influence in Jackson County for thousands of votes. A hue and a cry was raised that these votes had been stolen, that there had been crooked work in Jackson County. Years later this claim proved entirely valid.

Stark was campaigning in St. Joseph after that primary and Arthur V. Burrowes, the *News-Press* news editor, told me to interview him and ask him, point blank: "Are you satisfied with being nominated with stolen votes from Jackson County?"

I called on Stark in his room at the Hotel Robidoux. Stark was in the company of fifteen or twenty of his supporters. When I requested to interview him privately, Stark said, "No, anything you want to ask you can ask in front of my friends."

"Well, some of this is rather personal," I said.

Again Stark replied, "No, anything you have to ask, you can say in front of my friends."

I began the interview, finally asking the $64 question, "Major Stark, are you content to be nominated largely on stolen votes from Jackson County?"

Stark was a military man and I could see his face going tense and livid. Before Stark could say anything, however, one of his followers, Jake Bretz, a deputy liquor control supervisor, jumped up, grabbed me by the collar, and shouted, "Are you trying to blackmail our governor?" In highly impolite terms, I told Jake to let go of my collar and Stark answered he wasn't going to answer my question.

At that point Maurice Hoffman, prosecuting attorney of Buchanan County, told Stark it would be very poor public relations to refuse to answer the question. He suggested that he, Stark, and I go to his office at the nearby courthouse and take care of the interview there.

Stark, away from his friends, followed Hoffman's advice and answered the question in a diplomatic manner. He said, in effect, that he was not aware of any stolen votes in Jackson County, that he was just hoping to run the state of Missouri as a representative of all the people. It was a typical politician's answer.

The aftermath: Stark was elected governor and one of the first people he fired was Jake Bretz. The disgruntled Jake let loose a vituperative blast at Governor Stark when he learned he was out in the cold.

I couldn't resist: I sent Jake a collect telegram: "Are you trying to blackmail our governor, Jake?"

A former state representative who knew what it was to be bounced around in politics, Jake took the message good-naturedly.

Prosecutions Don't Win Elections, Though

When New York Governor Thomas E. Dewey came to St. Joseph in the fall of 1940 I interviewed him at Hotel Robidoux during his campaigning for the presidential candidacy of Wendell Willkie.

Dewey, who would make his own run for the presidency against Harry S Truman in 1948, had made an outstanding record as a crime-busting district attorney in New York. He played havoc particularly with those involved in organized crime and still was vitally interested in the prosecution of crime in all areas.

Dewey turned the tables on me and asked about the crime picture here and wanted to know how successful prosecutors had been here in obtaining convictions. The Robidoux was only a block from the courthouse so I took him to the county building where he could look over the records of convictions won by Prosecuting Attorney Maurice Hoffman.

Dewey was impressed with Hoffman's high percentage of convictions and said the local prosecutor was entitled to congratulations.

A high conviction rate didn't help Dewey against Truman, though.

"Hell," Said the Soapy Senator

Over the years, in campaigns stretching from 1932 to 1944, I interviewed United States Senator Bennett C. Clark many times. The occasion I remember best was while he was taking a bath.

The senator arrived at Hotel Robidoux that evening and was asked for an interview by Virgil Jackson, a *Gazette* reporter, and me. He explained he had a very busy schedule with few minutes to spare but that he could be interviewed if we did it while he was taking a bath.

The offer was accepted. I, luckily, got the use of the only seating place in the bathroom after putting the lid down, but Virgil Jackson asked the interview question I most remember. The year was 1938. War clouds were heavy over Europe.

"Senator," Virgil asked in his most polite manner, "can you give me two or three short paragraphs summing up the international situation in Europe?"

"Hell," said the soaped senior senator from Missouri, "I'm thinking about writing a book on it."

Incidentally, Senator Clark for about thirty years fought a crusade over a matter he believed had deprived his father of the United States presidency. That crusade was to abolish the rules of the Democratic National Convention that required a candidate to receive two-thirds of the delegate votes before being declared the party's nominee for president.

At the 1912 Democratic National Convention in Baltimore, the senator's father, Speaker of the House Champ Clark, polled over half of the delegate votes on early ballots, but the two-thirds rule held. The result was that certain Clark delegates finally wavered and left his ranks. That brought about the nomination of Woodrow Wilson, who easily was elected president that fall.

One of those accused of being a prime mover in abandoning Champ Clark was William Jennings Bryan, who wound up as secretary of state in the Wilson cabinet.

Not long before his death, Senator Clark achieved his great desire. The Democrats changed the convention rules to allow nomination by a simple majority.

The Clark battle was won but it was far too late in the day for Champ.

Thrown Out with a Teetotaler Governor

One of the finest human beings any journalist ever knew was Forrest C. Donnell, who was elected governor of Missouri on the Republican ticket in 1940. He served for four years before going on to the United States Senate. Donnell, like President Truman, was something of a rarity. He was a totally honest politician.

He insisted on crossing every "T" and dotting every "I". He stood for no foolishness and was the essence of integrity. If he said something, he meant it.

For example, he was so scrupulously honest that when he wrote a letter and wanted to say, "Hilda sends her regards (Hilda being his wife)," each time before he sent such a letter, he called Hilda and asked her if it was okay.

When elected to the Senate, Donnell followed every rule and regulation so closely that it disturbed some of the senators who were used to running that body in their own way, and taking short cuts. There were no short cuts under Donnell's code; they did exactly what they were supposed to do under the law and under the rules of the Senate.

The Donnell character was exemplified in a long story that appeared in the *Saturday Evening Post*. It referred to Forrest Donnell as the Senate's "hair shirt". He did cause a lot of senators grief, because he was honest and some of them were not.

Forrest Donnell was a teetotaler. He had never tasted alcohol in his life, and he never allowed any liquor to be served in the mansion while he was governor. He was uncomfortable with any of his appointees who drank. As a fact, before naming some of his people, he asked them point blank if they drank. If they said yes, their chances of being appointed dimmed considerably.

I have one distinction. I was once kicked out of a saloon with Forrest Donnell. It happened in the 1944 Republican National Convention in Chicago. It had been a long day of convention sessions, and a group of the Missouri delegates had gone to the Hotel Sherman (in the loop of Chicago), and were relaxing in the Shamrock Room.

Included in the group were two St. Joseph people besides myself; David W. Hopkins (the former congressman) and Leo V. Anderson (president of the Board of Police Commissioners). We were having our share of drinks, and enjoying them. It was not sissy stuff, some were drinking boilermakers, others highballs and some straight whiskey.

Then, about twenty minutes till two in the morning, into the room came Forrest Donnell. No one had ever heard of him being in a saloon before, but there he was. He came over to the table when he recognized Leo Anderson and Dave Hopkins, and said, "Will you boys join me in a sarsaparilla?"

I'm sure that Leo didn't know exactly what sarsaparilla tasted like, but he said he would love to have one. Dave, a fast-thinking politician, said "Make mine a coke." I was a sissy and took a sarsaparilla, wondering privately if I would be able to spell it in a news story.

The governor was just starting on his sarsaparilla, and he hadn't been in the room more than ten or fifteen minutes when the bartender came over. He was a big, burly guy. He said, "Listen, it is almost two o'clock. I'm so damn tired of you drunks in here. Get out!"

Here was Forrest Donnell, the governor of Missouri, the only drink he had had (which wasn't finished) was a sarsaparilla, and he literally was being thrown out of a Chicago saloon!

Donnell said, "We are sorry that we disturbed you, and it won't happen again. We are leaving right now, and I hope that you have a good night's sleep."

This was typical of Forrest Donnell.

Ah, How Fleeting Fame

One of my prime assignments as a *News-Press* reporter came early in January of 1941 when the paper tapped me for its Jefferson City correspondent.

I arrived at the Capitol to find the General Assembly involved in a big fight over an attempt by some Democratic solons to keep Republican Forrest C. Donnell from being sworn in as governor even though he had been elected in November of 1940.

The Democratic challenge flopped when the Missouri Supreme Court declared that the failure to declare Donnell elected was illegal. But the governor-elect was kept out of his office until February 26—roughly fifty days after he should have been inaugurated.

During the interim there was one all-night joint session that opened at three-thirty in the afternoon and lasted until about six o'clock the next morning. It was rather maddening. Just when it appeared that something might be accomplished, someone would ask for a roll call. That was before the days of electronic roll calls and calling the roll of one hundred sixty-three House members and thirty-four senators took about forty minutes.

And not a single worthwhile thing was accomplished in that all-night session.

The man who lost that gubernatorial race was Democrat Lawrence McDaniel. During the time when it seemed he might be elected, hordes of job-hopefuls thronged around him. Two days after the high court killed his chances, I ran across McDaniel in the lobby of a Jefferson City hotel, playing a pinball machine.

He was all by himself.

Dripping Derbies Derail Democrats

Someone had the idea it would be great to run a special train from St. Joseph to Sedalia when Al Smith was to speak at the Missouri State Fairgrounds during his 1928 campaign for president.

57

In the meantime, an enterprising merchant on the lower end of Felix Street also had a great idea. Al's symbol of his campaign was the brown derby. Democrats everywhere were wearing brown derbies.

The shopkeeper had hundreds of old black derbies in storage that he had not been able to sell. He came up with the novel idea of having a clerk paint them brown, using regular house paint. When he put those "brown" derbies on sale, they sold better than any hot cakes ever sold. Almost every man at the courthouse was sporting a brown derby, and the same was true at the Democratic city hall.

The day of the big trip on the special train to Sedalia arrived. The train was jammed with happy and jubilant Al Smith supporters. It was still Prohibition, and many passengers on that train had their bottles of booze with them.

At Sedalia, however, a catastrophe struck. It rained, and it rained. It was a tremendous downpour and at the outdoor meeting there was no cover, except for a small area under the speakers stand. Al Smith still spoke out and his loyal friends, including the big contingent from St. Joe stood in the rain and listened. They applauded everytime that he said, "If I am elected I will bring back beer, I will bring back whiskey, I'll end Prohibition."

It went over big, and the people were soaking wet, but then to their horror, the brown derbies began to run from the rain. You never saw such a sorry looking group of men in your life. The brown derbies dripped onto shirts and onto coats. They dripped onto ties and onto shoes.

Loyal Democrats could not leave during the speech or do anything except mop up the damage that had been done by that brown paint. Certainly it was a far from an exuberant group that came back on that train from Sedalia.

One the way down, there had been plenty of liquor; now it was all gone. One the way down, there had been several high stake crap games, but the losers had no more money to lose. It was a sorry entourage that disembarked in St. Joseph, and the most brown-stained group in the history of the west. It was a fiasco, which grew into a bigger fiasco six months later when they realized that Al Smith did not have the votes to become president.

A Case of Reverse Superstition

Many years ago, interviewing an authority on Theodore Roosevelt, I learned that on the day Roosevelt was inaugurated as president in 1905 he wore an opal ring that Abraham Lincoln had been wearing the night he was assassinated.

He said Roosevelt was the most superstitious man who ever served as president and that he thought wearing that ring would insure him success as chief executive.

The expert on such matters used to lecture on college campuses on what would have happened if Roosevelt had been elected president in 1912 instead of Woodrow Wilson.

Maybe Teddy shouldn't have worn that ring after all.

Hoover Stays Mum on FDR

In the early fall of 1933 former President Herbert Hoover decided to come to northwest Missouri to look over the farm he owned in this area. He and Mrs. Hoover, a delightful and pleasant lady, were to spend the evening and night with Mr. and Mrs. Arthur M. Hyde at their home in Trenton. Hyde, a former governor of Missouri, had served as Secretary of Agriculture in Hoover's Cabinet.

The *News-Press* sent me to interview the Hoovers at the Hyde home. President Hoover was only six months out of the presidency. He knew he was a much-cursed man with many wrongfully blaming the Depression on him. But to me he was most gracious.

I sat with him on the sprawling porch of the Hyde cottage. What he didn't say was more relevant then than what he did say. He discussed things like the crop outlook in northwest Missouri, his long friendship with Secretary Hyde and other topics. But he said not a word about what he thought of President Franklin D. Roosevelt, who had succeeded him only six months before.

FDR was riding high. He was doing many things contrary to the thinking and ethics of Mr. Hoover, but Hoover kept silent about the New Deal and his thoughts of Roosevelt. The blasts would come later. For that moment, Mr. Hoover was being a perfect gentleman, a political rarity.

The Times They Have Changed

Newsmen and politicians weren't always at each others' throats. In fact, a vice-president of the United States once worried over this reporter's personal well-being.

He was Charles Curtis. Before being elected vice-president on the ticket with Herbert Hoover in 1928, he had represented the Kansas district just across the Missouri River in Congress.

I was interviewing Vice-President Curtis in the lobby of the Hotel Robidoux in 1932 when he campaigned here for the re-election of President Hoover. It was in the days before photographers used flash bulbs. Under the day's cumbersome system, the photographer set up his camera on a tripod, went behind it, draped a heavy black cloth over his head to keep out the light, then had someone light a match in front of the person to be photographed, got his focus from that light, and snapped the picture.

The photographer asked me to light the match in front of the vice-president's face and retired under the black cloth. Curtis quickly blew out the lighted match, muttering, "You'll burn your damn fingers."

Today newsmen and politicians often seem more likely to fan the flame than blow it out.

Whose Ox Is Being Gored?

We must cut government expenses. That is always a popular political battle cry. But doing it is always difficult.

In 1949 when I was working in Washington as executive secretary to Congressman Phil J. Welch, the Bureau of Animal Husbandry issued an order to cut its work force in St. Joseph by two inspectors. Over those two jobs Congressman Welch received more than seven hundred letters, telegrams and phone calls of complaint from stockyards and packing house interests here.

Welch heeded the complaints from his constituents and, by pulling the right strings, got an order dismissing the two inspectors rescinded.

The message was clear—then and now. Everyone wants government expenses cut—in someone else's backyard, not their own.

Ferd Frankenhoff and His Dime Fines

One of the most colorful characters that ever hit the political scene in St. Joseph was Ferd J. Frankenhoff. He got national publicity in the early 1930's when he began to assess ten cent fines in cases involving illegal possession of liquor.

The system worked this way. He would fine people $100 on the charge as required by ordinance, and then give them a stay of execution on $99.90 of the penalty. They only had to pay out ten cents.

By way of background, Ferd Frankenhoff had been a professional ballplayer, and a pretty good one in the minor leagues until he broke his leg. He was very discouraged, and the only jobs he could get were driving trucks. An Atchison boy, he came to St. Joseph and got a job driving a bread truck. He didn't waste his time. He attended the St. Joseph Law School at nights, finally earning his law degree and subsequently passing the state bar examination.

In 1928 he was elected police judge. It was quite a switch. The judge before him had been Benjamin Franklin Watson, who was a former chief of police, and a very strict individual. To give you an idea of just how strict he was, when his grandson appeared before him on a speeding charge, he told him, "Young man, the ordinary fine for speeding in this court is $15, but you're my grandson and everybody expects you to get off easy, so your fine is gonna be doubled. Your fine is $30."

Frankenhoff was not that severe. He believed in giving everyone a break. In those days, almost everyone who came before the police judge was very poor. Frankenhoff started out by giving people stays of execution on their fines, meaning they did not have to pay them. The police court clerk got tired of writing out stay of execution so many times every day, so he simplified it and just wrote "S.O.E." Jokers at the police station soon said that "S.O.E." stood for "slipped out easy."

Frankenhoff built up a tremendous personal political machine of his own by the thousands of favors he did for many people in police court. After serving in police court for three terms, he ran for circuit judge in 1934, and was elected in a hotly contested race.

Part of his campaign was based on the leniency he had shown people in the waning days of Prohibition in the early 1930's. He subscribed to a clipping service to see how much publicity his ten-cent fine got him. So many clippings kept pouring in that finally he had to tell the service to cut it out. He couldn't afford to pay for those hundreds of clippings that were coming in every week as a result of his ten-cent fines.

Judge Frankenhoff made a number of rulings in court that meant various state statutes were invalid and unconstitutional. He was very much in the news all over the state as a result of those rulings.

One time a story in the paper was critical of one of his grand jurors, saying that the jury was pressing to find out what could be done about stifling the Welfare Board. The story emphasized that one member of the grand jury had a daughter who had been discharged by the Welfare Board, and hinted of a possible personal vendetta.

Frankenhoff was furious. He called the grand jury into open court, summoned the reporter who had written the story, and castigated him in front of the grand jury for being absolutely unfair and saying that he had put some things into the paper that should not be there such as the fact that this juror had a daughter who had been fired from the Welfare Board.

The next day he would be apt to meet the reporter, and have a friendly visit and talk to him and perhaps bring him a drink. He was that way. He would blow awfully hot, and the next day would cool off and be the friendliest man you ever met.

In 1940 he ran for the Democratic nomination for governor and this should give you an idea how times have changed. His principal platform was that, if elected, he would pay older people $40 a month in Old Age Assistance. Just think what that contrasts to present figures which are so many, many times higher. Ferd's campaign could have done well but because of a lack of finances, he was defeated.

He practiced law and then he went into the Marines and played a very active role in combat in the South Pacific. He was no youngster at the time — in fact, he had served in the army in World War I twenty-five years before.

After coming back to St. Joseph following distinguished service as a Marine officer in World War II, he became a workmens' compensation referee, a post he held until shortly before his death. He was a colorful figure with a tremendous memory.

Everytime he met a person, he inquired about their family, and two or three years later, he would meet that same person, call them by name, and ask about their children, also by name! He had a great personality and he might have gone on to become a very colorful governor if he had had adequate financing. More than hundreds of dimes.

Bert Was a Triple Threat Genius

Bert Voorhees was a triple threat man. He was a sharp newspaperman who became an outstanding attorney and one of the top political leaders in Missouri.

In my early reporter days I had frequent contact with him and he was one of few people I ever knew I would unhesitatingly classify as a genius.

He was nationally recognized in whist circles and with his memory it is no wonder.

I witnessed one of his outstanding feats of memory in 1932. At that time St. Joseph had sixty-three precincts and the city political committee of each party had a man and a woman member from each precinct.

City office nominees in those days were selected at city conventions, and the delegates to those conventions were named by the city committee members. Bert's feat happened with the approach of the conventions.

The GOP committee members hadn't done their job. So Bert was called in. As courthouse reporter, I was sent to see Bert in the courthouse office of County Assessor Arthur B. Neudorff. Relying only on memory, Bert named two delegates from each of the sixty-three precincts. He knew also from memory the exact boundaries of each precinct and he knew just what Republicans lived in each precinct—and which ones could be relied upon to follow the wishes of the GOP organization with which Bert was identified.

It took him not more than two hours to name all of those delegates for appointment—and he even sprinkled in a few of the opposition factions so the convention wouldn't appear too "steamroller-ish."

That's how well Bert Voorhees knew and played politics. Not only did he know everything about Republicans here but also those in counties throughout the state. And he was an expert in keeping in touch with them.

No wonder that twice, in 1924 and 1928, Bert was chosen as chairman of the Republican State Convention, and that in 1928 he was elected Republican state chairman for Missouri—and directed the campaign that saw Herbert Hoover carry Missouri in being elected president and Henry S. Caulfield being elected governor, along with a full Republican slate of state officers.

Bert racked up another distinction that year. He was a delegate to the Republican National Convention, but he didn't vote for the nomination of Hoover. His vote, to the very end of the convention, went to Charles Evans Hughes, the famed chief justice of the United States.

A year or two after the convention, Congressman David Hopkins took Bert to the White House for a social call on President Hoover. Goodnaturedly, the President twitted Bert about being the lone delegate holding out for Hughes instead of for him. Bert did not apologize.

Bert first tasted politics as a newspaperman. When the *News-Press* was formed in 1903, he became its first political reporter. His early newspaper experience had included a stint as city editor of a Leavenworth paper. Besides writing politics here and covering the courthouse, Bert studied law in the offices of Culver and Phillip. He didn't bother to go to college to obtain his legal education, but he readily passed the state bar examination. And eventually the law firm became Culver, Phillip and Voorhees, one of the best known firms in the state.

When Bert was mentioned for state GOP chairman in 1928, it was clear that only a member of the state committee could hold that post. Bert wasn't a member, so John Schuder, cashier of the Burlington Railroad here, resigned so Bert could have his place.

Bert amply repaid the favor. He arranged for the nomination of Schuder as mayor of St. Joseph in 1930. Schuder was elected and re-elected in 1932 and 1934.

Bert Voorhees never forgot a friend.

Reporters relied upon him as a background source for hundreds of political and legal news stories. As Governor Caulfield's top man from 1929 to 1932, Bert ran the police department. There was a police board but everyone knew that Bert called the important shots. And most were glad that he did.

His greatest emphasis in politics was on one thing—loyalty. As with his memory, Bert was 100 percent on that.

John L. Raises a Little Hell

A Buchanan County courthouse official once turned down a chance for fame of a sort, deciding discretion was the better part of valor.

His name was Ben L. Arnholt and the opportunity he skipped was to fight a very angry John L. Sullivan, the great prize fighter known as the Boston Strong Boy in the years when he reigned as heavyweight champion of the world.

The time was just after the turn of the century. Sullivan, who had lost his ring title some years before, was on the road with his own stage show. John L. would box a few exhibition rounds for each show and he had a troupe of singers, dancers and a comedian.

When his act played St. Joseph, he hired a *News-Press* reporter, Bert G. Voorhees, to be his press agent and publicity man. Bert,

65

who later was to become a lawyer and chairman of the Republican State Committee, did a good job. John L. played to a packed house. However, the old champ made one error: He tried to leave town without paying Bert.

Bert went to his friend, Washington Township Constable Arnholt, and levied an attachment on the costume trunks of Sullivan and his troupe. John L. was informed at Union Passenger Station he couldn't take the trunks until he paid off Voorhees to get the attachment released.

John L. came to the courthouse. He went to the constable's office and said he wanted to "see that fellow Arnholt." He said he was going to knock Arnholt's head off.

Now Ben was no dummy. He was polite to Sullivan but did not tell him who he was. He just informed him that there was no way to release the attachments unless Voorhees' bill was paid.

John L. paid off and left town as Voorhees and Arnholt breathed sighs of relief.

What's In a Name? Ask Will

Parents sometimes can be thoughtless or at best extremely careless when naming their children. Often they don't realize the far-reaching impact and repercussions of an ill-conceived name.

A fellow George Sherman knew in the Navy constantly was the butt of cruel jokes and rude remarks in reference to his name. It was Harry Haas.

The old St. Joseph *Gazette* once had a lady printer named Clapsaddle, a source of great amusement to her co-workers, especially since printers are not best known for their diplomacy anyway. However, printers, while perhaps lacking the tact of ministers and shopkeepers, aren't dumb either. Discretion was the better part of valor where printer Clapdaddle was concerned and she functioned as efficiently as if her name had been Smith or Jones.

One St. Joseph matron who overcame the considerable handicap of her name considering her chosen avocation was Ms. A. J. Booze. Ms.Booze was a dedicated foe of alcoholic consumption in any form and so zealously did she pursue her attacks on John Barleycorn that she was elected head of the local Women's Christian Temperance Union. Subsequently, she headed that organization statewide.

A couple of professional men in St. Joseph overcame the handicap of names that tended to raise an eyebrow or two. One was an osteopathic surgeon named Dr. Bonebrake and the other was a medical doctor who did very well despite the name of Dr. Toothaker.

One dedicated St. Joseph Democrat, however, feared his name was just too much of a handicap and refused all overtures from the party and friends to be a candidate for county judge.

In those days, more than forty years ago, county judges didn't always have a sterling reputation for scrupulous honesty and since the courthouse was a Democratic stronghold, the individual in question put his party's welfare above his personal ambitions and refused to run because of his name.

He figured he would be giving the Republicans just too much ammunition if he became a candidate, even though his reputation for honesty was unblemished.

His name was Will Steele.

Coin Toss Decides Candidates

In the late 1930's and early 1940's, St. Joseph had a very smooth-running Democratic machine. The man at the helm was Mayor Phil J. Welch, who was pretty much of a genius in smoothing out disagreements and getting people to work together for the benefit of the Democratic party.

Maurice Hoffman was the prosecuting attorney of Buchanan County and planned to run for re-election in 1940. Joseph A. Sherman was the municipal judge and also was planning to run for prosecutor. Both were young and popular and a head-on battle looked inevitable as the primary loomed. It could have become vicious and harmful to Democratic unity in the fall election.

Mayor Welch wanted to avoid such an intra-party fight, so he called Hoffman, who lived just across the street from him, and Sherman to his home.

He talked cold turkey to them. "It won't be good for the party if you fellows tangle in a campaign. You both have strong political followings. I've got an idea of how we can work out this problem.

"There will be an opening this fall for the judgeship of division No. 3 of the Circuit Court. So I want you two to flip a coin. If it comes up heads, Hoffman will run for re-election and Sherman will run for circuit judge. And vice versa."

The two agreed. Hoffman lost and ran for circuit judge. Sherman won and made the race for prosecuting attorney.

Both won election by smashing majorities.

Mayor Welch had engineered a double triumph.

World's Shortest—and Best—Political Speech

As a reporter I have listened to thousands of political speeches, many of them by candidates seeking to convince the audience they were the finest examples of political ability since Thomas Jefferson, Abraham Lincoln, Theodore Roosevelt, Woodrow Wilson, John F. Kennedy, et al.

But there is only one of those speeches I can recite completely with accuracy. I heard it a number of times and on each occasion was even more impressed with it.

The man who delivered the memorable bit of oratory was Dr. H.F. Mundy, a Democrat who served several terms as coroner of Buchanan County. Each time when he was introduced as the next candidate speaker he would rise, smile and say:

"Vote for Mundy on Tuesday. Thank you."

He never lost an election.

No Pendergast Taint

As senator and thirty-third president, "Give 'em Hell, Harry" never made any bones about his connection with the powerful Kansas City political boss, Tom Pendergast, but at no time was he ever tainted by that long assocation.

Truman's loyalty to his friends was legendary. And as city editor of the Independence *Daily News*, George Sherman saw first hand the almost fanatical loyalty Truman inspired in those around him.

An Independence police officer named Mike Westwood did parttime work for the newspaper and he and Sherman had many talks about Westwood's role as a personal bodyguard for Truman whenever the president was in town. (Despite all of his Secret Service protection, Truman was aware of how much it meant to Mike, so Westwood was included in the president's security arrangements.)

"I have no doubt," Sherman said, "that Mike not only would have laid down his life for Truman but that he would have done it cheerfully and with enthusiasm."

Mike even disliked a popular joke making the rounds in the Truman era. It went something like this:

"Truman was standing in front of his mirror dressing for a state function. Gazing into the mirror, he said casually to his wife, "Bess, how many really important men do you think there are in the world today?

"'One less than you think, Harry,'" she promptly replied.

Although no one took it for more than a funny story, Mike didn't like it one bit. And there's no question that Truman managed to walk with kings without losing the common touch. Westwood tells of several occasions when Truman would see motorists stranded along the highway, would stop his motorcade and ask members of his entourage to help out. Usually, according to Westwood, the stranded motorists had no idea who their benefactor was.

Only a man of Truman's impeccable integrity, however, could have survived his Pendergast relationship. Pendergast was born in St. Joseph but did not sprout his political wings until he moved to Kansas City, where his older brother, Jim, already was a significant political figure. Young Tom quickly made his mark in the heavily Democratic North Side.

By the mid-Twenties, Tom was the political boss not only of Kansas City but also of Jackson County and was a power in state Democratic circles. In 1932 the extent of his political clout became evident. He personally selected twelve of the thirteen congressmen elected in Missouri that year. (The congressional elections were held at-large due to disagreements over the 1930 census.)

In addition, "Boss Tom" personally picked and arranged for the nomination of Francis M. Wilson as the Democratic candidate for governor. The enormity of his power was shown when Wilson died just a month before the general election. Pendergast picked little known Platte County Circuit Judge Guy B. Park, secured Park's nomination from the state Democratic committee and then saw to it that Park was elected.

Harry Truman was the beneficiary of the Pendergast power in the 1934 election when "Boss Tom" tapped the presiding judge of the Jackson County Court as his choice for United States senator. The Pendergast power carried over to 1936 when the Kansas City boss picked Lloyd C. Stark from the famed Louisiana nursery family and successfully masterminded Stark into the governor's office. Shortly after that, however, Pendergast's power began to crumble.

Truman's integrity was never more evident than when, as a member of the Senate Interstate Commerce Committee, he directed an investigation of railroad financial matters. His staff uncovered damaging evidence against many of Truman's friends in Missouri, but the senator would not use his influence to call off the investigation. If he had to make a choice between loyalty and integrity, there was no question in Truman's mind that integrity was paramount.

Subsequently, a government probe of the Pendergast machine uncovered evidence of vote fraud and questionable financial manipulations. In 1938 "Boss Tom" and more than one hundred of his colleagues were indicted for vote fraud and income tax evasion. Pendergast pleaded guilty to the tax evasion charge and, along with many of his friends, went to prison.

Truman won re-election to the Senate in 1940 totally on his own merit and without help from the crumbling Pendergast machine. In fact, in the 1940 elections the last vestiges of the Pendergast era were ousted by a reform group.

THE COURTHOUSE

And Other Arenas
of Governmental Doings
and Legislative Shenanigans

This structure, now demolished, served as the Buchanan County Jail from 1908 through 1986. It was from this jail in 1933 that a mob took Lloyd Warner and lynched him.

Glen Thomas was elected sheriff of Buchanan County after serving as chief of police of St. Joseph. He figured in solving many major crimes here and held the post of sheriff just one hundred years after it had been held by his grandfather.

(*Photos courtesy St. Joseph News-Press/Gazette*)

PART THREE

Sparta Loses to Blacksnake Hills

Replete in its architectural lines of classic beauty, the Buchanan County Courthouse must be regarded as the most intriguing historical and dramatic structure in this area. Over the years no stage, no movie lot, has topped the high drama that this courthouse has known.

Since its first days in 1874, countless thousands have gone through its doors in quest of justice and, very often, mercy. Some have emerged happy and free, their load in mind and life lightened; others have been headed for prison, and a handful sentenced to execution.

The courthouse has touched the lives of practically all who have ever resided here, in the issuance of marriage licenses, through voter registration, payment of taxes, civil suits, inheritance cases, witness and jury duty.

Few of the adults of this county have been immune to courthouse appearances. Since 1846 the block occupied by the present courthouse has been the seat of justice of Buchanan County. That there should be controversy at a courthouse is only natural and Buchanan County has always lived up to that.

Even the name of the first county seat, Benton—after one of Missouri's first United States senators—was changed in a matter of months to Sparta through the heavy influence of those pioneers here disagreeing with the policies and actions of Senator Thomas Benton. The county court made that name change.

Buchanan County was named for James Buchanan, but it received that name seventeen years before Buchanan become president of the United States.

At the time this county was named, Buchanan was our popular ambassador to Russia. People expected great things of him and

73

he lived up to those hopes by becoming president. The first Buchanan County seat of government was located in a rural area near the center of the county. There was only a very small settlement there when it was decided Sparta should be the site of the courthouse. It was at that time the name of Benton was given and quickly changed to Sparta.

The first courthouse was a log structure. It was used only a few years but it served important purposes in the educational and religious field, as well as for county business. Years later newsman Harold Slater went down to the farm on the Sparta road to the site of that original courthouse and found the remnants of the old courthouse were being used as a corn crib.

The county court had voted $6,000 for the erection of a courthouse in Sparta, but construction was never started. That was due to the fight that developed by those who wanted the courthouse moved to the more populous Blacksnake Hills, where Joseph Robidoux had founded the settlement that was to become St. Joseph. It took three elections but finally in 1846 the people decided the courthouse should be built in St. Joseph.

Joseph Robidoux donated a square block for the courthouse site, the block that is still used. His wife was unable to sign her name and so the deed conveying the land to the county is marked with her "X".

The building has served many purposes. When it was struck by the disastrous fire March 28, 1885, the courthouse contained the place of worship of the Latter Day Saints, the lecture room of the Northwestern Medical College, the concert hall of the Mendelsohn Society, a number of lawyers' offices, and even the living quarters of some attorneys.

The courthouse was rebuilt after that 1885 fire in which its dome collapsed. During the months the rebuilding project consumed, the county offices were scattered around downtown buildings.

Incidentally, the courthouse served as the county jail in 1909 while a new county jail was under construction. The prisoners were housed in the east side of the courthouse basement. There was not a single escape during the nine months prisoners were held there. The two-foot thick stone foundation walls possibly discouraged some who may have had the idea of fleeing.

Another use was found for the courthouse following the State Hospital fire in 1879. Male patients of the state hospital were kept at the courthouse for three months after the blaze.

Harold Slater took over as courthouse reporter for the *News-Press* in 1929. At that time there were still a number of Civil War veterans around the building, one of them being colorful Lyman Forgrave. Forgrave had been a Union drummer boy in the War Between the States and in the 1910's and 1920's served fourteen years as a justice of the peace of the courthouse.

He was different from most Union veterans in that he hated the Grand Army of the Republic with a vengeance. He thought it was strongly Republican. Need it be said the Lyman was a dyed-in-the-wool Democrat?

Incidentally, for some years when he was past the age of 70, Lyman still was playing the drum publicly. He was a member of a fife and drum unit that appeared at public gatherings, particularly political ones. That fife and drum corps epitomized the picturesque trio so deeply associated with the Revolutionary War.

With times tough in the Depression days, a number of men loafed about the courthouse corridors for want of something better to do. Some had wives who worked and kept them in smoking and drinking funds. A few were marriage license runners.

Here's how the "runners" worked—they would see a couple go into the county recorder's office and figure they might be obtaining a marriage license. They would approach the emerging couple, ask them if they planned to wed, and then explain they had a judge friend who would marry them immediately without all the fuss and bother of a conventional wedding.

If the couple bought the idea—and quite a few did—the "runner" would take them to a county judge or a justice of the peace to perform the ceremony. He could figure on a tip of $1 or so from the groom for his help and also expected the performing judge to give his part of his fee after the ceremony.

There is no courthouse switchboard now, but more than 70 year ago there was one until Cupid short-circuited it with one of his darts.

It happened this way: After the switchboard was installed, two of the three county judges got a crush on its female operator. They both sought to date her. Jealousy developed. When the switchboard operator become engaged to one judge, the loser prevailed upon the third judge to vote with him to remove the switchboard and leave the bride-to-be without a job. The marriage reportedly turned out to be a happy one anyway.

Speaking of the marriage ceremonies performed by the justice of the peace, several of those dignitaries had a gimmick to collect a better fee. The Missouri statutes set the fee for a marriage at $2. The groom usually didn't know that and so after the ceremony he would ask the justice, "How much do I owe you?" Those justices of a scheming nature would answer, "Give me what you think she is worth to you." Expressed that way, even the cheapest groom would come up with $5.

Slater happened to be on hand for the unique marriage ceremony by a justice while checking records in his courthouse basement courtroom. The justice was in the middle of the ceremony when a boy about 12 entered carrying a box of ice cream bars, Cheerios.

The justice frowned and gave a negative shake of this head. The boy then asked the bride and groom if they wanted a Cheerio. The groom graciously offered to buy a Cheerio for her. She said "No thanks" but the groom bought one for himself and stood there with it melting in his hand as the justice completed the ceremony.

Recalling an exceptional act of thoughtfulness: Duckworth Tootle, scion of one of the best known and most prosperous families in the history of St. Joseph, liked chicken fighting. He made no secret of it.

In 1931, Walter Powell, also well known locally as a chicken fighter authority, was arrested on a charge of murder by conspiracy. He was taken to the county jail and ordered held without bond.

The arrest of Powell saddened Duckworth, so he decided to do something to make Powell's stay in jail easier. On the north side of Faraon Street, directly across the street from the jail, was a ramshackle brick barn that was a remnant of the days when the Tootle Home was an imposing house on that block.

Duckworth got hold of several roosters, established them in that barn, and saw to it they were fed and watered daily. His sole idea was that the crowing of the roosters each morning might cheer up Powell, his fellow chicken fighter. It probably did, but Powell eventually got out of jail on bond, was tried and acquitted, and probably was forever grateful to the thoughtful Duckworth.

Our nominee for the most considerate man: More than 40 years ago, each of the 12 townships in Buchanan County was entitled by statute to elect a justice of the peace.

Those justices in the 11 rural townships received no pay, no expense allowances. They were entitled to fees if any cases were filed in their courts but such cases were rare. Often justices served a full four-year term without having a case brought before them. That is why some township people regarded the office as a joke and elected men to it who were held in comedy esteem in the neighborhood. Finally, one of those rural justices got a highly important case. It involved a former presiding judge of the county who had been charged with jury tampering.

The case went to to rural justice on a change of venue from a justice court in St. Joseph. The case was of such importance the *News-Press* looked into the background of the rural justice. It turned out it was the first case filed in his court in more than three years.

A news story pointed out the justice several times had been arrested, mostly for peace disturbances, but one time for being found in a bawdy house. He had pleaded guilty to that charge and had been fined.

The justice was incensed when he came to the courthouse the next day, and called on the reporter whose byline had been on the story. He wanted to know why the story had been published. He was informed it was a matter of public record. Then he explained, "Let me tell you the truth about that. The two policemen arrested me there, but I wasn't guilty. I was just down at that place to see a friend. I wasn't guilty but I'll tell you why I entered that guilty plea. If I hadn't pleaded guilty, it sure would have embarrased those two policemen who arrested me, and they're pretty nice fellows." P.S. When the hearing was held the justice ruled the former presiding judge was not guilty.

Two major things are missing at the Buchanan County courthouse. One is the inquest into the death of Jesse James and the other, surprisingly, is the cornerstone of the courthouse, laid with full ceremony the afternoon of August 20, 1873.

The report on the inquest into the death of Jesse James disappeared from a courthouse file more than 50 years ago. It was beautifully written in longhand and was enclosed in a heavy brown paper cover. Over many years it was a curio that was shown to the courthouse visitors. Someday it may emerge from its hiding place, and when it does, it undoubtedly will become a collector's item that will attract high bidding.

The newspapers of the day gave full coverage, columns of it, to the ceremony that marked the laying of the cornerstone of what the described as the most magnificent structure west of the Mississippi River.

The papers told how Rosenblatt's brass band led the ceremonial procession to the courthouse site. They listed the fraternal groups that took part in the festivities, gave a full account of the speeches and mentioned the articles that were placed in the cornerstone ranging from a 1738 German coin to cards of the various business houses. But the stories failed to state just where the cornerstone was.

Over the years there have been numerous quests to locate the missing stone, with a tenacity reminiscent of those who sought the Holy Grail. Officials have had excavations made along various segments of the walls of the impressive structure.

Two late officials, Presiding Judge Jake Neighbor and Circuit Judge Sam Wilcox, spent many hours in painstaking research and among other things, sought Masonic records that might reveal just where the ceremonial stone was located. All to no avail.

Scribe Slater's fifty-plus year love affair with the courthouse has never wavered, lasting even well into his retirement. The veteran newsman still spends two or three days a week at the scene of some of his most memorable journalistic experiences.

However, not all of Slater's courthouse time is spent commiserating with cronies over coffee about "the good old days." In fact, to paraphrase a popular slogan about country boys, law enforcement officials may have taken gambling away from the courthouse gang, but they haven't succeeded in taking the courthouse gang away from gambling.

The story-behind-the-story on those regular courthouse visits is that Slater and his pals like to compare notes on how they are doing in the Missouri and other lotteries!

A Couple of Courthouse Characters

Over the years, the Buchanan County courthouse has produced perhaps more than its share of characters. Many of them are mentioned throughout the pages of this book.

Two others reporter Slater recalls vivedly were the "courthouse bootlegger" and the "courthouse magician".

It was 1929 and Prohibition still was the law of the land, but that didn't keep Cyclone Thompson from doing business almost at the doorstep of the county jail. Some of his best customers were deputy sheriffs.

Cyclone was an unusual little fellow and carried his illegal booze in a market basket covered by potatoes, turnips and onions. He went through the building on a regular route. He didn't hawk his wares but he didn't need to. Everyone knew who he was, what he was selling and the price. (It was a dollar a pint, a healthy price for those days.)

Mysterious Carson was an out-of-work magician who would pick up an occasional dollar by demonstrating how he could free himself after being locked in the sheriff's vault. Later Slater learned his secret. Mysterious Carson had a very flexible screwdriver, without a handle, that was hidden in his belt.

Both men were regular "fixtures" around the courthouse in those days and it would have worried courthouse patrons, including the sheriff's deputies, if either of them failed to show up.

Times were different in those days. Everyone was touched in one way or another by the Depression and though times were tough, the atmosphere was less strained than today and the prevailing philosophy was more one of "live and let live".

Occasionally, however, the county court would decide to run the moochers out of the county building by having them arrested as vagrants, which they practically all were. On one such occasion the first victim was "Crooked-Neck" Clark, whose head due to an accident was bent over one shoulder so that he looked like a crippled bird.

Crooked-Neck was arrested and hustled before a justice of the peace. He pleaded guilty before Justice Maurice Mason and was sentenced to three days in jail. Clark was undismayed and even put the bite on the judge right there in court, and replied, "Judge, would you like to let me have a couple of cigarettes?" Irritated that Clark hadn't gotten the message, the judge gave Clark an additional two days in jail. Crooked-Neck just grunted.

Before the Civil War, slaves often had been sold at auction on the lawn at the courthouse site, with members of the county assessor's staff inside placing taxable valuations of them just as they did on horses, cattle, sheep and hogs.

Over the many years, the Buchanan County courthouse has been the source of literally millions of stories, a variety of the humorous, the joyous and the sad. Naturally, many of those stories provided laughs.

One day a doctor failed to appear as a scheduled witness in a circuit court trial. The judge was upset. He called a deputy sheriff before the bench and handed him a subpoena for the missing doctor. He emphasized it was an order to bring the doctor into court.

The deputy returned in half an hour; there was no doctor with him, and the impatient judge wanted to know why. "Judge," reported the deputy, "I couldn't bring Doctor Thompson to court. He's sick in bed with a trained nurse." The judge grinned and thanked the deputy.

Yes, the courthouse is a great kaleidoscope of life, a constant flowing stream of action, the great marketplace of intrigue and involvement in so many different forms of human endeavor.

It is the great silver movie screen over which flickers much of the life of this community.

Jimmy McGreevy figured in a courthouse classic close to 75 years ago. Jimmy was a feisty little saloon keeper who was a power of sorts in Democratic politics. His saloon was at Fifth and Francis Streets but most of his political muscle was in the South Side.

The Democrats were holding a county convention at the courthouse and witty and colorful Mike Moran was to preside; McGreevy was there in force. He had leased two street cars for the evening to bring his cohorts from the South Side to the county building in order to control the convention, and add greater luster to the name of McGreevy.

McGreevy was all over the convention floor, objecting to rulings by Moran, declaring his own political beliefs, and trying to tell the convention what it should be doing. He talked loudly and rather roughly. He made one mistake though. He got near the bench where Moran was presiding. Mike did the unexpected. He picked up the speaker's pitcher of ice water and, surprisingly poured its contents over the head of McGreevy, proclaiming, "I baptize thee, Jimmy McGreevy, a little troublemaker."

McGreevy reportedly was quiet during the remainder of the convention session. Mike Moran had created a legend that was to live as long as any man at that meeting was to keep breathing.

Moran, who had served in the Missouri State Senate, was an outstanding orator. His knowledge of the law was not considered great by his peers, but they admitted that when it came to convincing oratory in the courtroom or on the political stump, Mike had no equal in this entire area. Mike had one major fault. He drank considerably—very, very considerably.

Politician Produces a Piano "Duet"

Every courthouse has its store of legends and one of those in Buchanan County is what might be called "The Piano That Went Astray."

The event happened many years before I became courthouse reporter in 1929. It involved a highly popular county official who was married but who happened to have a very demanding girl friend. When Christmas time rolled around she told him she would be satisfied with nothing less than a piano as his Christmas gift to her.

He acquiesced, went to a music store and left precise instructions. He explained the bill for the piano must be sent to his office and that the piano must be delivered to the home of his girl friend. Under no circumstances, he emphasized, should either the piano or the bill be sent to his home.

Unfortunately there was a mix-up. When he arrived home Christmas Eve, a new piano graced his living room, and his wife was waiting for him with a plethora of questions.

"Why," she interrogated, "did you buy us a piano? Neither one of us plays nor do our sons. Have you ever heard of either of them saying they wanted to become piano players?"

Now in politics quick thinking is a must, and this particular official rose to the occasion. "Why, darling," he said, "this piano is a beautiful piece of furniture, and I thought it would add so much to the beauty of our home."

They kept the piano; the official had to go to the expense of buying another for his girl friend. Part of the legend was that this time he rode out on the truck with the piano to make certain it was left at the right place.

Naturally, the whole story leaked out at the courthouse and

folks there were still relating it years later when I was courthouse reporter.

The episode had one side effect; it gave the poor fellow a nickname. You've guessed it. It was Paderewski.

The Penalty for Kissing a Felon

Twice while courthouse reporter, I covered weddings performed in the county jail, both of parties who were in the jail as a result of felonies.

At one wedding, the bride had a black eye. She explained to the officiating minister that one of her cellmates had become unhappy with her that morning and had tossed her head-first into a bathtub, thus explaining the darkened orb.

The other jail wedding united a man under sentence for burglary and a woman who had been sentenced on a narcotics charge. Incidentally, it was the second time the groom had been married in jail. Maybe he found the atmosphere especially romantic.

The bride had formerly operated her own bordello and her name was about as well known as that of the mayor. The wedding was performed by a justice of the peace who at the conclusion of the ceremony kissed the bride. I reported the kiss in my newspaper account of the wedding. I'm not sure the society editor would have done it.

The justice of the peace was waiting for me when I showed up bright and smiling at the courthouse the following morning. He wasn't bright and smiling. He was wrathful.

"I didn't get a minute of sleep last night after your story," the justice fumed. "My wife kept asking me all night why I kissed that dreaded woman. She wouldn't believe my story that as the officiating authority I was required under the law to do that. She's never going to forget it and it's all your fault."

I told him the next time he had a jail wedding I wouldn't mention that he kissed the bride, but my promise didn't pacify him. He shouted he would never again kiss any bride!

One Way to Convince a Jury

William C. Cole was a practicing lawyer here who first was elected to Congress in 1942. He tried many cases and had a highly unusual experience in one of them.

He was representing a well-known policy writer charged with first degree murder in the stabbing death of a popular gambler in a cigar store-card room at 711 Edmond Street. An argument that erupted while the victim was in a 25-cent rummy game brought on the tragedy.

The policy writer had gone to a nearby restaurant and taken a boning knife used on hams. The knife driven into the victim's chest snipped off a main artery leading to the heart.

Cole argued for his client that the stabbing was accidental. The knife was thin and razor sharp. In his demonstration to the jury in an effort to prove the stabbing was accidental, Cole cut himself accidentally on the leg during the course of his argument.

His pants leg was cut and he suffered a gash on the thigh. Court was adjourned so Cole could go to the hospital for treatment and also have a chance to get another pair of pants.

The jury bought part of Cole's argument. It found the defendant guilty of manslaughter, not murder, and he got off with a year in jail.

Cole always argued that his own wounding was entirely accidental.

Owen Even Convinced His Clients

Probably the most colorful of the attorneys who was practicing at the St. Joseph bar in the era of the 1930's and up to about 1942 was Stephen K. Owen.

Stephen K. Owen was most famous for his defense tactics in criminal cases. He won scores of victories. In 1942, he was elected probate judge and he served in that capacity until his death in 1960.

Steve was primarily a showman. Some of the cases that he defended brought surprising verdicts. I still remember one murder case in which the state thought it had an air-tight case against a fellow accused of murdering his wife, but that was before Steve made his argument to the jury.

When the jury came in with a verdict of not guilty, the defendant was so surprised that he fainted dead away.

You had to see Steve in action to really appreciate him. One thing it seems, in looking back, is that his clients always had mothers. The mother would be sitting in the courtroom, close to the counsel table, probably in the first row of the spectator section.

These mothers ran to a type. They were tiny, grey headed ladies. They wore black hats, and usually black shawls. They had on very plain clothes, and they kept dabbing their eyes with handkerchiefs all during the trial.

Then Steve would get up and make his final plea to the jury. He was a tremendous cross-examiner and he would get his points across tellingly for a final summation. He would tell the jury:

"Members of the jury, you are led into that jury room, and a lot of people are waiting to hear your knock on the door...waiting for the time for you to come out and say what your verdict is. I'll be waiting and my client, the defendant, will be waiting. That little woman will be waiting (pointing to the mother in the spectator section, who was dabbing her eyes at double speed). She wants to hear that knock on the door, hoping that you will come out and say that her boy is not guilty. She wants her boy to go home with her and have supper with her tonight. I think, in the interest of justice, that you will bring in that verdict of not guilty. That is the right thing to do, and it will mean so much to my client, and to his dear little mother."

About that time, Steve would be a little overcome and he would dab his own eyes a bit. The jury would retire, and surprisingly, a number of times, the verdict was "not guilty".

I would like to tell another story about Steve Owen. Over in the county jail one night, they brought a fellow in who was accused of a couple of hold-ups. He told his cellmate that he needed a top flight attorney because he was in a bad jam. The cellmate happened to be George Neff, who was one of the leading burglars in St. Joseph.

George Neff told the fellow that he needed Steven Owen, because he was the best. Neff said, "I'll tell you how good he is. The last time that he defended me, when he got through talking to the jury, I thought I was innocent." No lawyer ever received a better recommendation!

Escapes from the Escape-Proof Jail

A bottle of black shoe polish was the only "tool" used by one man to escape from the old Buchanan County jail, "moth-balled" in 1987 after seventy-eight years.

Another man who escaped from that jail paid for a few weeks' freedom by the loss of both feet to freezing and eventually his life in the electric chair of the state of Georgia.

They are among the forty-one men who escaped from the jail, which had been in use nineteen years before the first escape in 1928. No woman ever escaped from that 1909 vintage jail, which was sold to the county with a guarantee it was escape-proof. It wasn't, but every man who escaped eventually was recaptured.

It was while George Moran was sheriff fifty years ago that an accused young forger with flaming red hair used the liquid shoe polish for a successful hair color transformation. A jail trusty, he got into his street clothes after dying his hair, mingled with a group of high school youngsters being given a tour of the jail, and walked out with them undetected. He was nabbed in Brookfield, Missouri a few days later.

Charles Coates, under a life sentence here for robberies, was the leader of a group of four that escaped from the jail in November, 1940, after threatening to kill the night jailer, elderly Cam Hillix. Coates' robbery spree here came to an end after he was arrested for a holdup at the McMichael drug store at 33rd and Mitchell Avenue.

Earlier he had escaped from two other Missouri jails and a state prison and had been a major trouble maker during his stay in the jail here.

Coates fled from here to Memphis, Tennessee, where he married a girl, and then went on to Georgia. He killed a Georgia state highway trooper who stopped him for a driving violation. An intensive manhunt resulted and Coates, starving and nearly frozen, was tracked down in the Georgia mountains on Christmas Day. It was necessary to amputate his frozen feet. He had to be carried into the courtroom in a chair but the jury gave no sympathy. It decreed death and, after four reprieves, Coates was carried to the electric chair in May, 1942.

Some unusual weapons have been used in the escapes from the jail. One thug got his freedom after threatening to cut the throat of a night jailer with a sickle. Why would there be a grass sickle in a county jail? It was in a storage room there for use by trusties who trimmed the courthouse lawn.

Incidentally, the fellow who made the first escape in 1928 wasn't timid in talking about it. He was in jail on a burglary charge at the time but later became a good and useful citizen. He was a very thin fellow. His theory was that he could squeeze his body through any opening he could get his head through.

To make his escape he sawed out only one ten-inch bar in his tier. That made an opening about ten by eight inches. The prisoners in the tier with him were very cooperative. They helped him by soaping down his body and literally pushing his slippery torso through the opening. They then tossed his clothing out to him. He climbed the tall jail fence and was free — for about six days.

A bit of history: The 1909 vintage jail was built on the site of another old jail. While construction was going on, the state, county and city prisoners were kept in the basement of the courthouse. Otto Theisen, who was sheriff in that year, 1909, was intensely proud later of the fact no prisoner escaped from that substitute jail. He admitted that the two-foot thick rock foundation walls of the courthouse probably discouraged any prisoner who had an idea of breaking out.

Surprise Witness Helps Convict Rapist

One of ths most unusual cases I covered as courthouse reporter was a rape trial in which the only corroborating witness was a mile from the scene of the attack.

The attacker had not selected a romantic spot. He assaulted the young girl on the top of the sewer inlet into the Missouri River. The location was north of Mitchell Avenue.

The trial boiled down to the victim's word against that of the defendant. The state then produced as a surprise witness the attendant who had been on duty on the Grand Island bridge a mile away. He had watched the attack through a pair of strong binoculars and he testified how the girl had attempted to fight off the attack.

The jury found the defendant guilty and assessed a three-year prison sentence.

Local Trial Inspires Hollywood Classic

For a city of its relatively small size, St. Joseph over the years has had more than its share of clever and able attorneys, both on the side of the prosecution as well as those representing the accused.

Perhaps the most novel and certainly the most dramatic defense ever devised by a lawyer for a client was the brainchild of Bart M. Lockwood, a former city counselor, former assistant prosecuting attorney (it was he who filed the murder charge against his former co-worker, Prosecutor Oscar McDaniel) and earlier a criminal defense lawyer. Bart was well versed in the law, had a flair for the dramatic and the ingenious mind that some lawmen believe is a hallmark of anyone successful in the legal profession.

In the early 1900's Bart was defending a woman accused of poisoning her husband. The state had presented a comparatively strong case and included in the evidence displayed on a table in the courtroom was a bottle, purportedly containing the exact poison found in the victim's body. The bottle had be introduced by the state as a key piece of evidence in the case.

Bart cleverly set the stage for what was to become one of the most dramatic scenes ever witnessed in a courtroom. He questioned witnesses closely and obtained positive statements that yes, the bottle contained the very poison which caused the victim's death. Once that fact was firmly implanted in the minds of the jurors with ample corroborating testimony, Bart strode to the evidence table, picked up the poison bottle and with a flourish, drank the contents!

There was a moment of shock-induced silence in the courtroom, then a murmur of voices and finally a babble of excited commentary, causing the judge to bang his gavel for silence. Without missing a beat, Bart turned back to the jurors and continued his argument for the defense. Bart's concluding statement was "...that couldn't have been poison this defendant used or I wouldn't have swallowed it!" It didn't take the jurors long to bring back a verdict of "not guilty."

Bart was never accused, officially at least, of any sleight-of-hand with the poison bottle, but the story-behind-the-story is that somehow he had learned that a police evidence officer had switched bottles because he thought the actual poison might be dangerous to leave around. I am convinced that Bart was tipped off to the switch, but no proof ever surfaced.

The story made headlines all over the country and although Bart didn't get any screen credits, the incident became the cornerstone for a key episode thirty years later in the Edward G. Robinson film entitled, "Illegal."

Typically, the movie version was even more theatrical. In the Hollywood scenario, Robinson played the role of a crooked criminal lawyer in a poisoning case and actually drank the poison. As it turns out, he successfully gambled on a quick verdict and had hospital attendants waiting nearby with a stomach pump.

Dr. Gleason's First (and Last) House Call

Not unlike similar seats of government in towns and cities across this great country, the Buchanan County courthouse was a popular gathering place for loafers, ne'er-do-wells and just plain characters.

Two of the perennials who graced the spacious, murky halls of the massive old structure were known as Hal and Gleason. The "Laurel and Hardy" type twosome (Gleason was a big friendly guy with buck teeth and perpetual grin and Hal was of only average size) were courthouse regulars.

Gleason would work if it walked up and tapped him on the shoulder, but that hadn't happened in quite a while. Hal was more fortunate. He had a wife who worked. She gave Hal forty cents a day spending money. Everyone at the courthouse knew about it and was aware of exactly how it was spent. Hal would eat a quarter lunch at the Buffalo Saloon and with the remaining fifteen cents he would purchase three large, important looking cigars. Obviously at a nickel apiece they weren't exactly of Cuban vintage.

One afternoon when they were putting their heads together trying to figure out a way to get a little beverage money, Hal had an inspiration. His wife was sick and couldn't go to work. He figured it was just a cold, so he turned to Gleason and said, "Gleason, have you still got your good Sunday suit?"

Gleason did and Hal revealed his plan. "Look," he said, "I've got an idea. My wife doesn't know you and she's sick. I'll tell her tonight that I've got a close friend who is a doctor and I'll say that because of our friendship my doctor friend will make a house call and charge only four dollars. I'll tell her my doctor friend will examine her and find out what's wrong."

Gleason was a willing conspirator. "When can we do it?"

"Tomorrow," Hal replied.

At his home the next day, Hal introduced Gleason to his ailing wife as " . . . a very distinguished surgeon and physician. He will examine you and find out what's wrong, but my love, I've got to have four dollars to pay him because he only works on a cash basis."

"Go over to my purse," his wife said, "Take four dollars out and give it to him."

Gleason wasted no time getting at his task. "All right, young lady," he said in his best bedside manner, "I'll have to examine you."

As Gleason is looking in her throat and checking her pulse, Hal's wife says she's feeling a bit faint and will have to lie down, which as far as Gleason was concerned, is just what the doctor ordered.

By this time, Hal has figured out that Gleason's examination, intensive touching and probing is going far beyond the bounds of medical propriety and he decides that Gleason is just fooling around. One word leads to another and before long the two bosom companions and co-conspirators are engaging in fisticuffs, not a very dignified thing for a 'distinguished physician and surgeon' to be doing with his patient lying just a few feet away.

The fray got so out of hand that neighbors called police. Both Hal and "Doctor" Gleason were arrested and taken to city court where an unsympathetic judge fined them both for disturbing the peace.

Guess who came up with the cash to bail the villains out? It was Hal's ever-loving wife, who had recuperated enough to come to court.

County Judges "Scalp" Buffalo Bill

Oldtimers always ranked William F. "Buffalo Bill" Cody as one of the most distinguished callers at the courthouse.

The oldtimers would recall how Buffalo Bill would come to the courthouse to get his show and parade license each time he brought his circus here. He didn't walk into the courthouse; he thundered in wearing his big hat and buckskin coat and trousers.

His routine would begin as soon as he entered the front door:

"Where are those dirty, train-robbing county judges? I know they'll try to hold me up again on the license charges and their demands for circus passes. They ought to hang all the county judges here."

The oldtimers said he was no less vitriolic as he thundered his way out of the county building, shouting he had been held up by the county court once again and that he was never coming back.

But he came back each year as long as his circus was on the road and each year he provided a delightful show in reciting what he claimed to be the evil doings of the county judges.

At that time, which was before 1915, Buffalo Bill was said to be the best known man in the world as his circus had played abroad, including Europe, and in all parts of the United States.

And that long, flowing white hair made him a man who once seen was never forgotten. I know; I saw him once in a circus parade.

A Tragic Killing Ends Happily

This is a story of murder followed by a romance that flowered in the jail.

Nearly half a century ago, St. Joseph had two sister prostitutes who were among the best known members of their trade here. Sometimes each operated her own bawdy house; other times they worked out of the same abode. The mother was living with one of the daughters.

One night the daughter lost her temper and beat her mother to death with a brick. Their home was just a block off the South Sixth Street Tenderloin district. Police investigating the death said the brick-wielding daughter was too drunk to make a coherent statement. They filed a murder charge against her and sent her to the county jail.

At the trial, the defendant took the witness stand to picture herself as a devoted daughter who had only kindness and love for her mother with never a thought of violence. Her attorney explained to the jury that the mother became ill that night and that the devoted daughter who stood accused had been helping her to the bathroom when the mother fell accidentally and struck her head on a brick doorstop.

The prosecutor pointed out that the dear old lady must have fallen against that brick twenty-five or thirty times to sustain all her fatal injuries. The jury voted a ten-year prison term for the daughter. The members had not been impressed by the defense lawyer who claimed "Everyone loved this dear old lady, no one would hurt her, especially not her own daughter." No amount of oratory could alter the fact the mother was struck numerous times.

The story-behind-the-story is that while in jail awaiting trial the daughter met a jail visitor and fell in love with him. Although sentenced to ten years in prison, they married anyway and he waited for her.

It's doubtful, however, that they kept a framed picture of Mom resting on the mantle.

A Libber Before Her Time

Long before ERA or women's liberation jumped onto the front pages and the evening television news screens, Buchanan County had a woman sheriff. I was a courthouse reporter at the time. I covered her period in office and she did a good job. It happened this way:

Sheriff Otto Theisen died in December of 1934. The county court named his widow, Mary, to serve as interim sheriff before ordering an election to be held early in February of 1935. She did not run in the special election, although her friends urged her to do so.

Sheriff Mary showed that a woman could handle the job as well as any man. She had good deputies and used good judgment. She was simply a darn good sheriff.

Or sheriff-ess, as she might be called today.

Ada Topped 'em All

One of the most unusual prisoners that I knew when I was courthouse reporter was a lady named Ada Roberts. Ada ran a chicken dinner place on South Twenty-second Street and she was in jail for violations of the Prohibition laws. Ada served liquor with her chicken dinners. As a matter of fact, Ada served a lot of liquor *without* chicken dinners.

Ada didn't waste her time in jail. She had a sewing machine in her cell and she made hats—big, floppy women's hats. By the time Ada got out of jail, almost every deputy sheriff's wife was wearing one of those hats.

She was a hard act to top.

Mike Made the Grade and Called the Shots

For years Mike Costello was just about as much a part of the county building as its dome.

Mike was a road contractor and, coincidentally, his brother was married to the sister of Tom Pendergast, the Kansas City Democratic boss. Mike was a big, friendly fellow, with a cigar always plunked in his face. He did much of the road grading for the county and was liberal in giving jobs to perennial drunks in his road grading camps.

Costello, a staunch Democrat, got the road work, regardless of which party was in power. A newsman once started a story with, "County courts may come and go, but Mike Costello always makes the grade."

Mike's outpost was the first floor juncture of the first floor corridors. Once he explained, "Standing right here, I can see the sheriff's office, the treasurer's office and the county court bench. I know everything going on that I want to know about."

Apparently, what he saw he translated into political muscle. After one election he named all but two of the new sheriff's deputies—and the new sheriff was a Republican.

Legislative Shenanigans

Humor, someone has said, is life exaggerated. And I found that a sense of it helped understand the workings of legislative bodies and their members.

When I was covering the 1941 and 1943 sessions of the Missouri General Assembly a representative from the Ozarks, deep in the heart of Missouri, was the subject of most conversations in the Capitol halls and the local watering holes in Jefferson City. His name was Browning, and someone had convinced him that one way to make a name in the Legislature was to vote against every bill that came up. So he did.

If a bill had come up to declare Labor Day a holiday, he would have voted against it. If someone had brought up a bill to order the raising of the United States flag on the Fourth of July, he would have voted against it. In fact, Browning even voted against a bill to pay his own salary—obviously radical behavior for any elected representative of the people.

Likewise obviously, his service in the Legislature was brief. In a way, that was too bad, because Browning certainly was colorful. He was a good little fellow who had a bizarre idea. Some of his friends even had cards printed: "The Browning for Governor Club." But Browning disappeared back into the Ozark hills and his dream of becoming governor went down the drain—and the cards became collector's items around Jefferson City.

Incidentally, one of the most unusual bills during that time was introduced by a man from St. Joseph, Paul Turner. The bill would have made it a misdemeanor for women to wear open-toed shoes. Not surprisingly, the bill did not even get to a committee.

That is one of the blessings of our legislative system. Many of the bills die in the pipeline.

No Place to Pin a Badge

While covering sessions of the Missouri General Assembly in the Forties, I listened one night to testimony at a committee hearing on a bill to legalize nudism in Missouri, to permit the operation of nudist camps and farms.

One witness hailed from deep southern Missouri. Nudism, he said, was a wonderful thing. He had practiced it for many years, he was held in high respect in his community and many of his closest friends were nudists.

"The home folks think this much of me," he said. "I have been elected to the town board, I have been a member of the school board and right now I'm deputy sheriff of my home county."

An elderly legislator from the Ozarks spoke up. "Sir," he said, "you say you are a nudist and a deputy sheriff. I want to know one thing: Where do you pin your badge?"

The roar of laughter from the committee drowned any answer—and chances for passage of the bill.

FBI Agent Richard Martin, acting on co-workers' information, uncovered the body of six-year-old Bobby Greenlease.

Chief of Police Edward C. Burke thought the Greenlease investigation should have been continued to find out what became of Tom Marsh.
(*Photo courtesy of Joan Stokes*)

ON THE DARK SIDE

The Warner Mob Killing, the Greenlease Murder, a Gallows Tripleheader and Other Cases

Weather Forecast
Fair and warmer tonight
with a low of 47.
Complete Forecast on Page 2

ST. JOSEPH NEWS-PRESS

CITY EDITION

VOL. 76, NO. 247   ST. JOSEPH, MO., WEDNESDAY EVENING, OCTOBER 7, 1953   28 PAGES   FIVE CENTS

Body of Kidnaped Greenlease Child Is Found in St. Joseph

Greenlease Home Called From Here

However, Youth Who Phoned Not Implicated

About 7 a. m. Friday Chief of Detectives Verne V. Starmer received information a call had just been placed to the Greenlease home in Kansas City from a telephone booth in the Robidoux Hotel, source of the information cannot be divulged.

Chief Starmer along with Detectives Hannibal Morrison and Harry Hopkins went to the hotel and found a young Negro youth beside the booth.

The officers questioned the lad and he told them he had seen a middle aged man come out of the booth and leave with a red-haired woman. The officers took the youth in a squad car and made a check of the hotels in an effort to locate the pair. When they were unable to do so the boy was brought to the police station where he was questioned further by Chief Starmer.

Admitted Making Call

Then the boy changed his story and admitted he had placed the call. He said he did not know where the Greenlease boy was but he and some friends were talking about it, and he decided to make

The body of Bobby Greenlease was found in the shallow grave, marked by a shovel handle, near the center of picture. House is at 12 01 South 38th street. Men in the picture are FBI agents. (More pictures on page 7)

Tattoos May   **Spending Spree**   **Says State**

Shallow Grave on South 38th Street

Two Arrested in St. Louis, One a St. Joseph Woman

Maryville Man Shot at Heady Home

Many Complaints on Activities There

Sheriff C. A. Jenkins and his deputies have received complaints for the last few months about activities at the home of Mrs. Bonnie Heady, 1201 South Thirty-eighth street, the woman in the Greenlease kidnaping case.

A man reputedly was shot there on May 30. He was a Maryville, Mo., man and was shot in the hand. Sheriff's Deputies Lloyd Cole and Jack Stamp where he told a story of a round of drinking which ended when a woman at the house drew a revolver from a dresser drawer and shot him in the hand. He was treated at Missouri Methodist Hospital but declined to prosecute.

FBI Makes Announcement

Boy's Parents Had Paid Ransom of $600,000 Last Sunday

(BULLETIN)

Only one bullet wound was found in the body of Bobby Greenlease during the preliminary part of the autopsy this afternoon at the Meierhoffer Funeral home. Dr. Edward I. DeMott was making the autopsy with Dr. H. F. Woods, coroner.

By HAROLD M. SLATER

The body of kidnaped Bobby Greenlease of Kansas City was found in a shallow grave in St. Joseph this morning.

FBI agents found the body in the yard at 1201 South 38th street.

The body had been buried in a plastic bag with lime. The six-year-old boy had been murdered.

A confession of the kidnaping was obtained from two persons arrested at St. Louis, one of them a St. Joseph woman, Mrs. Bonnie Emily Heady, 11, of the 1201 South 38th street address.

The new grave had been disguised as a flower bed. The body had been buried in a plastic body with lime, the purpose being to eat up the flesh.

PART FOUR

The Greenlease Murder

It was one of the world's most heinous crimes, the biggest news story I ever covered and it had a casual beginning.

It was October 7, 1953; I was city editor of the *News-Press* and was home on vacation. My wife, Marguerite, and I were reading when a friend, Emma Sidenfaden Byrne, called to say she had heard on Kansas City television that the body of kidnapped Bobby Greenlease had been found in the yard at 1201 South 38th Street in St. Joseph.

Newspapers and broadcasts had been humming with stories about the Greenlease case since Bobby, age six, had been kidnapped from a Kansas City school on September 28, 1953. Ransom negotiations and possible clues had been headlined worldwide.

The address where the body had been found was only a mile and a half from my home. I told the *News-Press* office I would go to the grave site and cover the story.

The yard in which the body was found was the home of Bonnie Brown Heady. I knew of her from her square dance club publicity in the days before she was divorced a couple of years earlier. She was short and dumpy, a pudgy five-foot-three or so. She was dark-haired and not given to smiling.

Little Bobby's body was still in the grave, covered with the blue plastic in which he had been buried along with a quantity of quick lime. A crowd had gathered around the house and deputy sheriffs were on duty to keep out all except those with official business.

At the grave in a flower bed I learned the details: Mrs. Heady, 41, and an ex-convict named Carl Austin Hall had been arrested in St. Louis, had admitted the murder and the ransom had been recovered. The ransom actually was $600,000. It turned out, only half had been recovered, the rest stolen in St. Louis after Hall's arrest.

I went to the *News-Press* office, wrote the story, then went to the funeral home where positive identification was made of the Greenlease boy by a dental chart. After that I returned to the Heady home, by then swarming with FBI agents and other officials. Chief Deputy Sheriff Lloyd Cole, a long-time friend, was guarding the gate. He warned me I might get ordered out but gave me some advice. "Keep quiet. Keep your coat on. There are so many FBI men here they don't know who they all are. They may think you are one of them," Cole said.

When I went to the Heady home that morning I noticed almost a full case of Old Stag whiskey on a kitchen table. But the souvenir hunters had been there by that afternoon and only two fifths remained.

The FBI was fingerprinting and checking everything in the house, even the paneled recreation room on the second floor where Mrs. Heady and her then husband on occasion had entertained their square dance club.

Deputy Cole let my son, Robert, and two of his college classmates tour the house before the FBI put an absolute clamp on all visiting.

Hall had sprinkled lime into the grave to hasten the deterioration of the boy's body. The prize boxer dog owned by Mrs. Heady nosed his way into the earth and got into enough of the lime that it burned his mouth and caused his death.

The investigation of the crime was as intense as any crime probe ever made in this community. State murder and kidnapping charges had been expected but when it developed Hall and Heady also had taken the boy over the Kansas state line to kill him, federal charges were filed. The pair had been in jail in St. Louis and were brought to the Jackson County jail in Kansas City to await trial.

I was present in court in Kansas City early in November when Hall and Heady pleaded guilty to the federal charges. Judge Albert L. Reeves, a brilliant jurist near eighty years old, ordered that a jury be impaneled November 16 for a trial to determine if their punishment should be death or imprisonment.

Mrs. Heady, once a sales clerk in several women's wear shops in downtown St. Joseph, told people at the Jackson County jail she wanted to be executed "instead of spending my life working in some penitentiary laundry."

The federal court trial that started November 16 drew a vast array of top journalists from the United States and some from Europe. Famed Bob Considine was at the press table, but the most famous person was Thomas Hart Benton. The great muralist had been retained by *Life* magazine to produce drawings of the proceedings. Judge Reeves had forbidden any cameras in the courtroom.

Bonnie had short legs and she looked uncomfortable as she sat at the defense table with her feet dangling a full six inches above the floor. She had met Carl Austin Hall in a bar at the Hotel Robidoux four months before they had carried out the heinous crime. Hall had infatuated her. He went home with her that night and lived with her until the murder was committed. He told her of making plans to acquire a lot of money so they could live in a luxurious life style. She had been drinking heavily and fell into his scheme although she did not know at first that it included murder. She finally agreed even to killing the child.

No crime ever was more cold-bloodedly planned. The afternoon of the day before the abduction, Hall had spaded up the flower bed at 1201 South 38th Street where the body was buried. Earlier he had purchased flower plants to disguise the grave. Also, he had bought the quick lime. He was leaving nothing to chance.

He had decided by a mathematical formula to set the ransom at $600,000, then a record ransom sum. He believed eighty-five pounds was as much weight as he could carry handily in a duffel bag. Then he determined that $600,000 in ten and twenty dollar bills would weigh eighty-five pounds.

Hall was the son of a wealthy Kansan living in the southern part of the state. On his father's death, Hall inherited more than $200,000. He was wild and a big spender who enjoyed showing off his money. An example: once when he was told that a major Kansas City hotel was filled and could take no more guests, he showed off to a friend by going to the desk clerk and telling him, "I just bet fifty dollars you could get a room for me. My friend here called that bet and said you couldn't. You get me that room and I'll give you the fifty dollars." The clerk suddenly found an available room.

After Hall wasted away his inheritance, he held up a Kansas City cab driver. For that he received a five-year term in the Missouri state penitentiary.

In prison he began to think of a scheme for getting rich through a kidnapping. Before deciding on Bobby Greenlease as his victim, he had considered kidnapping the boy's older sister, Virginia

Sue, then about sixteen. But he decided she could be difficult to abduct and might make a scene that could bring his arrest even as he was kidnapping her. So he elected to take the boy instead.

Hall and Heady had several drinks at a bar the morning they drove to Kansas City to commit the crime. Because the plan involved calling at a convent school to get custody of the boy, Hall purchased breath sweetener mints so the nun who answered the door would not smell liquor on Bonnie's breath.

The two had driven to Kansas City several times to learn the routine of the Greenlease family, including exactly the time when Bobby would be taken to the exclusive private school known as the French Institute of Notre Dame de Sion.

On the day of the abduction, Hall parked Bonnie's station wagon on a drug store lot, then had Bonnie taken to the convent school in a cab. She told the nun who came to the door that she was a sister of Mrs. Greenlease, that Mrs. Greenlease had suffered a heart attack and they wanted Bobby to be with her.

Before leaving Bonnie, the nun suggested she step into the school chapel to say prayers for the recovery of Mrs. Greenlease. Bonnie was in that chapel about four or five minutes before the little boy was brought to her and they drove away in the cab that was waiting outside. One wonders what was going through the mind of Mrs. Heady as she carried out her continuing role in that vicious crime while waiting in a chapel.

Bobby was talkative as he rode in the cab with Bonnie and later in the station wagon in which he was taken into Kansas. Hall had procured a rope with which to strangle the boy, but when it turned out to be too short, he killed Bobby by firing several shots into his head. Bonnie said she didn't want to see the boy killed, so walked away from the car while Hall performed the murder. He had blood on his shirt and coat when he came back to Bonnie.

The cruel and conniving Hall had convinced Bonnie before the kidnapping that it would be necessary to kill young Greenlease. Otherwise he might be able to identify them or provide clues leading to their arrest.

After murdering Bobby they drove to a saloon in North Kansas City and had some drinks. Bonnie meanwhile had helped Carl lift the body into the station wagon and cover it with the sheet of blue plastic. Also, she had helped wipe the blood from Hall's face and hands, then turned his coat inside out after he removed it so no one would see the blood on it.

They drove back to St. Joseph and buried the body in Bonnie's back yard. Originally, Hall had planned to drop the body into the Missouri River, but he abandoned that idea after deciding the body might surface and be found before they could collect the ransom. Before they buried Bobby, they removed a religious medal from his body for use in a ransom note proving their authenticity as the kidnappers.

Hall went back to Kansas City that afternoon to mail the ransom note. Back home, he and Bonnie watched television for a report on the kidnapping. But the channel they watched did not carry the story that night. That surprised them.

When they went to a greenhouse to purchase chrysanthemums they specified only blooming plants. That was to allay suspicion by any passerby who might notice the fresh grave.

Bonnie was drinking more and more. That, she said later, was an effort to placate her conscience as she realized more and more what a horrible thing they had done.

After sending a series of ransom notes with their demands, Hall picked up the $600,000 ransom where it had been dropped in a duffel bag along a lonely Jackson County road. He and Bonnie drove on to St. Louis, where Hall rented an apartment, installed Bonnie there, then went out on a spree around town.

He kept the cab driver with him as he spent money recklessly, then had the cabbie procure a prostitute to be his companion as they painted the town red. The cab driver saw the money Hall had and tipped off a friend, Police Lieutenant Louis Shoulders.

At that time there had been no news stories about the $600,000 ransom having been paid. Shoulders thought Hall had been in some black marketing, possibly in the motor car field, and started investigating.

Shoulders and an aide arrested Hall, got a confession from him and took Bonnie into custody at the apartment where the ransom was stashed. Shoulders was a national hero for a few days when it was announced that he had solved the kidnapping and murder and supposedly turned in the ransom. His status fell to that of bum shortly afterwards, however, when it was learned that $300,000 of the ransom was gone.

Shoulders denied guilt but the probe that followed resulted in Shoulders drawing a three-year federal prison sentence for perjury. His police officer companion drew a two-year perjury sentence.

Ironically, under present interpretation of the law, Hall probably could not have been convicted. That was because Shoulders in a St. Louis jail used third degree methods in wringing the confession from him. One thing he did to get Hall to talk was to bang his head repeatedly against the bars of his cell.

The great part of the missing $300,000 never showed up. As years passed though, it became rather generally known that Shoulders had passed that $300,000 on to a shady acquaintance in the rackets at St. Louis. That character knew how to "launder" the money and get it circulated without personal detection.

When the investigation first started, Richard Martin, an FBI agent in St. Joseph, drew a dangerous and frightening assignment. It was about three o'clock in the morning when his FBI superiors called him at home, told him to go to the Heady home at 1201 South 38th Street, break in and wait for a phone call.

At that time Hall had been saying that a fellow named Tom Marsh, well known to police here as a derelict drifter, actually was the man who murdered young Greenlease. When Martin, later to become a state legislator and municipal judge here, pried open a window to gain entrance to the Heady home, he had to realize that Marsh might be waiting in the house or that some neighbor seeing someone forcing their way into the house might shoot him.

Martin sat by the telephone and waited several hours before he was instructed to go to the back yard, to dig into the flower bed and see if there was something in it encased in a sheet of blue plastic. Thus, he was the person who actually found the body of the victim of the vicious murder.

Bonnie, a chubby and matron-like person, displayed practically no interest during the trial as the federal prosecutor built an air-tight case against her and Hall. The murderers offered no defense. The only hope of their attorneys was to try for lengthy prison terms rather than the death penalty. Neither Bonnie nor Hall paid much attention to what their attorneys were doing in trying to save their lives. Bonnie professed to be deeply in love with Hall and said that was the only reason she went along with him on the crime foray.

The jury was out for an hour before it returned its verdict of death. Bonnie smiled. Hall seemed to be trying to look repentant. Judge Reeves sentenced them to be executed on December 18 in the gas chamber of the Missouri state penitentiary at Jefferson City.

The gas chamber at the Missouri penitentiary contains two harsh metal chairs. Bonnie and Hall sat side by side as they waited for the pellets to set off the lethal gas. They were permitted to exchange a kiss and Bonnie renewed her request that they be buried together. But that was not to be.

Hall's body was buried in southern Kansas in the area in which he grew up. Bonnie was buried at the Clearmont, Missouri, cemetery in the Nodaway County area that had been her girlhood home. It was a bleak December morning when Bonnie was taken from a Maryville mortuary to the cemetery.

It was the only funeral I ever attended to which admission was restricted to those who had passes signed by an attorney. Authorities thought there might be a great outpouring of the curious, but there wasn't. The people had been sickened by the cruel tragedy and wanted to do nothing as much as forget Heady and Hall.

As a precaution against crowds showing up, a heavy piece of road equipment had been placed across the road leading to the cemetery. It wasn't needed. Only a few newsmen and a scattering of chilly people showed up. There was no service. Two of the newsmen were pressed into service to help carry the casket to the side of the grave that had been dug. No one seemingly had even thought of having pallbearers.

But one great mystery still remains: what happened to Thomas Marsh?

When Hall first was arrested he insisted that Thomas Marsh actually had fired the fatal shots into Bobby's head. When he changed his story and said he alone had fired those shots, he insisted that he had never known a Thomas Marsh and that he had given that name as a spontaneous thought. "I just picked the name out of the thin air in trying to pin the murder on a fall guy," Hall told authorities.

But despite his disavowal of ever knowing a Thomas Marsh, it seems highly likely that Hall did know him. Marsh was serving time in the Missouri state penitentiary at the same time Hall was serving his robbery sentence and some police officers theorized that Hall and Marsh had engaged in criminal activities together after release from prison.

Marsh was well known to St. Joseph police. He was a wino and petty criminal, a derelict who drifted mostly between the Skid Row of Kansas City and the similar area here.

Just a few days before the Greenlease murder was uncovered, police here and in Kansas City could have picked up Marsh in a few minutes any time they needed him. Since the day Hall first tried to blame the murder on Marsh, however, not a trace of him has been found. It is as if he were swallowed up by earth. Fifteen years after Hall and Heady were arrested, the father of Marsh said he hadn't heard from him since. Other relatives claimed the same.

Marsh would not be an easy man to disguise or escape detection. He was almost a roaming gallery of tattooes. On his left shoulder he had a tattoo of a skull and crossed bones, a small heart was tattooed at the base of his left thumb; there was a dagger entwined with a snake on his left forearm, three chain links with the initials F.L.I. on his right forearm, and a large cross inscribed, "In memory of sister" on his inner right arm.

The late Chief of Police Edward C. Burke held to the theory that Hall had killed Marsh after a crime series to keep him from testifying against him in the event of arrest. Burke theorized that Hall might have disposed of Marsh's body in an abandoned mine shaft in southeast Kansas, an area with which Hall was well acquainted.

Burke always felt that Hall should have been questioned more about Marsh. He felt that when the authorities solved the big crime they pretty much lost interest in Thomas Marsh. That, he often said, was too bad.

Following her arrest, Bonnie told people at the Jackson County jail that Carl Hall intended to marry her. She said the wedding was to be October 12, 1953, in Chicago. Bonnie, however, was probably dreadfully wrong about Hall's intentions.

Arvid Owsley, who was sheriff of Jackson County at the time, talked at length with his prisoner, Hall. He said that Hall was very tired of his drunken paramour and that sometime after collecting the ransom his plan was to kill Bonnie and cut her body into pieces. Hall told Owsley that he had purchased two garbage cans into which to place the dismembered body and planned to bury those cans and contents near a small stream in St. Louis County.

In my entire life I never felt as sorry for anyone as for the little nun of the French Institute of Notre Dame de Sion who had turned Bobby over to the deceitful Bonnie. That nun was a witness at the Hall-Heady trial. She was sweet, demure and crushed. But she told her story in a way that proved her great character and inward strength. Tears were in the eyes of most of the people in that federal courtroom at Kansas City as the tiny nun, clothed in the habit of her order, told how Bonnie had deceived her into believing she was Mrs. Greenlease's sister. When she left the witness stand, those in the courtroom witnessed one of the greatest and most admirable examples of charity, compassion, consideration and thoughtfulness they will ever see.

Mrs. Greenlease, beautiful mother of Bobby, walked up to the nun, put her arm around her shoulder and told her not to blame herself in any way for the tragedy. She told the nun that if Bonnie's plan hadn't worked that day, the abductors would have found some other way to get hold of her son.

Mr. Greenlease, the father, told an interviewer after the verdict, "Death is to good for them but that is all the law allows."

The criminally clever Hall had insisted that the ransom money be from all twelve of the Federal Reserve districts. Bank employees who assembled the money for the payoff worked all night to list the numbers on the bills, but their work paid practically no dividend. How many people were going to check the number of each ten or twenty dollar bill they received? Few ever turned up.

An amazing sidelight of the Greenlease case was the speed with which justice acted. Hall and Heady died in the gas chamber in ten days less than three months from the day they kidnapped and murdered the boy. In contrast, the last case in Buchanan County in which the defendant paid the supreme penalty lingered in the courts for four and one-half years before the death in the gas chamber.

Another sidelight of the tragedy was the near frantic search that was conducted one night in the alumni office of Northwest Missouri State College, now Northwest Missouri State University. A woman who worked in that office told me that notices had been prepared around the first week of October, 1953, to send to all alumni and other former students inviting them to be honor guests at the homecoming football game at Maryville.

After Bonnie Brown Heady was arrested and charged with the crime, someone happened to think that one of those invitations probably was addressed to her. So the search was made to locate the letter. One can easily imagine the fear of the college authorities that the invitation might be delivered to Bonnie in the Jackson County jail and how the news story would develop to report she was invited to be an honored guest. The letter never got to Bonnie.

And so the books were closed on Heady and Hall, a sordid and sickening saga of the very worst in human behavior.

A Fitting Epitaph

Being among the few media representatives on friendly terms with Prosecuting Attorney John Downs, George Sherman and a St. Louis *Post-Dispatch* reporter were two of the first people admitted into Bonnie Heady's home after the FBI agents had finished.

It was a small home, Sherman recalls, but neat and clean. The bed was made and a pair of Carl Austin Hall's pajamas lay across the bedspread just as though he would be wearing them that evening. The only hint that he might not return was a travel timetable on a bedside stand.

The most notable feature of the home was a top floor, paneled recreation room, resplendent with a large and well-stocked bar. (Mrs. Heady's liquor dealer claimed she consumed two fifths a day.)

The FBI had been typically thorough, fingerprinting every possible place, even the walls where someone might have put a hand. A stack of wood was in the basement and apparently the agents had examined each stick.

One rumor, never verified, was that the agents had found a "black book" with the names of several prominent citizens who had been "guests" in the home along with some of Mrs. Heady's female friends. Most media representatives discounted the story. There was some indication, however, that pornographic materials had been found in a desk in the living room.

Mrs. Heady must have had a real passion for shoes. Her closet was literally filled with them. Her dressing table contained numerous bottles of what appeared to be expensive perfumes along with the usual powders, creams and lotions.

The most striking item in the home, however, from Sherman's point of view, was a trophy that one of Mrs. Heady's prize Boxer dogs apparently had won at a dog show. Sherman thought the inscription more appropriate for the owner than the dog. It read:

"Perfect Bitch of 1953."

A Night of Infamy

It was a night of horror, a night of community disgrace, a shame that will endure through many years. It was a return to the law of the uncivilized jungle.

I am referring to the night of November 28, 1933, when a young black man, Lloyd Warner, was taken from the Buchanan County jail, beaten, stabbed repeatedly and the body then set on fire. I was at the jail, on assignment to cover the event which many knew was certain to occur. Warner had been charged with raping a young white woman.

I couldn't turn off the thoughts that night as I waited in the front office of the county jail. As a newsman I realized, overpoweringly, that a major story—although a highly tragic one—was breaking and was to be covered.

But as I saw the mob and heard its roars, I thought this was akin to what led to Calvary and the Crucifixion of Christ. It was a demand for blood, an unjustifiable demand. Perhaps my thoughts also should have been attuned to the Constitution of the United States and the fact that one man's guaranteed rights were being stripped away.

But here was a story to be reported.

That morning I had been in Division No. 3 of Circuit Court when Lloyd Warner was brought before Judge J.V. Gaddy to face a charge of rape. He pleaded guilty at that arraignment. After the plea was entered, some technical questions were raised, due in part to the fact that the state might ask for the death penalty. Because of that, the plea was left standing temporarily and Warner was taken back to the county jail.

Early that afternoon talk was heard around town that a mob might storm the county jail to take Warner away from the sheriff and deal him "summary justice." Editor Arthur V. Burrowes heard the talk and asked me to go to the jail that evening and stay there as long as necessary if anything occurred. He told me he might be sending me on a wild goose chase and expressed the fervent hope that he was. He did want the paper protected if there was to be a major news story. There was nothing in the paper that evening about the mob talk, but there was a front page story about Warner pleading guilty and sentencing being delayed.

As darkness began to fall a crowd began gathering near the entrance to the jail. The jail was immediately behind the two-story sheriff's residence and was of matching red brick. There was a little alcove about ten feet across the main door to the jail and entry was through a storm door on the alcove. There was a brick wall directly across from the jail door. There was an open space straight across from the jail door with the brick wall forming sort of an arch over it.

The weather was against justice that night. It was a mild fall night, close to shirt sleeve weather. Undoubtedly most of the people who gathered around the jail wouldn't have been there had the weather been cold, blustery, or otherwise unpleasant.

The first group around the jail apparently was made up only of folks who thought of themselves simply as sightseers. They chatted, laughed and joked. But the crowd grew quickly. Within an hour after dusk there were between 1,000 and 1,500 people milling about and talk of mob action began to circulate loudly.

That night I saw first hand the tragic phenomenon a mob can produce. I saw ordinarly mild men suddenly decide, in the presence of a mob, that they were leaders. No one before had paid them much attention but now they, in ignorance, took on the mantle of spokesmen of the crowd.

I remember particularly three. One was a middle-aged dishwasher at a restaurant on lower Edmond Street. Another was an ordinarily peaceful street car conductor. On duty he had difficulty getting action when he ordered his streetcar passengers to "Step up front in the aisle. Make way for the oncoming passengers." But it was different that night. When he spoke of violence, many in the mob were ready to heed his words.

The third person I remember was a young fellow who was almost pathetic. He made his living by selling apples on the street for a nickel or a dime apiece. That night he was shouting for action and declaring "Our women must be protected." Later he was to serve a prison term himself for rape.

It was close to eight o' clock when a small self-appointed delegation from the mob came to the front door of the jail and demanded to see the sheriff, insisting he must turn the prisoner over to them. Sheriff Otto Theisen came to the jail door. Sheriff Theisen was a stocky little Dutchman with a round, friendly face and still a few locks of gray hair. As a young man he had a reputation for being handy with his fists, but he had mellowed and now was peaceful and friendly to all. He'd buy you a drink or give you anything he had.

He told them that Warner was not in the jail and offered to let a delegation into the jail to make a search for Warner. The three or four men making the demand weren't buying that. They said they wanted Warner and that if the sheriff didn't turn him over to them they were going to break in and take him.

Outsiders would have had a hard time locating Warner. The jail staff had him in an ideal location for hiding. Between the jail tiers on each floor there was a narrow passageway to permit workmen to enter to make repairs. A solid steel door, heavily locked, is at the only entrance to that passageway. That door is narrow, considerably above ground level and almost unnoticeable. Warner had been placed in a passageway as soon as the first segments of the mob gathered. He was handcuffed to a plumbing pipe.

The request for the prisoner refused, the mob grew noisier and more threatening. The early good spirits and conviviality vanished. The cry for blood was loud. A harried man facing tough problems, Sheriff Theisen asked me to call the governor of Missouri for him and request him to call out the National Guard to help.

I knew Governor Guy B. Park well. I had covered his election campaign just a year before. I reached him by phone at the Mansion that night. The governor told me he would call out the National Guard and also ask the Missouri State Highway Patrol to assist the sheriff.

The tank unit of the National Guard responded to the governor's order. It sent two tanks to the jail in the hope the mob could be dispersed. But the Guard efforts were futile. The mob wouldn't even let the guardsmen get out of the tanks. When the men tried to open the doors at the top of the tank to get out, the mob wouldn't let them. They crashed down those lids as soon as they were opened. The guardsmen sat there in frustration, prisoners in their own tanks.

The front door of the jail was in a difficult position to be defended. That heavy brick portico made it impossible for a tank to get within eight feet of the door.

Sheriff Theisen had a few tear gas bombs in the jail. He had deputies throw them into the mob, but the bombs were old and some didn't go off. Someone in the mob noticed one of the bombs hadn't gone off. He picked up the sputtering gas shell and tossed it back into the jail office. The fumes of that bomb drove those in the jail office—the sheriff, some deputies, some policemen, a few firemen and two reporters—back into the center area of the jail.

I returned a few minutes later planning to use the phone in the jail office to let my wife know what was going on. As I crouched behind a steel filing cabinet to make the call, I heard a ping over my head. A deputy sheriff shouted, "Someone out there is shooting, get out of that office." I set what must be a Guinness record for speed in evacuating a county jail office.

Separating the center section of the jail from the office was a solid steel door at least a half-inch thick. I doubt the mob could ever have gotten through that door. But it tried. A log chain was attached to the heavy iron front door of the jail and, using a Chevrolet truck for power, the mob tore that door from its moorings. Some razing work had been going on at the grounds of the old Tootle home directly north of the jail and some members of the mob found an iron pole, once the center pole of a circular fire escape, and used it to batter away at the heavy steel door behind which officials and others in the jail had sought protection. With that sturdy iron pole, a few men made a deep dent in the steel door. But it held.

There was bedlam in the jail. In addition to Warner, there were eleven other black prisoners in the jail that night. Those blacks weere fearful of what might happen to them once the mob got into the jail. They feared the mob would make no distinction, that they might lynch any or all of them. The white prisoners were equally disturbed, fearing the mob also might grab them.

Blacks were shouting, "Give him up. Think of the rest of us. They might lynch us. Give him up." The whites in the jail joined in with similar pleas.

The jail population was in an uproar. About 10:45 that night Sheriff Theisen conferred with other officers in the jail and said he had made a decision. It was to give Warner to the mob. A deputy sheriff took Warner from his hiding place and brought him down to the center section of the jail. Warner knew what was going on. He pleaded for a chance to be heard.

I talked to him and asked him if he had attacked the white girl. He said he had not, that it was all a terrible mistake.

Theisen explained he was surrendering Warner for the sake of the safety of the other blacks in the jail. He said it boiled down to "one or many".

A deputy sheriff noticed that the handcuffs still were on Warner and commented the cuffs were worth something like fourteen dollars. So the cuffs were removed before Warner was turned over to the mob and led out into Faraon Street at the side of the jail.

Someone shouted, "Let's take him out to near 21st and Francis Streets where he attacked the girl and hang him there." Others seemed to agree, but instead Warner was led down one block to Fifth and Jule Streets. On that single block trek I thought of how much this mob action was like what had happened nearly 2,000 years before when the executioners took over Christ.

I kept as close as I could to Warner on that walk because I had a story to cover and did not want to miss anything. As Warner started out an unidentified man drove an ice pick repeatedly into his back. Warner slumped and was practically being dragged along when he was taken to the southeast corner of Fifth and Jule Streets to a tree in front of the Dr. A. V. Banes building.

Someone produced a rope and Warner was strung up. Somebody came up with a bucket of gasoline and sloshed it over Warner's body. A lighted match was tossed and the body—Warner was apparently already dead—was ablaze. Tossing that gasoline was a foolhardy thing as well as a very cruel deed, for the flaming gasoline might have caused severe burns to many on hand, even though some of them probably deserved such a thing. The excess gas ran down the Fifth Street gutter toward Francis Street as the body of Warner burned to a crisp.

The crowd started drifting away, many of its members probably ashamed of what had happened and realizing they were guilty themselves of the crime for merely having been present.

The body was cut down and left in the street until a black undertaker arrived and took it away for eventual burial in the city cemetery.

A terrible and tragic chapter in the history of St. Joseph was written that night.

There was an immediate uproar by the citizens of St. Joseph. Possibly among those who cried the loudest for something to be done to ease the disgrace to the reputation of the city were some who had stood by and watched the tragedy unfold to its dreadful conclusion. Undoubtedly many of them realized, but didn't want to admit, that they had been members of that mob.

The people demanded an investigation. Attorney General Roy McKittrick ordered one of his assistants from St. Joseph, William Orr Sawyers, to head up that probe. Assisted by Chief of Detectives John T. Duncan and other members of the police department, Sawyers questioned many about what had happened in the jail that night.

Judge J. V. Gaddy also moved into action. He summoned a county grand jury especially to investigate the lynching. The grand jury too interviewed scores of witnesses before returning its indictments. Twice I was called by the jury as a witness. Identification of mob members was sought. The grand jury definitely was out to indict and witnesses had to be sure and careful not to put uninvolved persons into jeopardy.

The first man to go on trial for murder as a result of an indictment of the grand jury was Walter Garton, a dish washer at a cheap restaurant who on the night of the lynching suddenly thought he had acquired a magical gift of leadership. It had been Garton who had attached the long chain that was used to pull out the iron front door of the jail. He was a pitiful sort of fellow and sat through the court proceedings as if he were in a daze and didn't really know what was going on. The courtroom was jammed each day for the Garton trial. The chief defense attorney was William Meyer, who had achieved his law degree while serving as head of the ROTC here.

The defense argued that Garton was no more guilty than other members of the mob who had not been charged. The jury accepted that argument. It found Garton not guilty. A lot of people probably breathed a sigh of relief, for their clergymen had told them that as observing members of the mob, they were just as guilty as those who engaged in the action.

Undoubtedly, the jury took into consideration the physical appearance and mental aspects of Garton. He just didn't appear to be rational and the situation he was in drew sympathy. After he was acquitted, Garton was sent to a state mental institution at Anamosa, Iowa. I never heard of him again. He was the only person to be brought to trial on a murder charge over the lynching The other murder indictments were dismissed.

One of the major side tragedies of that night was the manner in which mob members played havoc with the home of Sheriff Theisen adjoining the jail. The furnishings were ripped up, the piano scratched and scarred, paintings slashed and many things of value stolen by idiots who thought they were gathering souvenirs. The home was left a shambles. Even a lace tablecloth was cut into pieces by those who wanted "just one souvenir of that night of horror."

The young man who sold apples on the street to make a living stole Sheriff Theisen's revolver from the home. He drew a jail term for that. Later that same self-proclaimed defender of the rights of women was found guilty of raping a girl. The crime was the same with which Warner had been charged, but for him justice was more lenient. He drew a two-year penitentiary sentence.

During the Garton trial I was saddled with a most unpleasant duty. Prosecuting Attorney Frank L. Kirtley called me as a witness. Then, while interrogating me, he asked me to step down from the witness chair and place my hand on the shoulder of the man who had attached the log chain to the jail door. I had no choice. I put my hand on the shoulder of Garton, feeling very sorry for him in realizing he was a fellow who wasn't very smart and had been the victim of circumstances.

The acquittal of Garton ended the only legal action over the heinous lynching. But the stigma lingered on.

They Paid the Final Price

They herded us together at four thirty that morning in a large and dreary, white-washed room in the old Jackson County jail, a room garishly illuminated by a series of bare light bulbs, including those clustered around the gallows. There, an hour and a half later, I was to witness my first legal executions. Three young men were to be hanged simultaneously for one of the most spectacular murders and bank robberies in the history of Kansas City.

The execution date was July 25, 1930—a distant date, yet the memory of it remains crystal clear. For ninety minutes some two hundred witnesses stood in that somber death chamber awaiting the springing of the trap at precisely six o'clock. There were no chairs, no benches, not even something to lean on. The instructions for witnesses were explicit; be there no later than four thirty. It was a wait in solemn silence; no one had much to say.

The doomed men were Tony "Lollypop" Mangaricina, John Messino and Carl Nasello. They had been convicted of the death of Police Officer Happy Smith during their wild flight by motor car from the robbery of the Home Trust Bank. Happy Smith was the traffic patrolman on Twelfth Street at the Hotel Muehlebach corner. He was one of the best known and most popular members of the Kansas City police force.

What made their crimes even more sensational was that they occurred while the Republican National Convention was in session in Kansas City nominating Herbert C. Hoover for president. A blast of machine gun fire from the car of the fleeing robbers had cut down Happy Smith and injured others. But even as he fell, mortally wounded, Happy Smith performed his final bit of police duty. His revolver shot smashed the windshield of the bank robbers and made their car careen against another.

That sideswipe provided the clue that eventually brought the men in the car to the gallows. In the collision, the door handle from the criminal car was broken off. The serial number inside that handle led to the identification of the murderers' car and of those in it. The robbery-murder had taken place in the summer of 1928. There had been a trial and numerous appeals, including one just six hours before the triple hanging.

The jail in which the hanging took place was at Fifth and Cherry Streets, adjoining the old Jackson County Courthouse. The gallows had been erected with the trap at floor level from the death cell. Mangaricino, Messino and Nasello were led directly out from the death cells, with no need for the customary thirteen steps. The handsome trio wore dark trousers and white shirts and were shackled with the usual death harness locked around them. Deputy sheriffs and a Catholic priest walked out to the trap with the doomed men. The three nooses were only about eighteen inches apart as only a single trap about four feet long was being used. The men exchanged their final words as they stood stomach to back in close formation. They gave each other their final goodbyes, with two saying, "So long, Lollypop." They had claimed to be innocent.

Sheriff Jefferson Smedley conducted the executions. Maximum security had been provided for there was fear that a major demonstration might erupt in the area of the jail.

About twenty minutes after the trap loudly slammed the three were pronounced dead. The crowd drifted silently out of the gallows room. Leaving the jail, they saw large flat bed trucks loaded down with floral pieces, including one especially large one designed as a huge clock with its floral hand set at a few minutes after six, the time of the hanging.

Altogether I covered more than twenty legal executions, other hangings at the Jackson County jail, a hanging at Fulton,

Missouri, several at the Kansas State Penitentiary at Lansing, and a number in the gas chamber of the Missouri State Penitentiary at Jefferson City.

At one hanging in the old Jackson County jail I heard a fervent plea by a rabbi seeking to halt the execution of a young slayer of a policeman. Dramatically and emotionally, the rabbi said the doomed man was mentally unbalanced and not responsible. The noose had already been adjusted around the victim's neck as that plea concluded. The plea failed and the hangman's trap clanked open.

Another remembered hanging at that old Jackson County jail was of a man named Kaufmann. He had run a newspaper ad for a housekeeper and when a young girl applied he raped her and then murdered her. The murder was committed in Swope Park. Kaufmann put on an insanity act on the gallows. He told the spectators that he was the Son of God and that they were allowing one of the greatest crimes of all times if they did not demand that his execution be halted. No one paid any attention.

At a Kansas City execution of the slayer of a young girl, the uncle of the girl victim presented a disturbing factor as the execution time neared. He had his admission card as an official witness and he showed up staggering drunk and in stocking feet. He had spent the night in bars, seemingly as a very good customer, and it was now six in the morning. In a loud voice, he went about the chamber emphasizing two things. One, that he was the girl's uncle. Two, that he had lost this shoes someplace during his convivial night and that he sure would like to find out where they were. Otherwise, the execution proceeded without incident.

At the Lansing penitentiary I was present as a newsman when one of the handsomest men I have ever seen was hanged in a big warehouse for the murder of his wife and two children. The family members were found dead in a trailer home that burned at Troy, Kansas. The husband-father said he had been out of town when the fire occurred. There was a great show of sympathy for him for a few days before officials got a tip that resulted in a full investigation revealing the three had been killed in the trailer before it was set on fire.

That tip came from a St. Joseph doctor, whom he had talked to about having an abortion performed. The probe brought out evidence that the man had a girl friend and that he had wanted to do away with his wife so he could marry the girl friend. One of the incriminating bits of evidence was the picture of the girl friend he was carrying in his wallet when arrested for investigation.

117

He died on the gallows without uttering a word when given the opportunity to talk. When he was told he could have anything he wanted for his final meal, he elected to take Polish sausage.

At another execution at the Lansing prison, a priest prayed on the scaffold with the doomed man. Then he placed a crucifix in his hand. Minutes later, when that hand was cold in death, the priest at the foot of the gallows removed the crucifix.

By far the most dramatic execution I ever covered was that of George McKeever, who was hanged at Fulton, Missouri, December 18, 1936. It was one of the last executions by hanging in Missouri as the following year the state law was changed so that all legal executions were in the gas chamber of the Missouri State Penitentiary at Jefferson City. Before the law changed, deaths were by hanging in the county in which the conviction was secured.

McKeever and another man had shot and killed Sergeant Ben Booth of the Missouri State Highway Patrol and Sheriff Roger Wilson of Boone County when the officers had stopped them on a main highway in Columbia to question them about a Kansas City murder. Sergeant Booth was the first member of the Missouri Patrol to be killed in the line of duty.

McKeever was tough and arrogant. He had spent two years on Death Row in the Jefferson City prison during the appeals that resulted in this death sentence being confirmed by the Missouri Supreme Court. He was a bitter, snarling man when he was brought from the state prison to a holding cell in a Fulton city building. When they searched him there even to his shoes, he grumbled, "What's wrong with you guys? You think I've got bombs in my shoes?"

Fulton hadn't had a legal execution since before the Civil War when a woman slave was hanged for the murder of her master. Consequently, officials had to take some unusual steps to prepare for the execution of McKeever. They acquired a two-story barn near the edge of the town, literally sawed off one end of the structure and then built a gallows with the traditional thirteen steps near the open end of the building. It was there in a heavy snowstorm that McKeever, wearing a little cap, was hanged at six that morning.

The sheriff, an elderly man, became violently ill that morning and was unable to conduct the hanging. So he deputized Colonel Marvin Casteel of St. Joseph, commander of the State Highway Patrol, to carry out the death decree. It wasn't a pleasant duty for the colonel, but he was a man who never allowed unpleasantness to interfere with duty.

The night before the hanging Colonel Casteel had several conversations with McKeever in the holding cell. It had been so little used that one had to walk over a pile of coal in the basement to reach it.

McKeever told Colonel Casteel that he was worried that he might be buried in the shabby manner of a pauper. Casteel told him that wasn't so, that they had purchased a nice casket for him. McKeever said he wouldn't believe that until he saw it. The colonel was an unusually considerate fellow. He had McKeever manacled, placed in a patrol car, and then took him to the furniture store where the casket had been purchased.

It was past closing time at night, but someone let the group in and McKeever got to see the casket. He picked up the pillow in it, held it against his face and said, "It feels real good." Ten hours later his head was to lie on that pillow in death.

Back at the holdover cell, McKeever decided to help the patrol to clear up a number of crimes. He sat with Casteel in a far corner of the cell and listed a number of robberies and burglaries of which he had personal knowledge. But to others McKeever still was bitter in his talk. He showed his contempt for the proceedings by urinating as the sheriff was carrying out his mandatory duty of reading the death warrant to him.

Later that night just outside that cell I heard the most powerful sermon of my life for the need for repentance. A young priest from St. Joseph, the Reverend Francis Barry, was chaplain of the State Highway Patrol. He was at the death cell that night as part of his duty. A big and friendly man, Father Barry broke the ice of McKeever's tough behavior and talked earnestly to him.

"George," he told him, "I'm going to offer you the cheapest and best insurance policy that anyone ever had the opportunity to accept. I ask only that you repent and make your peace with God after expressing your sorrow for any crimes you have committed and asking Divine forgiveness. What you do in the few hours of life you have left could be the most important in your life. If offers you a chance for salvation. Think it over, George, for this is a chance that will never come your way again."

McKeever bought the idea. State troopers and other peace officers backed away from the immediate cell area so Father Barry could baptize McKeever and then hear his confession. Only God knows how much good McKeever's repentance did.

Invitations, almost as formal as those for weddings, were issued for the execution. A canvas fence about twelve feet high had been erected around the open end of the barn that contained the gallows. It served no purpose. Those without the invitations just crawled under the canvas and a number of young boys were among those who saw George McKeever hanged.

The first man I saw executed in the gas chamber at Jefferson City was little Adam Richetti, the tough running mate of the notorious gangster "Pretty Boy" Floyd. That was in 1937 when the gas chamber was brand new, a huge barrel-like metal cylinder with its two chairs for the condemned awaiting the fatal fumes.

Richetti was executed for his role in the infamous Union Station gangland massacre in Kansas City, a crime in which Floyd also had played a major role. Floyd was shot dead in a Midwestern farm as he tried to crawl under a henhouse to avoid capture by the lawmen who had moved in on him.

Spectators looked into the gas chamber through small glass windows as pellets dropped into a crock of acid to produce the fumes that bring death. Richetti put on an insanity act in his last-minute effort to escape death. He fought for life until his very last breath, trying to blow away from his nostrils the poisonous fumes that had begun to swirl around him. Suddenly, his head dropped. He had paid the price.

A highly dramatic night at the Missouri State Penitentiary was when Oscar Ralph Ashworth, kidnapper of a twelve-year-old girl, technically came within eleven minutes of dying in the gas chamber. Actually, it was about three hours earlier when the news broke that he probably was to be temporarily spared. That was on a cool October night in 1938.

Ashworth had taken the girl to a quarry north of St. Joseph. He had not molested her. He left this locality and was extradited from a northern state.

He was arraigned before Judge Ferd J. Frankenhoff. Frankenhoff, who as municipal judge was known for leniency, was at the other end of the spectrum the afternoon. Ashworth entered a guilty plea. Frankenhoff sentenced him to death and less than ten hours later Ashworth was dressed in at Death Row at the Jefferson City prison. There was no appeal on his plea of guilty. The parents of the kidnapped girl asked for leniency for Ashworth, but justice stood fast with the death penalty.

The evening of the day of the scheduled execution, Ashworth was taken to a cell adjoining the gas chamber, stripped down to shorts and socks and prepared for death. A minister conferred with him. Parked near the death chamber was a hearse that had been hired by Ashworth's family to take his body to a Maryville mortuary.

It was to be a double-header execution. A young St. Louis man named King, who had killed a cab driver, was scheduled to die in the second chair one minute after midnight. I was there with Merrill Chilcote, news editor of the *News-Press*. Shortly after we arrived at the prison we were informed that three St. Joseph attorneys — Abe Goldman, Leonard Johnson, and Earl C. Borchers — were driving to Jefferson City to file a plea for a writ of error with the Missouri Supreme Court to halt the execution.

Then came word that the three had been delayed in the area of Moberly by a severe storm. That word had been relayed to both the office of Governor Lloyd C. Stark and the Supreme Court. Because of the emergency, some extra time was to be allowed.

Chilcote and I waited in the room where convicts meet their visitors. Never one to waste time, Chilcote was writing quips and verses for his "Jackpot" column as we awaited the final word on what was to happen.

Periodically, reports were received by the warden on the progress of the attorneys through the storm and it was ten minutes to midnight before the plea actually was filed and execution stayed. The technicalities of the complicated legal situation had resulted in the execution time for Ashworth being set back for two hours so the necessary paperwork could be completed.

The doomed King pleaded that he too be allowed those two extra hours. His request was granted. Then trouble erupted for carrying out the death edict of King. In the gas chamber directly under the chair of the victim there is a large crock of acid into which the chemical is dropped that produces the gas. That night, after the drama of Ashworth being saved from death, the acid crock broke. Stores were closed as it was after midnight, but a prison official persuaded one store owner to open his business to sell them the needed crock. With that in place, the lethal pellets were dropped to bring death to King. Ashworth meanwhile had been escorted back to his cell in Death Row.

As we left the prison that night in the heavy rain, we saw a woman kneeling in the cobblestone paving in front of the main entrance praying aloud that her son, King, be spared. It was too late. Her son already was dead.

A couple of months later I interviewed Ashworth in Death Row. I talked to him of his reaction of that night when he came so close to death. "I'm not a religious man," he said, "but that night when I was brought back to my cell from the gas chamber room I got down on my knees and prayed all night to God in gratitude for having spared my life."

I inquired about his physical reaction. "For a week after I felt like I had been out in the bitter cold in a drenching rain and that I had been soaked so that my every bone and muscle ached. I felt as if my body was almost frozen solid."

Several year later when I was visiting in Jefferson City I met with Colonel Marvin Casteel, then director of the Missouri prison system. He took me out to the Renz prison farm across the Missouri River from the capital city.

There I saw Oscar Ralph Ashworth for the last time. He was driving a huge tractor in the farm field and professed to be delighted when Colonel Casteel called to him. He came off the tractor and said it felt good to have visitors from St. Joseph. He explained that he was a trusty at the Renz honor farm, that he was getting along fine, and appreciated what Colonel Casteel had done to make his time in prison as pleasant as possible under the circumstances. It was a strange feeling to see Ashworth out in the open after last having talked to him in the squalor of Death Row. He was grateful to Governor Stark for having commuted his death sentence to life.

The commutation had come after the Missouri Supreme Court had in finality denied his appeal. Stark's reason for commuting the penalty was based on the fact he hadn't harmed the girl he kidnapped and that he had gone through a great ordeal when death hovered almost on his shoulder for hours in that cell next to the gas chamber.

A couple of years after that visit, Ashworth fled the honor farm. He has never been heard of since, but some surmised he made his way to South America. That was more than forty years ago.

Murder on a Lawyer's Advice

This is the story-behind-the-story of a Buchanan County murderer who was never prosecuted even though he turned himself in and confessed to the crime.

Colorful and popular Assistant Prosecuting Attorney Bill Sawyers found himself squarely in the middle as the result of a careless, off-the-cuff comment.

It was a typical busy morning in the prosecuting attorney's office when a quiet middle-aged man approached Sawyers and said in a casual, almost off-hand manner:

"Mr. Sawyers, I'm having a little trouble. There's a fellow hanging around my wife all the time. Twice I've found him in the house. The other night I came home unexpectedly and I found him in the bedroom with my wife. I just don't know what to do about it."

Still not thinking about the situation as anything but a casual conversation, Sawyers replied, "By God, if it was my wife, I'd kill him."

That ended the conversation and Sawyers didn't think anything more about it until later in the day when the man returned, approached Sawyers with a degree of enthusiasm and informed the assistant prosecutor, "Well, Mr. Sawyers, I followed your advice. I did what you told me to do — I killed him!"

Sawyers was stunned. He had no choice but to charge the man with murder but he was in a bad spot. The man had asked his advice and followed it to the letter. After huddling with his boss, Sawyers filed formal murder charges against the killer and bond quickly was arranged.

A series of continuances of the case followed until public attention was diverted elsewhere and the case was quietly dropped from the docket. Bill Sawyers was spared the embarrassment of the assistant prosecuting attorney being called to the stand as the key witness for the defense.

His popularity grew and he enjoyed a long and fruitful career in politics, which included service as a probate judge and state senator. That career easily could have been destroyed before it ever blossomed, all because of one careless remark which may have cost a philanderer his life.

Too Many Crooks Spoil the Broth

If ever there was a perfect example that crime doesn't pay, it would have to be infamous train robber and thief, William LaTrasse of Kansas City. LaTrasse spent forty-five of his seventy-six years behind bars and during those long hours in prison cells he had ample time to reflect that his "victims" in several instances profited more from his exploits than he did.

The story-behind-the-story on LaTrasse might never have come to light if Harold Slater hadn't casually mentioned that one of LaTrasse's victims was the father of a classsmate of his at Christian Brothers, the local Catholic high school. Up to that point, LaTrasse had remained silent, refusing to give any interviews but Slater's comment touched a responsive chord.

"Are you a Brothers' boy?" LaTrasse asked, then volunteered proudly that he had attended DeLaSalle High School in Kansas City.

"From that point," Slater said, "it was like turning on a spigot," and LaTrasse poured out his life story, which included several interesting tidbits.

There's no record of LaTrasse pursuing the classics in the prison libraries, but had he done so, undoubtedly he would have been most sympathetic toward Diogenes, the Greek philosopher who roamed the world with a lamp in search of an honest man.

Slater's interview with LaTrasse was in the month of January, 1958, at Lansing State Penitentiary in Kansas where LaTrasse was serving two life terms for participating in a gambling holdup in which two men were killed in a shootout.

Once he found a sympathetic ear in fellow "Brothers' boy" Slater, LaTrasse told the full story of the spectacular train robbery forty-eight years earlier on Christmas Eve, 1910. Although it was the only train robbery he ever staged, his one-man effort captured the imagination of the newspaper public and made headlines all over the United States, turning the one-time petty crook into an instant celebrity.

LaTrasse told Slater that his total take from the robbery was between $3,600 and $3,700 but that when his victims reported their "losses" to a Missouri Pacific railway executive, the amount collectively claimed exceeded $50,000. "They had me dead to rights. I had no reason to lie then anymore than I have now," LaTrasse told Slater. "I told them the truth when I said the take was $3,600 to $3,700."

LaTrasse lived by his own warped code and in his own misguided fashion was a man of principle. His personal code of ethics precluded him from taking from women passengers. "I didn't bother any of the women passengers, I didn't ask them for their money and I didn't take any money or anything else from them," he told Slater. "This may sound funny," LaTrasse added, "but one newspaper story really hurt me and that was when a lady passenger told a reporter I had taken $34 from her all in change, that it was her Christmas money and all she had to buy presents. I hadn't taken a penny from her or any other woman on the train."

Very little planning went into his Christmas Eve train robbery. He told Slater he had been drinking and acted on impulse. When Slater suggested it took nerve to do what he did, LaTrasse shook his head and replied, "No, it was just damned foolishness."

LaTrasse said he bought a ticket on the Leavenworth-to-Kansas City run, boarded the train and walked to the rear of the observation car. "When the train started, I announced to the passengers it was a holdup, and I waved a pistol to make the point emphatic," LaTrasse recalled.

He hadn't even brought along a satchel or a sack to hold the loot. He simply stuffed the bills and change into his coat and overcoat pockets.

After going through three passenger cars, he ordered his victims to stand aside and then pulled the signal cord in approved conductor style, bringing the train to a halt in the Kansas City, Kansas, railroad yards. Once the train had stopped, he simply stepped off and disappeared.

He tried to hide out in Chicago, but acting on a tip from a former cellmate at Missouri State Penitentiary who claimed LaTrasse had told him he was going to pull off a train robbery, police soon tracked him down.

Shaking his head in disbelief at his bad luck, LaTrasse insisted that he had never told his ex-cellmate any such thing and had acted on the spur of the moment when he pulled off the daring daylight robbery.

After his arrest in Chicago, LaTrasse was brought to the Wyandotte County Jail in Kansas City, Kansas, to await trial, but quickly escaped and headed for Murphysboro, Illinois. It was one of four escapes LaTrasse pulled off during his long criminal career.

With the police hot on his trail after fleeing the Wyandotte County Jail, LaTrasse figured out a novel way to hide out for the next six months to let the hue and cry die down. He decided the safest place to hide from the law would be in jail! His plan was to get himself arrested in Illinois on a petty larceny charge where he could quietly spend five or six months in a local jail under an assumed name while Missouri and Kansas law enforcement officers wore themselves out on a cold trail.

His plan was to get caught stealing something worth less than $30. Anything more valuable would be grand larceny rather than petty theft, would result in a prison term and a fingerprint check, the last thing he wanted if his plan were to work.

He found just what he was looking for outside a clothing store in Murphysboro. It was a man's suit on a clothing dummy in front of the store and it carried a price tag of $22.50, well below the $30 figure which meant the difference between petty theft and grand larceny.

LaTrasse boldly stripped the suit from the dummy, then slipped onto a nearby alley to put in on. He didn't mind a bit when Murphysboro police grabbed him in the alley, but once again he was sorely disappointed by the lack of integrity displayed by his victim.

The Murphysboro merchant wasn't any more honest than the passengers on the Leavenworth-to-Kansas City train. The merchant reported the value of the suit as $32, two dollars over the felony limit. LaTrasse drew a one-to-20 year sentence at Menard penitentiary in Illinois.

It didn't take long for the word to reach Kansas and LaTrasse was hauled back to Lansing to finish out his robbery term.

That was in 1912 and just a year later he escaped from Lansing, heading for the east coast where he paid $35 for a round trip ticket as a passenger on a mule boat bound for Europe. He had no intention of using the return portion of the ticket.

Then came World War I and LaTrasse, still a fugitive, joined that motley array of misfits and malcontents that made up the French Foreign Legion.

Curiously enough, LaTrasse was a good legionnaire. He was wounded and promoted to sergeant, which earned him a pay increase to the princely equivalent of $1.25 per month.

Forty years later at Lansing prison he spoke with pride of his French Foreign Legion unit.

"At the siege of Verdun, we turned back the German forces commanded by the Crown Prince of Germany. Our company won 27 citations for valor." One of those citations went to LaTrasse.

Returning to the United States at the end of the war, LaTrasse once again was arrested and returned to Lansing to serve the balance of his train robbery sentence after an absence of seven years from prison.

He stayed locked up for eleven years that time, but he still hadn't learned his lesson. On his release, he went to Kansas City and held up a gambling game.

He picked up $500 from the players, stepped outside and said, "Never saw so many machine guns in my life." The police had been tipped off and had surrounded the place.

LaTrasse was sentenced to ten years for that robbery and wasn't released at Jefferson City until 1940.

He stayed out of trouble two years, then he and two other men held up a dice game in the rear of a beer place at Parsons, Kansas. They met opposition and a father and son were fatally shot.

LaTrasse didn't fire the fatal shots, but he was equally guilty with those who did. He wound up being sentenced to two life terms in the Lansing penitentiary. Incarcerated there in 1942, he made a sensational escape over the prison wall three years later.

He reminisced, "I used a ladder I had made with mop handles and adhesive tape to get over the wall. I had to make an 18-foot drop and suffered a broken foot and fractured vertebra. The pain was intense. After three days of hiding in farm fields, I asked a passing motorist to take me back to the prison. I had been without food or water the entire time I was out."

It was to be his last hurrah.

From that time until his release from Lansing on parole thirteen years later, he was a model prisoner. An arrested tubercular himself (no pun intended), he worked those years as a volunteer nurse in the tubercular unit of the prison hospital. He won praise for his efficiency and compassion and was declared, "a very reliable man" by none other than Warden Tracy Hand.

Ill luck dogged his entire criminal career and about his only wish that came true was his last one, which was to die outside prison walls.

Past the age of 76, he was paroled from the two life sentences on December 31, 1958. When he left prison all he had to show for his long criminal career was the cheap, shoddy prison-issue suit he wore, a toothbrush and $25.

Less than three months later he died, a free man in Denver, Colorado.

Just as Diogenes couldn't seem to find an honest man, William LaTrasse, the Brothers' boy gone bad, couldn't seem to find an honest victim!

Back Shooter Claims "Self-Defense"

One of the most dramatic, most telling arguments, I ever saw in a criminal case, was made by Joseph Sherman, St. Joseph's prosecuting attorney in the early 1940's.

The defendant was accused of shooting, and killing, a black soldier. The defendant had lost some money in a gambling game at a place on the lower end of Francis Street. After he lost the money, he came back with a gun, and shot and killed a different black soldier, not the same one he had been gambling with. The victim had no connection with the gambling game at all; he was just a fellow who happened to be there.

The defendant claimed that he shot in self-defense. He said that he was fearful of his life, and that this man had a reputation of being tough. (I guess that once a fellow is killed, he always has a reputation of being tough.)

The jury listened, and then came time for the closing arguments. Joe Sherman came before the jury. He held up a heavy brown shoddy army overcoat. In the middle of the back, there was a great hole torn by the gunshell. It was black and bloody around the edges. Sherman held up this coat before the jury with the bullet hole in the back and said, "Gentlemen of the jury, this man was fighting for your country. I thank you."

He sat down and the jury went out. When they returned, the defendant drew seventeen years.

Ironic Twist to Lawman's Murder

Once there was a man in St. Joseph who was murdered because he didn't wear his regular hat.

His name was John Brown. He had been constable of Washington Township, and had an office at the courthouse for about four years. He was known as a western gunman. He came here out of Oklahoma, sort of a Matt Dillon type character, wearing a huge cowboy hat. He was tall and commanding and on the silent side.

When he first came here, he was the lawman at Winthrop, Missouri, located directly across the Missouri River from Atchison, Kansas. In Missouri, Winthrop had more saloons than any city of its size anywhere. I believe at one time with a population of two hundred, it had something like fourteen saloons.

The saloon men down there, before the advent of Prohibition, hired John Brown to be their law. He took care of the job admirably, and was eventually elected constable. He served with distinction, a man whom everybody in town recognized by his trademark, the big Stetson hat. He was constantly around town carrying on his duties and his politics.

One night, he had a date with a lady friend. (He was single, I might add.) Because it was difficult to put his big, brown hat under a seat at the Missouri Theater, to which they were going that night, he wore a cap, instead of the usual distinct hat. He took the lady home, then went to the garage at the rear of his house at Fifth and Antoine Street. A sixteen-year-old boy tried to hold him up. The boy panicked and fired, fatally wounding Brown.

The boy would never have thought of trying to hold up John Brown if he had seen that big hat (John's trademark). He would have known that he would have no chance; that he was facing a gunman with a killer reputation.

But he didn't know, and John Brown was killed because he wore a different hat that night.

129

On Death Row by Request

Once when I was on duty in Jefferson City I was visiting at the penitentiary and saw a fellow in a solitary cell there. I knew he was not under death sentence, but there he was right down on Death Row.

He was in a solitary cell there, so I asked about it. A guard told me that he was there at his own request, explaining that the cell occupant was guilty of just about the worst crime that can be committed against inmates in a prison—stealing their mail.

Very few things mean as much to a penitentiary inmate as the mail he receives. The fellow guilty of that knew he was certain to be stabbed to death no matter how careful he was. So he asked to be put in solitary on Death Row for safety reasons.

I kept in touch with his case. It turned out he voluntarily stayed in solitary for nearly four years before he finally decided it would be safe for him to venture out into the relative freedom of the prison yard.

I never heard about him again, so presume he served out his time without being stabbed to death for his violation of one of the most sacred penitentiary codes.

The Truth Saves a Killer

More than forty years ago a bully named Bert ran roughshod around St. Joseph. I won't mention his last name because a number of his relatives are still living.

Bert was a pure troublemaker. He would get drunk and slap young fellows around—or anyone else who happened to be handy. Then he'd dare them to do anything about it.

One day, at a pool hall near Eleventh and Grand Avenue, Bert kicked around the wrong young fellow. The young man walked home, then walked another mile or so to his sister's home where he obtained a gun. He came back to the pool hall where Bert had collapsed and was lying on a pool table. The young man shot and killed him as he lay passed out.

The next morning policemen brought the youth to Central Police Station for questioning by Chief of Detectives John T. Duncan. "Boy," asked Duncan, "what are you in here for?"

"I killed Bert —————— last night," the young suspect said. "He's slapped me around for the last time. I killed Bert—————."

"Boy," said the chief of detectives, "you did a good night's work."

After a month or two, the young fellow was brought to trial on a murder charge. Barney Reilly, one of the most colorful lawyers in St. Joseph history, defended him. Barney was a former baseball star on the St. Joseph Western League club, an athlete at Yale and had been manager of the Royal Theater in St. Joseph. Everybody knew Barney, a towering white-haired guy, and a tremendous orator.

They tried the case. The State called Chief Duncan to say that the defendant had admitted the murder to him. Barney cross-examined him, then said, "Chief Duncan, what did you tell him? Didn't you tell him that he'd done a good night's work?"

Duncan was a good policeman, but above all, he was an honorable man with a sense of honesty. He wanted a conviction in the case but, with Duncan, the truth came first.

"Yes," he said, "I told him he'd done a good night's work."

The jury went out but could not agree on a verdict. The State never tried the case again. That one statement, the members figured, precluded any possibility of conviction. The defendant went free and eventually became an outstanding citizen of St. Joseph.

It Just Wouldn't Look Right

On a daily news beat, pathos could crop up anywhere. Like the Buchanan County jail.

I was at the jail one morning when the sheriff's deputies were preparing to deliver a prisoner to the state penitentiary at Jefferson City to begin serving a life sentence for murder. His tearful sister was there to tell him goodbye and to give him a farewell present.

It was a nifty looking sailor straw hat. I don't know what became of it, but I know that no warden at Jefferson City—or anywhere else—would allow a convict to wear a straw hat.

A hat like that just wouldn't look right with a suit that had horizontal stripes.

FRINGE BENEFITS

Some of the World's Nicest People Come a Reporter's Way, Too

Captain John Downs stands with Col. Charles A. Lindbergh in front of one of the F4U Corsairs made by the Vought-Sikorsky Company which the Lone Eagle represented during World War II. Downs flew a South Pacific dawn patrol with Lindbergh.

PART FIVE

The "Rand" Is Quicker Than The Eye

One of the top fringe benefits of being a newspaper reporter is the pleasure derived from meeting certain delightfully different people. Like Sally Rand.

My friendship with Sally got its start six or seven years after Miss Rand had captured the major attention of the 1933 Century of Progress World's Fair at Chicago.

It reached its climax in 1977 when I was tapped to write the Sally Rand story for *Missouri Life*, a slick and beautifully produced magazine published and edited by Bill Nunn. In between there had been a number of random meetings with her, all of which produced interviews in her inimitable fashion.

Sally was twenty-nine—far from a spring chick as a stage dancer—when she first won that world acclaim at Chicago. When I had a number of interviews with her for the 1977 magazine article she was seventy-three and still working forty weeks a year in burlesque and nightclubs. She weighed one hundred and five pounds, had a thirty-four inch bust, a grandson — and distinctions that ranged from being held in a Chicago jail to lecturing at Harvard.

Here is Harold Slater's feature story from the March 1977, issue of *Missouri Life* magazine:

The One, The Only
SALLY RAND

On April 3, 1904, twenty-two years to the day after the infamous train and bank robber, Jesse James, was blasted to his reward in St. Joseph, a baby girl was born in his home state of Missouri to give him a run for his status as the Number One publicity getter for his state up to then.

She was Sally Rand, and she was destined to do more for the fan than George Westinghouse. George used his to cool; Sally used hers to inflame.

To some people she's a vaguely familiar memory, or a name from the past with a faintly risque taint. To others she's a stripper, or a consummate burlesque artist, or an entertainer with pungent and pithy oneliners. And to others she's a lady of charm and wit, an amazing living legend.

One thing is certain; she's a paradox.

Coming from the southwest Missouri "Bible Belt," the most staid area of a state noted for its staidness, she has carved out a career that ranges from a Cook County jail in Chicago to a lecture hall at Harvard.

And for considerably more than forty years, she has been a traveling "signboard" for her beloved state of Missouri.

No one meets Sally Rand without knowing in a few minutes that she is from Missouri. She is as proud of her state as a Boy Scout is of his first five merit badges.

Sally Rand is a phenomenon in many ways. She is as sensitive as she is saucy. Others may think of her fan dancing as something primarily sensuous. Sally doesn't. She feels it is a true art developed from her early days as a ballet dancer.

Friends will tell you that she cried when some brash students at Harvard asked her to strip after she had lectured there on the theater. But, on the other hand, she can be hard as the rocks of her native Hickory County when the occasion demands. She has demonstrated that as a champion in the art of putting down the obstreporous during her performances in places ranging from theaters to fairs to night clubs.

Part of the paradox of Sally is that she didn't become a national figure until she reached the age of 29 and burst into the major limelight when she fan danced at the Century of Progress in Chicago in 1933. At that age most show girls are casting around for a nice safe place to retire, possibly in an area with comfortable homes for the aged nearby.

Now seventy-three years old, she still works forty weeks a year, just as she has done for considerably more than two score years. She continues as an exotic stage attraction when most women her age are thinking largely of what nice new flannel gown they have to wear. Retire? Forget it, she told this interviewer. She has no more thought of retiring than Jimmy Carter.

Does she still enjoy the demanding routine of several stage appearances everyday?

"I love it," she said, when reached at the Royal Ascot at Detroit by this writer. "It sure beats doing needlepoint on the patio."

Sally was playing a six-week stand at the Royal Ascot. She went there after a lengthy stand in New York City and after playing a benefit at Columbia College in Columbia, Missouri, where she had been a student more than fifty years before when it was Christian College.

She was awarded her degree from that college when she was fifty-two, some thirty years-plus after she had departed its campus. Life has had a habit of playing the game with Sally that way.

She started out as a milliner's apprentice and had a variety of stage and movie experiences before she hit the fan dancing idea early in 1933. They tossed her into the pokey at Chicago when she gave her dance at the Paramount Club there, but that didn't deter Sally. She showed that Missouri instinct of never giving up, despite threats of more arrests and longer jail stays.

That same year, Sally stole the center stage of the Century of Progress Exposition at Chicago. Other acts and presentations at that exposition paled before Sally's showmanship.

If there was one single person who made the Century of Progress a whale of a success, it was Sally.

Being a practical person, she divides her life between A.F. and B.F.—After Fan and Before Fan.

She made her name a household word and has kept it that way. In Missouri, the question posed by that old song that started out with "I Wonder What's Become of Sally, That Old Girl of Mine?" is academic. Everyone. . . well, almost everyone. . . in the state knows. It is part of the heritage.

Getting back to that date connection with Jesse James: Bob Ford, for $10,000 reward, shot down his fellow robber James in St. Joseph April 3, 1882, just twenty-two years to the day before that Easter Sunday in 1904 when Sally Rand was born in Elkton, Hickory County, Missouri. Her name was Helen Gould Beck.

Legend has it that she picked up the name of Rand from a Rand-McNally Atlas while engaged in either a ballet or burlesque dancing stint in Kansas City.

Over the years—in the opinion of many—Sally Rand has eclipsed old Jesse, albeit it in a far different field, in bringing publicity to Missouri.

Only the late President Harry S Truman seems to rank ahead of her as the top publicity producer from this state, although some might rate ex-St. Louis Cardinal Stan Musial as being close to Sally.

It does seem quite a coincidence that Sally with her particular brand of entertainment should come from the Show Me State.

There are those who credit Sally with saving what few remnants of burlesque we now have. Certainly, she has tried hard, but there another Rand paradox bobs up. Friends say Sally doesn't care to work with strippers. The Missouri girl who over the years has made women gripe and men gape regards strippers simply as skin merchants, friends say, and doesn't even like the pasties they wear. One thing is certain: she never uses pasties herself.

One of the intriguing things about Sally's act is that no one seems certain after the show just how much of Sally they really saw. She can work magic with those fans.

She put it in her own words with "The Rand is quicker than the eye."

The fact her audiences now include grandchildren and great-grandchildren of the persons who first saw her fan dance in Chicago two generations ago is pleasing to Sally. It is proof to her that she still has the stage knack of keeping the public entertained.

A true performer in every respect, she aids greatly in her own promotion. She is generous with her interviews, cooperative and pleasant. And who do you think first suggested to restaurants in towns where she was playing that they include on their menus a Sally Rand salad—that is, one without dressing?

Well, no one other than Sally herself.

Even legislative halls have not been missed by Sally in her journeys. Some thirty-nine years ago, Sally, fresh from her Chicago triumphs, was formally introduced to the House of the Missouri General Assembly at Jefferson City.

The introduction was by scholarly little State Representative O. B. Whittaker of her own Hickory County.

Sally got as much applause as a bill to hike legislators' pay would have received, She even intrigued hardboiled Representative Browning by her conduct and comments. And Browning wasn't an easy man to impress. He had a record of having voted against every measure before the legislature—even the bill to pay his own salary.

Such triumphs came naturally for Sally.

Eighteen years after Sally Rand made her big score at the Century of Progress, Missouri officials decided her appearance at the Missouri State Fair would give that event a good attendance boost.

They were absolutely right, but the plan didn't work entirely smoothly at first.

The year was 1951 and there were certain self-professed moralists, among them a number of women, who protested. They didn't think Sally's act was in keeping with the conservatism they expected of a State Fair presentation.

The protests carried quickly to the ears of Missouri Governor Forrest Smith and he decided he would view Sally's show before there would be any all-clear signal.

Now Governor Smith was a man who in his many successful campaigns always stressed in his speeches that his Bible was well thumbed, that he was a man of true religion.

Adjusting his spectacles, the governor viewed Sally's dance and then announced there was nothing immoral, lewd or lascivious about it. So the show went on.

The result was a real boom for Sally. The State Fair drew a gate thirty two percent higher than that of the previous year and her presentation even eclipsed in popularity such events as the traditional ham breakfast for dignitaries, the baked custard pie competition, the auto races and the baby show.

Since then, Sally twice more has been brought back to the Missouri State Fair and the gate results have been electrifying.

Sally's performances even now are not restricted to the boondocks. She plays the big towns as well, including New York City where last fall she was the stellar attraction at the Beacon Theater at 74th and Broadway.

In addition to a stage star, she qualifies as a top physical culturist. That she takes real good care of her body is attested by the fact she still has legs that an 18-year old girl would envy, keeps her weight between 103 and 105 pounds, has a 34-inch bust and wears a size 7 junior petite. And please remember those measurements were pretty much the same as the ones she had more than half a century ago when she was a young ballerina in Kansas City.

What does she think of Women's Lib? She spouts one of the one-liners for which she is famous:

"I like being a girl. I always have."

She's a grandma, a glamourous one, and lives in Glendora, Cal, when not on the road.

Seemingly her only concession to age is that she asks for—and gets—more blue moonlight from the spotlight when she performs now. It is softer on the body view and the facial features that have known tens of thousand of make-up jobs over the years.

Her voice is gravelly and her comments provocative. She has an opinion on everything, and there is no lack of conversation when she is around.

To Missourians her loyalty is great. When the Democrats held their national convention in Atlantic City, N.J., in 1964, Sally was playing at a burlesque house there.

Several Missourians, this writer included, and Vonceile Marriott and Dorothy Wylie from St. Joseph, went to see her and sent a message backstage during intermission that they would like to say hello to her again.

Her answer was immediate, "Take the right stage door and go down the hall to my dressing room," her note read.

After old times had been reviewed, Miss Rand was asked if she would attend a Missouri delegation party that United States Senator Edward V. Long was giving the following evening.

Demurely dressed, Sally was on hand for that party, and who do you think got the most attention? It wasn't any politician, although there were scads of big names on hand. If Lyndon B. Johnson, about to be nominated for president that evening, had showed up at the party, Sally would have given him a run for the money. She just charmed everyone with tales going back to her childhood in Missouri, "When I ran around in the hills barefoot up to my chin."

Sally, who played movie roles under Cecil B. DeMille starting in the late 1920's (in one epic film she was handmaiden to Mary Magdalene) once summed up her thoughts about age with:

"It's fun growing old as long as you can stay young."

Fists of Iron and a Heart of Gold

Jack Dempsey was one of the greatest fighters who ever climbed through the ropes of a boxing ring. He was also a man who never forgot his early friends.

Benny Sembler, a well-known St. Joseph figure in his youth, had known Dempsey when the Manassa Mauler was earning that nickname by fighting his way up through battles in western towns and mining camps. Benny, a promising lightweight then, had been on some of those fight cards with Dempsey.

Between 1930 and 1948, Dempsey came to St. Joseph four or five times, sometimes to officiate at boxing and wrestling matches at the Auditorium and, at least one time, to promote the sale of U.S. war bonds. On his visits here, Benny usually acted as host and guide and the former champ delighted in telling about Benny once buying him a much-needed pair of shoes when they were both young fighters in lean financial times.

On those visits Dempsey also visited the late Henry D. Bradley, publisher of the *News-Press* and *Gazette*, who had been a young sports writer in Toledo, Ohio on July 4, 1918 when Dempsey had knocked out Jess Willard to win the heavyweight championship.

In 1943, Dempsey, then a lieutenant commander in the Navy, came to St. Joseph to promote war bond sales at Rosecrans Field and the Missouri Theater. One eleven-year-old boy, a hero worshipper of the old champ, looked forward for days to seeing Dempsey at the Missouri Theater.

But three days before Dempsey was to come to town, the boy came down with the chickenpox. He was heartbroken that he would be unable to leave home for the big day. But bighearted Benny heard about the boy's predicament and sent word to the boy that he was going to take Dempsey back to Kansas City after his appearances here and they would drop by the boy's home to visit him.

Dempsey showed up at the boy's home, autographed his baseball glove, then told the boy to tap the ex-champ on the jaw.

"That way," Dempsey explained to him, "you can tell fellows at school that you punched Jack Dempsey in the jaw and he was afraid to hit you back."

The little boy was the writer's son, Robert L. Slater, now vice-president of the St. Joseph Light and Power Company.

Joe Louis Gets His Answer

Joe Louis, the Brown Bomber and longtime champ after Jack Dempsey, had wondered about something for years. He got his answer in the news rooms of the *News-Press*.

Some years after Joe had been such an outstanding champion, he came to St. Joseph to referee a fight on Gust Karras's wrestling show at Municipal Auditorium. Karras brought him to the city room the day of the fight. I mentioned to Louis that Henry D. Bradley, retired *News-Press* publisher, had covered the Jack Dempsey-Jess Willard fight in Toledo when he was a young sports writer.

Joe was introduced to Henry. He had a question for the ex-publisher. "Some people in boxing say Dempsey's fists were dipped in plaster of paris before that fight," he said, "that he actually was hitting Willard with what amounted to two chunks of concrete?"

"Not so," said Bradley. "I was in the dressing room and his fists were wrapped only with tape in the conventional manner. There was no plaster of paris."

Joe looked relieved. Dempsey was his idol.

Chief Leo Was Aptly Named

If ever a man was aptly named it was Leo J. Urbanski, colorful chief of the St. Joseph Fire Department from the late 1920's into the 1950's.

Leo means lion, and that is exactly what Chief Urbanski was. He was a man unmatched for courage.

Curiously, Leo legally was a native of England although he never saw the land and despite the fact that neither his parents or their forebears had a drop of British blood.

Leo was born on the Atlantic Ocean, on a ship that was carrying his Polish parents from their native land to the United State. It was a ship operating under the flag of Great Britain and under international law that made Leo a native of England. It didn't bother him.

He had wanted to be a fireman so badly that he took the lowliest job on the department to get a start. That job was driving the wagon that went from station to station to pick up the manure of the fire horses and take it to a dumping place.

Leo was a natural firefighter. He didn't stay on that first job long. He soon was serving in the front lines at conflagrations of all sizes, shapes and kinds. Firemen in those days were paid $60 a month and worked a 24-hour day.

The firemen were off work one 12-hour shift each week and got one hour off for each of three meals a day, providing it was convenient. On busy days they had to skip those meal hours and there was no compensation for the sacrifice.

Leo Urbanski first attained hero status when he rendered yeoman work as a visiting fireman at the great Topeka flood in the early days of the century. He was in numerous rescue operations there.

In the early 1920's when several men were trapped in a caisson that was being dug along the Missouri River bank by the Light and Power Company, it was Leo Urbanski who volunteered to be lowered by a rope into the caisson and effect the rescue task. The men in the caisson had been overcome by fumes.

Leo become assistant fire chief, and then in 1928 he succeeded to the post on the death of another colorful chief, Horace G. (Darby) Regan. For many years while he was chief, Leo stayed on duty around the clock, sleeping at Central Fire station, and going out on every regular alarm. Not until he married did he forsake the fire station sleeping quarters.

Reporters found Leo an invaluable source of news. He was a generous man, a good host, but when it came to spending city money he was just a little tighter than a drum head.

When he would go to a fire chiefs' convention as a representative of the city, he saved city funds by sleeping at fire stations along the way. One city councilman, George Dodd, in looking over the bills for one of those trips, told Chief Urbanski he didn't have to skimp on lodging and that he ought to eat more expensive meals on his trips. "It's city money and I'm just not going to waste it," said the chief.

The top honor that came to Chief Urbanski was when he was chosen for a Ralph Edwards "This Is Your Life" radio show. The show personnel spared no expense in bringing to Hollywood many of the people who had figured in Leo's life, including some whose lives he had saved. But they couldn't get one show prop they wanted. They called the *News-Press* to see if one of the old fire horses could be found and sent out for the show. It was too late. The last of the horses was in much greener pastures.

Only one word described how Chief Urbanski guarded the Fire Department pension fund: Zealously.

One of his firemen was a father of nine. Frequently when fighting fires this particular fine man sometimes would wander into the more dangerous areas of the conflagration. Whenever that happened, Leo Urbanski would see him there and would shout, "Get back to the sidelines, Jim. Let the rest of us do the dangerous work. If you get killed with those nine kids it would bankrupt the pension fund!"

The Tragic Life of Pat Ellis

Pat Ellis had nothing in his favor but Mrs. Lanzel Degginger. She kept him from dying in the electric chair.

I first met Pat when I was a police reporter, He was only about seven or eight years old and he was literally living out of the garbage cans of cheap restaurants on South Sixth Street. He had parents but they seemingly were not interested in the little boy with his badly crossed eyes.

Pat had a persecution complex and he had a right to have one, as he was a boy who knew what it was like to be cuffed around. Some accused him of stealing, but he actually was just rummaging around in garbage cans to find food.

Pat's father was a police character on South Sixth, known by the somewhat inelegant name of "Pook-Eye". His mother also was a character on that same Tenderloin. The father's nickname stemmed from an eye that seemed ever to be in a staring position., The father's speciality was bootlegging on a small scale; and once, by some difficult to explain process, he had been elected chaplain of a fraternal unit here.

On one occasion when Pook-Eye was arrested for investigation he was entirely sober when Chief of Detectives John T. Duncan talked to him. The chief decided, however, to let the suspect cool off in a holding cell and then talk to him again. Two hours later Pook-Eye was roaring drunk when they brought him up to Duncan's office, although he hadn't been outside that police station cell.

Duncan ordered an investigation, being unable to figure out just what had happened. Tha answer was simple. Pook-Eye had asked the desk sergeant to have some coffee delivered to him in his cell. He suggested it be ordered from his favorite cheap restaurant on South Sixth and that it be charged to his running account there. A friend at the restaurant, who knew Pook-Eye's tastes, had laced the coffee heavily with alcohol. The police issued an edict: No more coffee from that restaurant was to be brought to the police station, not even for the policemen on duty.

Pat used to regularly wind up in juvenile court on minor complaints and Mrs. Degginger, a deputy county probation officer, got interested in him and helped him in many ways. She had him placed in several homes so he could have decent food and shelter, but Pat invariably would run away, usually after becoming convinced he was just going to be kicked around some more.

Each time the next thing you knew Lanzel would be out looking for Pat and trying to help him once again. His family continued to show no interest in him; but when he was fourteen years old some false papers were signed by them, wrongfully attesting he was past seventeen so he could enlist in the army.

Pat was big for his age, but he still had the attitude that the world was never going to give him an even break. The army sent him to a training center in Louisiana. He met another young soldier who invited him to visit him at his nearby home. There the young host showed Pat some trunks stored in the attic. Pat decided there probably was lots of money and other valuables in those trunks. So one day while he was alone in the house with the boy's mother, he killed her and looted the trunks. It turned out the trunks contained nothing of value.

The crime was crudely committed. Young Ellis was quickly arrested. Louisiana does not deal leniently with murderers; and although Pat actually was only fifteen years old, he was sentenced to die in the electric chair.

He still had one friend, Lanzel Degginger. No one heard from his parents or other family members, but Lanzel renewed her salvation efforts for Pat. She persuaded the *News-Press* to do a story about the tragedy of the boy's life, detailing the background that showed he actually was a boy who had never had a chance.

Two St. Joseph businessmen were touched—Robert Duncan and Barton Pitts. They hired the best attorney they could get in Louisiana to handle the appeal. They made arrangements to personally call upon Pat in his Death Row cell. The death verdict was upheld for months but, certainly due in part to the intercession of Duncan and Pitts, the Louisiana governor finally commuted the sentence to life imprisonment.

Lanzel kept on helping him. She sent him food packages and other gifts. He served about seven years before he was paroled.

Ellis went to Colorado and started a new life. He wrote to Mrs. Degginger several times a year, always at Christmas time, and reported on his progress. He had a good job, was married and had two children. Then the letters stopped coming and Mrs. Degginger heard no more from or about him. Not long before her death she said, "I still pray that he gets through life with a better finale than he had a start."

She did her part of that prayer.

A Remarkable Man Was Judge Vories

He was in the golden autumn of his life when first I knew him.

His name was Lawrence Archer Vories and he was a circuit judge of Buchanan County from 1917 until 1939. He was a most remarkable man both for his extensive public service and his humane manner.

Named for the original editor of the *Gazette*, in 1845 the first newspaper established here, Judge Vories had been elected prosecuting attorney of Buchanan County in 1890. He was mayor of St. Joseph, 1897—1898, the Spanish-American War period, and in the early part of this century he had served in the Missouri Senate.

In the 1930's he still was addicted to the wing collars that had been popular forty years earlier. There was nothing flamboyant about the man. An ever friendly person, he went about his duties in a quiet and efficient manner, many times going out of the way to protect people of lesser means from the unscrupulous who sought to take advantage of them.

His home was a huge tract at the northeast corner of 22nd and Duncan Streets. His orchard there was the highest assessed orchard in Missouri. Because it was in an area largely given over to residences, Judge Vories had it assessed as residential property, not as an orchard. He thought that in fairness he should pay for the privilege of keeping that orchard inside a city, and so he did.

Today the Vories house and orchard are gone and there are about twenty residences on the land where the Vories' apple trees once grew.

I remember calling on Judge Vories at his home one time to request help for a young father who had stolen because his wife and baby son were hungry. Police caught the fellow leaving a grocery store, a roll of bologna and two loaves of bread under his arm. It was in the middle of the night; it was burglary and called for a two-year prison sentence.

Judge Vories listened. The culprit had never been in trouble of any kind before. He couldn't get a job; he was desperate.

The judge saw that he was paroled a few days later and the fellow has never been in trouble since.

Never did I hear Judge Vories raise his voice or show the slightest evidence of anger. And I saw him about six days a week over a nine-year period.

He was most human as well as most humane.

There comes to mind a time when a major murder trial was being conducted in his division No. 2 courtroom. Some persons were anxious to get the trial over as quickly as possible, partly because they hoped for a heavy sentence as revenge for the slaying.

But Judge Vories was not to be rushed. Nor was he to break a promise he had made long before the trial. At noon during a hectic day of the trial, he announced the court would be closed that afternoon.

"I promised my wife, I would take her to the circus this afternoon. She's looking forward to it. The court is recessed," he said.

That was Judge Vories—a gentleman of breeding, friendliness and character long to be remembered.

He Was an "Honest S.O.B."

One of the more colorful and controversial prosecuting attorneys in St. Joseph was John Downs, who later served as a state senator and was instrumental in Missouri Western State College being located in St. Joseph. In fact, Downs Drive at the college is named in recognition of Mr. Downs' efforts in getting the school for his home community.

John was outspoken, often blunt as a prosecutor and as a legislator and was not overly popular with the local newspaper but he was always good copy.

As a legislator, noting that every newly elected representative had some favorite piece or pieces of legislation to introduce, a fact which he believed had the effect of systematically eroding individual freedom, John immediately came up with a suggested piece of legislation of his own.

"I think we should pass a law." Downs emphasized, "that says that for every new law we pass, we should take two old ones off the books!"

Unfortunately, John's proposal was never adopted.

Co-author George Sherman, who was a reporter during John's tenure as prosecuting attorney, has several fond memories of the Downs' era.

Perhaps one of the more illuminating occurred after John left public service and entered private practice.

During his time as prosecuting attorney, he was a devastating crusader against the illegal gambling houses which had flourished in St. Joseph for years, primarily because certain public officials for a gratuity would look the other way.

John was scrupulously honest and refused to accept anything that would even resemble a favor or a gratuity, let alone a bribe. Obviously, the gamblers found this totally honest politician to be a new and highly frustrating experience.

The story-behind-the-story, however, is that after he had left public office and returned to private practice, one of the gambling fraternity who had been hit the hardest by John's crusade came to him with an important piece of legal business.

To say that John was surprised would be an understatement and he couldn't help but say to the gambler, "...You're the last man in the world I ever thought would bring me any business."

The gambler's answer is a classic: "...I still don't like you, you S.O.B., but I know you're honest. Will you take the case?"

148

"I'll take it," replied John, still somewhat flustered and as close to being at a loss of words as any lawyer could ever be.

Another vivid memory of the Downs' era as prosecuting attorney involved a case where Mr. Downs was prosecuting a three-time loser.

Attorney for the defense was Lewis Randolph, Jr., who was almost as elequent and emotional in the courtroom as his brilliant and illustrious late father, Lewis, Sr.

Young Randolph had the defendant's pregnant wife and several small children in the courtroom. Drawing heavily on his oratorical skills because that was about all he had going for him in the way of a defense, Randolph stressed what a shame it would be to take this father away from his wife and children, then swung around and pointed dramatically to Prosecutor Downs, exclaiming emotionally, "...and this blackhearted Irishman wants to send this poor man to a long stretch in prison!"

The foreman of the jury snapped to attention as though he had been stung by a wasp and two or three other jurors also looked as though they had just been jarred out of a hypnotic trance.

They were out a very short time and returned with a resounding verdict of guilty.

What young Randolph had overlooked in his otherwise brilliant and moving summation was that the foreman of the jury was named "Sweeney" and there were several others on the jury of Irish descent!

A third incident involved *Gazette* Reporter Sherman finding out information on a lead Prosecutor Downs was following in connection with the Greenlease kidnapping. Only John's secretary knew where he was and why and she wasn't about to tell anyone.

As it turned out, Reporter Sherman had studied Gregg Shorthand in high school and also in business school, but had never used it and no one was aware he had the slightest inkling of what those funny little marks and symbols meant.

As Downs' secretary was adamantly refusing to give any information on the whereabouts of her boss, reporter Sherman glanced over her shoulder and saw that she had written in shorthand that Mr. Downs was at the Missouri State penitentiary checking on a "Tom Marsh" in connection with the kidnapping.

It wasn't until years later when Downs was no longer a prosecutor and Sherman no longer a newsman that the ex-reporter revealed how he had obtained the information for what was then an important story.

In later years, Mr. Downs held one of the highest presidential appointments up to that time of any St. Joseph resident. He was appointed by President Carter as United States Minister to the International Civil Aviation Organization, headquartered at Montreal, Canada. It was an appointment that required the advice and consent of the United State Senate, and at state affairs was higher in the pecking order than admirals.

Downs had a keen knowledge of aviation and was awarded the Distinguished Flying Cross for strafing operations against land and sea targets while serving as a fighter pilot in the South Pacific during World War II.

Downs' fondest memory of those days was meeting and flying with the famous Lone Eagle, Charles A. Lindbergh. Lindbergh had incurred the wrath of President Roosevelt by speaking out against United States intervention in the war in Europe. The president also resented Lindbergh's claim that the German air force was vastly superior to that of either the United States or Great Britain.

While Lindbergh opposed U.S. intervention, he wanted to do his part if his country did enter the war. But Roosevelt wanted no part of him. As Vought-Sikorsky Company's representative, however, the Lone Eagle did get opportunities to participate in the war by field testing Vought-Sikorsky aircraft under actual wartime conditions.

Downs, a Marine Corps captain, was based on the island of Enirau where Lindbergh arrived to check out the F4U Corsairs, which were built by Vought-Sikorsky. It was scheduled to be strictly a strafing mission but Lindbergh sympathizers had smuggled a five hundred-pound bomb aboard the Lone Eagle's aircraft. In his book, *The Wartime Journals of Charles A. Lindbergh* (Harcourt Brace Jovanovich, Inc., 1970), Lindbergh said visibility prevented him from dropping the bomb on a gun emplacement he had selected as his primary target. Instead, he blew a gaping crater in the center of an important coral air strip in Japanese-held territory. It was a three-aircraft mission with Captain Downs, the Lone Eagle and a Lieutenant Vaughn.

Downs describes Lindbergh as friendly and informal with a keen scientific mind. He especially remembers Lindbergh's astute knowledge of aviation and aerodynamics.

At that time, aircraft had not broken the sound barrier and the pilots were concerned that breaking the barrier might cause the aircraft to disintegrate. When diving in the F4U Corsairs, Downs said, they could actually see the sound waves building up around their wings. At the same time, the control stick would vibrate so violently that it would bruise the pilot's knees. No one knew the cause and Downs asked Lindbergh.

Lindbergh was reassuring. Sketching on a piece of paper, he pointed out where the sound waves were causing pressure on the ailerons, causing the control stick to vibrate. He indicated how a few simple changes in the fasteners could solve the problem.

Downs said that in all casual encounters with the Marine fliers Lindbergh dispensed with formalities, insisting that everyone call him just "Charlie."

George Sherman

The Lone Eagle Stays Aloof

When he visited St. Joseph, Charles Lindbergh was too much of a Lone Eagle for the likes of some locals.

The famous flier came to town shortly after his epochal solo flight to Paris. When he landed at Rosecrans Field, he wouldn't shake hands with several local politicians. Somewhat shy, anyway, Lindbergh had his own reasons. He felt if he shook hands with a few at the field, he would have to shake hands with everyone there. And that would be tiring and time-consuming.

Besides, of course, he wasn't participating in any popularity contest and he wasn't running for any office.

The Softhearted Sheriff and Thieves' Honor

One of the most unique stories in the annals of law enforcement anywhere took place in 1910 at the Missouri State Penitentiary at Jefferson City when twenty-two prisoners walked up to the gate seeking to be admitted!

The prisoners were not accompanied by a guard or guards; they were not shackled and they'd rather have been almost

151

anywhere else but in this case it was a point of honor. The gate guards were flabbergasted when a spokesmen for the group said "We're under sentence. Here are the papers. Will you book us in?"

The prisoners, several of them with long criminal records, actually were protecting the sheriff whose responsibility it was to deliver them to the penitentiary.

Otto Theisen was the sheriff. He was relatively new to the job and it was his first experience at delivering prisoners to the state institution. They were in a special railroad car and as the prison walls came into view, several of the younger prisoners were visibly upset. A number broke down and wept openly at the sight of the grim grey walls and guard towers.

Sheriff Theisen was touched and said to the men, "Fellows, I want to tell you something. You can see the walls of the penitentiary but I'm not gonna take you in. I've known most of you guys all my life. I went to school with some of you and I played with some of you as a boy. I associated with some of you as a man. I'm just gonna tell the engineer to unhook this car and then take us all back to St. Joseph. I'm just not going to take you into that penitentiary."

The men looked at each other in amazement, some even visualizing the dawn of hope. Then, almost miraculously, these men of questionable character and low morality responded to the incredible gesture of sympathy that had been extended to them.

One of the group, a several-time loser who was no stranger to prison life, spoke up. "Ott," he said, "you can't do this. If you take us back there they'll oust you as sheriff, probably sue you for everything you've got and we'll all still wind up in the penitentiary."

Despite the logic of the men and their pleas not to sacrifice his career in a useless gesture, Sheriff Theisen, who was known as a hardheaded Dutchman, remained adamant. "I'm still not gonna take you in there," he maintained.

"Okay," said the prisoner who had established himself as the leader of the group, "fellows, we'll go in ourselves."

There wasn't a murmur of of disagreement. Even though Otto Theisen and his badge of authority represented everything these men detested in life, his kindness had struck a responsive chord. As one, they turned, marched steadfastly to the prison gates and asked for admission.

Otto Theisen returned to St. Joseph and never again delivered a prisoner to the state penitentiary. He left that job to his deputies.

Wigglesworth Toole and His Inside Pass

The man's name was odd—Alpha Wigglesworth Toole—and so was his situation.

He was a bona fide prisoner at the Missouri State Penitentiary, but he spent nearly all of his time outside, including his sleeping hours, and he actually had to have a pass to go inside the walls!

At the time of his incarceration, Mr. Toole was about seventy-three years old and had been serving as deputy county treasurer, having been a trusted public official in various city and county capacities for nearly fifty years.

Mr. Toole had never been farther away from St. Joseph than Kansas City and was modestly proud of his public service and of his membership in one of the oldest families of the city. He could trace his ancestry to the Roosevelt family in New York, the same family that was to produce two United States presidents.

He also was quite proud of what some considered a rather difficult name. His job required him to sign thousands of county warrants every month and he insisted on signing them Alpha Wigglesworth Toole, rather than A. W. Toole, as well-meaning friends and associates often recommended.

His fall from grace came in 1932 when his boss, County Treasurer Oscar Shaw, a Republican, was defeated for re-election. Al, as everyone called him, knew that a change of the helm would also mean the end of his job.

So, in late December 1932 he called me into the vault at the county treasurer's office and made the shocking disclosure that he had misappropriated county funds.

"I want to tell you something," he said. "I'm going upstairs and tell the grand jury that I'm $6,207 short. (He knew the exact amount.) I'm going to throw myself at their mercy and they probably will indict me."

Editors at the *News-Press* were so stunned by the revelation that they wouldn't accept it, thinking it was some kind of trick or joke so I had to "sit" on his major scoop until the grand jury handed down an indictment. An audit revealed that Toole knew exactly how much was missing.

He drew a three-year sentence and during his stint at the penitentiary, he was not allowed inside the walls without a pass. The reason was that he was a skilled bookkeeper and his services were needed at a prison industry, a clothing shop, located outside the walls about two blocks from the prison.

Toole slept upstairs in a room over the downstairs office of the clothing shop. The only time he ever went to the penitentiary proper was once a month to collect what in convict parlance was his "tip". (A tip in prison language is the pittance the prisoners earn for the work they do while incarcerated. In Toole's case, it was about $6 a month. Most prisoners used the money for tobacco but Toole never smoked or used alcohol and instead used it to buy candy.)

Toole returned to St. Joseph a pathetic figure from the man who once had been so proud of his name that he would rather have writer's cramp than abbreviate it in any way.

The story-behind-the story, however, is that Toole never used a nickel of the misappropriated funds for his own purposes.

He confided to me that a young friend of his was in serious trouble and needed money desperately. So Toole "borrowed" the money, knowing it was wrong and that if caught before he could pay it back, he'd have to pay the price.

No man ever was a more loyal friend.

True Davis: A Man for All Seasons

He was a fresh-faced youth of fifteen when I first saw him, a student at Central High School decked out in a modish white suit, leading his own band. True Davis, Jr. started early on a career as one of St. Joseph's most prominent native sons and newsmakers.

Davis, it has been stated, is the city's only native son who is as well-known in the stockyards of South St. Joseph and other midwestern cities as he is in Washington, D.C. and the capitals and ballrooms of Europe. The statement is true. Still, he remembers his St. Joseph roots and his many friends here.

From those bandstand beginnings, True Davis worked in the public eye, making news by his accomplishments, not controversy. By the early 1960's Davis, owner of the Anchor Serum Company in St. Joseph, had already become not only an international figure in the animal vaccine world, but was also achieving international recognition in financial and political circles.

In 1963 President John F. Kennedy appointed Davis as United States ambassador to Switzerland. In recent times, presidential appointments have faced rough going but no such partisan nonsense surfaced on this and a later occasion when True Davis was evaluated for high government posts. Not a single negative vote was cast against this man who had been one of the city's major employers and also had played an active role in Democratic politics across the state and nation.

In fact, perhaps one of the most remarkable tributes ever paid to a presidential appointee was made on Davis's behalf by a prominent senator from the opposition party. On the floor of the Senate, he stated that " the greatest need in government is for more people like True Davis for important jobs."

That was a quarter of a century ago. And his reputation has grown with the years. In his younger days, Davis had been chosen to take directing roles in major state-wide political campaigns in Missouri. He made one state race himself—a vigorous campaign for the Democratic nomination for United States senator in 1968. He finished third, but lost no luster as the winner was the current political powerhouse in Missouri, Thomas F. Eagleton. Runner-up was incumbent Ed Long.

There was a host of publicity about those endeavors as there was about some of the many other honors showered upon him—selections as Outstanding Citizen by the Chamber of Commerce, the American Legion, the Veterans of Foreign Wars and other groups. But many activities and honors did not make the front pages or the air waves back home—such as adviser to the United States delegation to the World Bank and chairman of the Department of Commerce Expansion Council. He was named an Esquire of Missouri, served on the honorary staff of Missouri governors as a colonel and was on the American Royal Board of Governors. And his honors and titles in the national animal health field would fill a good-sized book.

So great was the demand for Davis' expertise that at one time in the 1970's he was on the board of directors of 29 concerns.

In 1965 President Lyndon Johnson named Davis assistant secretary of the Treasury. Next he served as president and chairman of the board of the prestigious National Bank of Washington. For many years now, he has been a resident of Washington, D.C. and, although approaching seventy, a time when lesser men already have spent several years in retirement, True Davis is still going strong, serving as an adviser to a number of leading banking institutions around the world.

But he is still True Davis of St. Joseph.

St. Joseph also has a "native daughter" who is as well-known around the world as "native son" True Davis.

While Harold Slater is honored as a personal friend of True Davis, co-author George Sherman's link to the city's most famous female is considerably more nebulous. In fact, he never met her personally but this world-acclaimed individual formerly served as a baby sitter for one of his best friends.

The friend is Pittman T. Mayse, formerly of St. Joseph and now a retired insurance man in Phoenix, Ariz.

Mr. Mayse's famous baby sitter was born in St. Joseph in 1914 and christened with the rather mundane name of Sarah Jane Fulks.

Two significant but unrelated events occurred in Sarah Jane's life in 1948. She won an Oscar and divorced her husband. She won the Oscar under the name millions recognize—Jane Wyman. It was for her role in the movie, "Johnny Belinda."

The husband she divorced was and is a rather famous fellow in his own right. Former President Gerald Ford once said of Jane's former husband, "He and I have something in common. We both played football. I played for Michigan and he played for Warner Brothers."

They also had something else in common since Miss Wyman's ex-husband went on to become President of the United States. President Ford's football reference was to Ronald Reagan's movie role as George Gipp, the great running back for Notre Dame during the Knute Rockne era. Miss Wyman most recently has expanded her worldwide fame as the stern, domineering matriarch in the popular television series, "Falcon Crest."

True Davis and Jane Wyman have something else in common in addition to their St. Joseph origins...their political persuasion. Miss Wyman's reason for the divorce after eight years of marriage to Mr. Reagan was because she and her conservative Republican husband "...engaged in continual arguments over their vastly different political views."

VIGNETTES

Fillers and Funnies—
and Some Philosophy—
from a Newsman's Notes

PART SIX

The Days of Those Superb Fire Horses

The St. Joseph Fire Department was motorized in 1923, but a few of the marvelous fire horses that had pulled the wagons around town still were enjoying their "retirement" in a nearby pasture a few years later.

For the present generation it would be difficult to realize how wonderfully the fire horses were trained — even to toilet manners. They were trained to perform those bodily functions on schedule and the result was clean stalls with fresh hay at the stations.

Fire Captain Joseph Traynor of Company No. 7, Tenth and Corby Streets, was one of the top trainers. The horses at that station took their exercises each evening when the weather was permissible by trotting up and down Tenth Street, without harness or riders. They galloped down to Church Street, three blocks south, then up to Lincoln, two blocks north of the fire house. They made a number of laps each evening. Small boys pleaded with the firemen for a chance to ride the animals but for safety reasons they had to be refused.

When a fire alarm sounded those horses would dash for the station and take their places before the fire wagons. They were trained to stop at marked spots on the station floor. Then the harness would drop on their backs and necks. Two snaps would be fastened on each and the horses would pull out with their wagon loads. Incidentally, the mechanism that provided for the harness to drop on the horses was the invention of a St. Joseph man.

Older St. Joseph residents, this writer among them, can recall the days when Fire Chief Pat Kane rode to fires in a racing sulky behind a high spirited horse. It was quite a sight, the horseshoes shooting out sparks as the chief, holding reins tight, drove over the numerous brick streets of that era.

Real Horse Sense

Turning back the pages of fifty years brings back colorful memories like the lunch wagon that was for years a fixture at the northeast corner of Tenth and Frederick Avenue.

During the daytime, the wagon and the horse that pulled it were kept in a feed lot at the southwest corner of Twenty-second Street and Frederick Avenue. About four-thirty or five o'clock, six afternoons a week, the wagon proprietor would hitch the horse to the wagon and trundle down to Tenth Street.

There he would unhitch the horse which, with harness dangling, would trot east on Frederick Avenue back to the feedlot at Twenty-second. There somebody would remove the harness and the horse would browse and eat until about two o'clock the next morning.

In the early morning dark, the horse, its harness dangling as before, would amble down Frederick to Tenth where the lunch wagon operator would hitch his steed to the vehicle and once again watch it meander out Frederick to that lot at Twenty-second Street.

That routine went on for years, and no one remembers the horse ever being in or causing an accident on its treks up and down Frederick — a first class example of honest to goodness horse sense.

The Czar Had Beautiful Blue Eyes

One of the most cherished interviews I ever had was with Alex Kerensky, the first premier of Russia following the overthrow of the Czar during climactic days of World War I in the 1916-1917 era.

Kerensky had been the jailer of Czar Nicholas and his family following the overthrow of the Russian government by the revolution.

I interviewed him in 1940. He then was living in New York City as an exile and he was at Maryville, Missouri as a lecturer to the Northwest Missouri teachers organization.

We talked that day in a Maryville schoolroom about what would result from Hitler sending the vaunted German army in the attack on Russia. The Hitler move only a short time before had been surprising. I talked with Kerensky about Napoleon's great mistake in trying to subdue Russia. His tragic loss in that campaign had been something of which all historians were fully aware.

But Kerensky thought it would be different this time. He figured Hitler's war machine would crush Russia. Fortunately, Kerensky's guess was poor. The great German war machine couldn't cope with the Soviet winter or the grim determination of the Soviet people at Stalingrad.

One thing about that 1940 interview I will never forget was the coat worn by Kerensky. This was a man who once had held life and death control over the whole Russian nation, a man who controlled billions of rubles, dollars and priceless artifacts. But that day in Maryville he was wearing a coat with a hole burned in one sleeve. . .

Fame and fortune indeed are fleeting.

I recall his answer when I asked him what it was like to have the Czar as his prisoner. "Czar Nicholas had the most beautiful blue eyes I ever saw," Kerensky said.

The Days of Ambulance "Runners"

Ambulance competition was pretty furious here in my police reporter days more than half a century ago.

At least five funeral homes offered ambulance service and the police department also had its ambulance, a rather battered vehicle that could do little more than pass the sanitation standards for a garbage truck.

When a call for an ambulance came in at old Central Police Station there would be a rush for telephones. It was before the day of really professional police officers and certain of the lower officers were "runners" for funeral home ambulance services.

Those chaps would get to a phone as soon as possible to tell their favorite funeral home where an ambulance was needed. Of course, they received some minor remuneration for their services.

The competition didn't stop with who got to the phone first. There also was occasional skullduggery at the scene where the ambulance was needed. That included one ambulance parking so as to block the doors of a rival ambulance and other tricks of the trade.

As for the police ambulance, well, it usually went out rather leisurely. It had no skilled attendants. The policeman in charge actually was on duty as a wagon guard for the police patrol, "The Black Maria," in which drunks and assorted lawbreakers were hauled to the police station and then up to the county jail.

The police ambulance did serve one unorthodox purpose. Some fellows, including an occasional newspaper reporter, used to sleep on its wheeled cot when the ambulance was not in use. Fortunately no one was sleeping on that cot one time when the ambulance heading north on Seventh Street from the station developed a faulty rear door, and the cot rolled out on Seventh Street and rolled south as the ambulance blissfully proceeded north.

Thankfully, I wasn't sleepy that day.

Bringing the Braggarts Back to Basics

A unique club existed here for a number of years and the good it did locally was something from which any other community might profit.

It was the "Big Feelers Club." It had no dues, no officers, no meetings, and it limited itself to a single pronouncement once a year. That event came on New Year's Day when the club announced the result of balloting on selecting the "Big Feeler of the Year"—the chap with the biggest ego that was badly in need of deflating.

The club was the brain child of a cadre of fun loving and sophisticated men, most of whom were involved daily in the business, professional and political scene of the city.

The club headquarters was the downtown Kinnison drug store. The sole ballot box was behind the prescription counter and the balloting was limited to a period of about a week before New Year's Day.

The balloting was conducted in the greatest of mock seriousness, and it was absolutely honest. The names of the young executives who tallied the ballots were never announced, but practically every man who dropped in at Kinnison's to exercise his right of franchise knew pretty well who they were.

The selection of the "Big Feeler" each year was announced solely by mouth, whispers to those who dropped in Kinnison's to see who the "winner" was. Also some of those had an interest due to the possibility they themselves might be the selection.

Every newspaper reporter in town knew about the annual election, but for obvious reasons—libel topping hurt feelings—the "victor's" name never appeared in print.

Over the more than thirty years the "Big Feelers Club" existed, only one man ever was re-elected. The "honor" he received originally did not chasten him. The fact there was one re-election may have served to induce other designees to have modified their ways for better public relations.

There was campaigning during the election period. One fellow seemed well on the way to being chosen when friends saved him the dishonor by telling potential voters they had once seen him talking to a man wearing overalls.

Another fellow was a front-runner for the title when word was spread that he once admitted he had dandruff on the collar of his blue serge coat. He lost out.

The "Big Feelers Club" dissolved without formality about forty years ago. A lot of its prime enthusiasts went away to war and then Kinnison's drug store closed its doors—and its ballot box.

It had served a useful purpose and its passing is still mourned in some circles—but not by anyone ever elected Big Feeler of the Year.

Judge Solves Pilfering Problem

At one time, the theft of coal from railroad cars was quite a problem in St. Joseph. There wasn't much in the way of welfare in those days and the people who took the coal needed it badly.

One day a habitual offender charged with stealing coal was brought into the court of Justice William Wyatt. The railroad man who made the arrest explained that the railroad didn't mind the people who picked up the coal that fell off the cars. What they objected to was the people who would climb up on the cars and toss off the coal, so that they could pick it up later on. Some of them threw off hundreds of pounds at a time.

The railroad detective said that the man in court was that type. They had caught him many times throwing coal off trains. That was why they had brought him in once again: to see if they could put an end to his thievery once and for all. The man's name (I'll never forget it) was Fitzhugh Lee.

Fitz had never been charged with a felony but he did do a little light pilfering when it suited his needs. Judge Wyatt, who usually just sent him to jail for three or four days at a time, came up with his own unique solution. He took a small piece of paper and he wrote on that piece of paper, "Fitzhugh Lee."

He gave it to the arresting railroad detective and said, "The next time that you see Fitzhugh stealing coal, just shoot him and then fill out this piece of paper. Say what time you shot him and where the body was taken. That will end the case." He told him to keep the piece of paper, so that the next time that Fitz gets in a coal stealing mood, "you can just get rid of him."

Fitzhugh Lee was never again arrested for stealing coal.

Anything for a Buck!

One of the characters I knew when working on the *News-Press* was a fellow who was sent to the penitentiary because he sold his own picture as that of a murderer.

His name was George Gorman. He was a thoroughly likeable fellow who made his living by selling stories to detective magazines and pulp-type fiction magazines. His writing style was flamboyant and sensational. He didn't always let the facts get in his way when he wanted to embellish a story.

One of the stories he sold to a detective story magazine was about a sensational murder. That magazine liked the story and asked George to get hold of a picture of the murderer and they would buy it from him. George couldn't get that picture so he sent in his own picture with a caption saying that was the murderer.

The magazine ran the picture and was embarrassed when it turned out the picture actually was that of the author. The publication filed charges for using the mails to defraud against George. The aftermath was that he was sentenced to Leavenworth prison for a year and a day.

Gorman didn't seem concerned about going to prison. In fact, he almost welcomed the opportunity. It seems he had a serious disease and figured he would have a better chance of being cured in prison than on the outside and at government expense.

Undoubtedly, he found considerable detective story material while he was in the "Big House."

This Criminal Should Have "Come Clean"

For years law enforcement officials have been urging criminals they've arrested to "come clean". This literally would have been especially good advice for one robber/rapist in the 1940's who was sentenced to a life term plus ninety-nine years for his crime.

He found out the hard way when one night he and three equally desperate criminals broke out of the Buchanan County jail and escaped in a stolen car.

After only a few blocks, the robber/rapist was forcibly ejected by his traveling companions. He made his way to the home of a woman evangelist, who returned him to the county jail and surrendered him.

Two of the other escapees were re-captured a week or so later but the fourth got away and subsequently was named as a suspect in the murder of a Georgia state trooper.

The story-behind-the-story as to why the robber/rapist was so unceremoniously dumped after only a few blocks by his cohorts turned out to be a matter of personal hygiene. His felonious companions told him that he had such a foul body odor that they couldn't stand him in the car with them, so out he went!

Whether that also was the reason the lady evangelist brought him back isn't known.

Sarah Bernhardt and Her "Silver" Slipper

A visit along the west side of St. Joseph, the business district that had been the original part of St. Joseph, was intriguing years ago when Dick Berry conducted the tour.

Dick was an oldtimer. He had been in the foundry business and was a school board member. He knew a little about the history of practically every old building in that area.

At the southwest corner of Fourth and Francis Street, he would point to a structure, since demolished, where Sarah Bernhardt, the Divine Sarah, one night had allowed well wishers to drink champagne from her slipper.

The great actress had appeared at the Lyceum Theater. The show over, she was escorted to the saloon on Francis Street for refreshments. When she left she was exuberant, although her slipper was very sodden.

And her male admirers were very happy.

Going to Bat for Ol' Diz

Dizzy Dean attained many distinctions, including the Hall of Fame, but the famed St. Louis Cardinal pitcher had one "honor" in St. Joseph that no other baseball player ever shared.

He had his own policeman bodyguard. He needed him. Chief of Police Earl M. Matthews was a baseball fan and he knew Dizzy was a valuable baseball property who needed guarding.

(After a few drinks Diz would become belligerent.) So in 1930 when Dizzy was pitching here, Matthews assigned Roy Rose, then a motorcycle officer and later a detective, to be Dizzy's personal bodyguard.

Where you saw Dizzy, you saw Roy. The policeman seemed to know no hours; Dizzy certainly didn't know any.

"The big thing was keeping Dizzy out of fights," Rose, now deceased, recalled. "Those were bootleg times and Dizzy would get quarrelsome after he sneaked a couple of drinks. I sort of ran interference for him.

"He didn't get hurt bad a single time, though. He was pleasant to me and told me later on several occasions he appreciated what I had done."

Dying Mom Deals Out "Life" Sentence

For more than forty years courthouse habitue Charley Fredericks always wore a black shirt. Some unkind souls claimed it was the same shirt day in and day out, but they might have been a bit more sympathetic had they known the story-behind-the-story.

Charley's apparent addiction to black shirts had nothing to do with personal preference. In fact, after forty years of nothing but black shirts, Charley would have been tickled pink to wear even a purple, or an orange or a lavender shirt or even no shirt at all.

The black shirt Charley habitually wore was a penance imposed on him by his mother more than forty years previously for a crime which Charley had helped to plan but which he never carried out.

It was in 1893 when a youthful Charley and a group of young co-conspirators, having imbibed a bit too freely, decided to hold up a train out in French Bottoms. They worked out details of their scheme but as the next day dawned the magnitude of what they were contemplating had a sobering effect on Charley and two or three of his fellow conspirators.

Charley confided in his mother and she reacted strongly. "You tell the law authorities immediately and don't you go through with this," she said, adding, ". . . this is a terrible thing. You go right now and report this to the police and to the sheriff's office."

Charley was a dutiful son and provided law enforcement officials details of the planned hold-up as his mother directed. They instructed him to go along with the plan and not to tip off his cronies. "Act as if you've never said a word," they instructed him, "and if there's any trouble, just fall flat and stay out of the way."

The railroad sent out a dummy train that night loaded with railroad detectives, deputy sheriffs and city police officers. Not far from the northwest limits of St. Joseph, the robber gang stopped the train and a brief gun battle ensued.

Charley did exactly as instructed by the authorities and laid low. One man was killed in the aborted robbery while several others were arrested and charged.

Because of his help, no charges were filed against Charley, but his mother was not so lenient. "You almost did a horrible thing," she told her remorseful offspring, "and for the rest of your life to remind you of it, I want you to wear a black shirt."

It was forty years after that ill-fated train robbery that newsman Harold Slater met Charley and although his mother had long ago passed away, Charley still was keeping his promise, still wearing a black shirt.

Funnyman Lou Never Forgot St. Joseph

Over the years many famous people passed through St. Joseph and some even lingered awhile before moving on to bigger challenges and achievements. To most of them the historic old river city was merely a way station on their road to more glamorous places. But one passer-through credited St. Joseph with being a major turning point in his career and his life.

He was Lou Costello, who later teamed up with Bud Abbott to entertain audiences all over the world. Costello spent a memorable winter in St. Joseph at a time when he considered himself a Hollywood failure. In 1930 Costello was on his way from Hollywood to an uncertain future back home in New Jersey when he stopped in St. Joseph and spent his last dime for breakfast. With his pockets empty, he landed a job at the burlesque house across the street from the restaurant.

In January of 1989, *News-Press/Gazette* Staff Writer Preston Filbert did a telephone interview with the famed comedian's daughter, Chris. Chris had written a book about her father entitled *Lou's On First*. The title, of course, was a take-off from the comic duo's most famous routine, "Who's on first?"

In the book, Chris Costello (Cristillo was the family name.) had written of her father's work at "the Lyceum Theater in St. Joseph." But Harold Slater, he of a prodigious memory, recalled that Lou never performed at the Lyceum Theater. Instead, Costello developed his baggy pants image at The Empress Burlesque House on South Seventh Street between Edmond and Charles Streets. The location later became, appropriately enough, a meat market and grocery store. Most recently, it has been the offices of the Burnham, Simpson, Comley and Associates Insurance Company.

Costello's daughter told Filbert that her older sister, Patty, recalled many times their father saying that " had it not been for that burlesque house (in St. Joseph), God only knows where I would've ended up."

After Slater correctly identified The Empress Burlesque House as the place where her father started his climb to the top, Chris Costello called Slater for more information.

She particularly wanted to know where her father had lived in St. Joseph but even Slater couldn't provide that information. The one man who was closest to Costello in St. Joseph and who would have known where he lived was Carl Castel. Castel was a theater musician at the time and later became editor of a labor paper but he had been dead for many years before Chris Costello wrote her book. Costello was a lonely man, Slater recalls, and much in need of the friendship that Carl Castel gave him.

Slater believes that Costello had a room in one of the several cheap rooming houses in the area of The Empress. The comedian who later earned millions was working for $20 to $25 a week in St. Joseph and spending most of it at a speakeasy around the corner. The speakeasy was located in Turner Hall. It was later razed and, ironically, now is the site of the St. Joseph Young Men's Christian Association.

Costello's daughter-biographer believes there is a definite trend today away from the explicit, raunchy comedy of an Eddie Murphy or a Richard Pryor back to the slapstick, wisecracking routines of the Abbott and Costello era. She says most of the fan mail today comes from enthusiasts who are under thirty years old.

The sleaze that spews forth from an Eddie Murphy, a Richard Pryor or a George Carlin is forgotten almost as soon as it is mouthed. In contrast, like the classics, old wine and vintage cars, the routines of comedians like Charlie Chaplin, Buster Keaton, Laurel and Hardy and Abbott and Costello, through the magic of films and video cassettes, will be entertaining and keeping fans of all ages laughing for generations to come.

But for one of the funniest of the classic funnymen, his winter in St. Joseph was no laughing matter.

The Book Most Stolen, Seldom Bought

Do big name authors make a lot of money?

I asked Homer Croy the question one day when he talked with a group of *News-Press* reporters. His answer would dampen any literary aspirations a bit.

The celebrated Croy was distinguished for his many books. His latest one, "Jesse James Was My Neighbor," had just been published. Homer had done a lot of research on the book and spent a lot of time writing it. He had made the grand total of $8,000 on it, he said, from a royalty of a quarter of a penny per copy.

"One movie company liked the title," Homer said. "They paid me $2,500 for the title—then made a movie that followed the book practically not at all."

One thing made him happy, though. A national survey showed that "Jesse James Was My Neighbor" was the book most frequently stolen from public libraries.

What Else Is New?

When Charles Evans Hughes, later chief justice of the United States Supreme Court, spoke in St. Joseph at a major Republican rally, I asked him what he considered the major crime in the nation.

He had an immediate and surprising answer: Perjury.

"Even though people are asking God to witness the truth of what they are saying, there is an unbelievable amount of lying by witnesses in court, in both civil and criminal cases," he said.

"The whole moral fiber of the nation is endangered by the amount of perjury that is being committed in our courts. For a great number of people, the oath to tell the truth has become meaningless."

If any man was in a position to know, it was Hughes. And one wonders what the chief justice would answer today to the same question.

The Army Invades S-a-x-t-o-n

"We've got an unbelievable situation here."

It was Steve Abbott of the Burlington Railroad on the phone that Saturday morning with what turned into one of the most unusual "war stories" of St. Joseph. It was in the early days of World War II and "We've got more than six hundred soldiers with orders to report for duty at Saxton," Steve told me. "They're there now."

Saxton was a Buchanan County town with a population of some twenty souls. It had two buildings—a grocery store and a school which also served as a lodge hall and community gathering place. The Burlington did not even have a depot in Saxton. It had a tool shed and a small paved place where passengers could get on or off the local when it stopped there—which was not often.

It's easy to imagine the townspeople's confusion when the Army decamped six hundred soldiers there. There was nothing for them to do and no place for them to go. Fortunately, the Burlington had a track clear enough for the detachment to wait there until someone could find out what had happened.

171

No one could conceive of any reason for six hundred soldiers to be sent to Saxton (S-A-X-T-O-N) until the railroad made a hurried check and discovered the answer:

The soldiers destination should have been Sikeston, Missouri (S-I-K-E-S-T-O-N), catty-cornered across the state deep in the Bootheel. It was a case of pronunciation on the telephone—a caller with a southern accent, perhaps.

It was a costly and frustrating misunderstanding, but the folks at Saxton were mighty relieved to learn that they were not being invaded. It was the biggest crowd they'd ever had, bigger even than a Democratic rally.

The Most Helpful Invention

Maybe she was right.

I was interviewing a woman here in the Thirties on the occasion of her one hundredth birthday, trying to avoid the often inane questions reporters come up with on such occasions. What, I asked her, did she regard as the most helpful invention during her lifetime?

Window screens, she said.

In her early life she had seen no automobiles, listened to no radios nor watched any television, plugged in no electrical appliances. She had not been warmed by central heating nor cooled by air conditioning. Yet her choice was window screens. She explained:

"Today we have no idea of how bad it was in summertime before there were window screens. Cooking was a torture, with flies and other insects coming in the kitchen through open windows. Even eating meals was an ordeal.

"The only way to avoid the hordes of pests was to keep the windows closed. Then you would just about suffocate. Window screens ended all that."

So much for the good old days.

Fond Memories of a Shabby Room

Many years ago a distinguished American author from the East came to the *News-Press* office with a most unusual request. He wanted to be taken down to a tawdry bawdy house where he had experienced his first encounter with a woman of the world.

He had been a country boy then, a callow youth inexperienced about the facts of life. He had never seen a nude woman, he said, but drawings he had seen had made him curious to see one. So he had gone to this bawdy house.

A newsman friend took him to the address where he retained fond memories of his adventure as a young visitor to the town. The building was still standing. It was still being used as a bordello, operated now by a black woman. She was courteous but curious when the author asked her if she would take him to a certain second story room.

So he told the new madam and the newsman his story:

In that long ago day of his adventure he had carried a pad of scratch paper and he told the madam at the house that he was an artist and needed a naked girl as a model for his sketching. She collected three dollars from him and sent him a girl to the second story room.

The prostitute stripped and he faced her with his drawing pad. She peeked over in a few minutes and saw he had drawn only a few straight lines. She asked him for the truth and he told her he was just a ignorant boy from the sticks.

"She was very nice," the author recalled almost a half century later. "She saw to it that I got my money's worth."

14 DEAD, 3 MISSING IN BLAST
AT PLANT OF ARMOUR COMPAN

Five-Story Building Is Razed by the Explosion Which Occurred at 3:15 P. M. Yesterday.

BURIED BY TONS OF DEBRIS

Rescuers Work All Night to Recover Bodies, Believing That Some Might Have Survived the Crushing Weight—Eight Injured Persons in Hospitals—Survivors Unable to Account for Disaster—Ammonia Fumes Hinder Firemen — Property Damage Nearly Half a Million.

An explosion, that form of disas-ter which St. Joseph has rightfully ...ed by the gases. It is not improb-able that some of the victims, who were not instantly killed by the

was dead, and the announcemen it sent a wave of horror thro the already large crowd. Not u then did it seem to dawn upon multitude what a terrible thing happened.

Armour police officers immed ly closed the plant property, wl is fenced on the east, to the pu Despite that, a number obta admittance by going around to back of the property.

Order Out of Chaos.

Led by Fire Chief Leo J. Ur ski, a small parade of fire tr

Continued on Page Two.

THE CASUALTY LIST

THE DEAD.

Arthur Paul Rogers, twe seven, 6208 South Ninth street. Earl Walter Hansen, thirty-823 Harmon street. Clement Ray Rickman, th four, 2826 Mary street. Mrs. Matilda Loar, forty

The Armour Tragedy
(See page 193.)

174

One "—if only . . ." and Other Stories on the Eternal Quest of Who, What, Why, When, Where and How Come

eight—Eight Injured Persons in Hospitals
-vivors Unable to Account for Disaster—
onia Fumes Hinder Firemen — Property
ige Nearly Half a Million.

on. that form of disas- | ed by the gases. It is not improb-
Joseph has rightfully | able that some of the victims, who
read in the last four- | were not instantly killed by the
·late yesterday after- | falling debris, met death from in-
·d a five-story build- | haling the fumes.
mour & Co. plant in St. | Gas masks were resorted to, and
ling in the loss of four- | the work went ahead. An hour
juring eight and leav- | later the gas was not nearly so
· missing; and causing | noticeable, and by 7 o'clock last
mage of $400,000—to | night it was giving the rescuers
| very little trouble.
hout warning beneath | The exact hour of the explosion
d beams of the build- | has been fixed as 3:15 p. m. Had
· the smokehouse, ten | the blast occurred a half hour ear-
r women were crushed | lier it is probable that at least
| twenty others would have been
ance to Escape. | trapped in the building.
no chance to escape | All the injured persons are at
rible death. The blast, | the Missouri Methodist Hospital,
eyewitnesses as a puff. | where they are being attended by
a loud report, jarred | Drs. C. S. Branson and J. T. Tuck-
the building to their | er. Armour plant physicians. With
and allowed the fire | the exception of one man, Orville
op. The heavy walls | Wise, all are given a good chance
burying their victims | for recovery.
n forty feet of debris.
and or more employes | **Back at Work Today.**
any were startled by | Three different agencies will in-
glance at the wrecked | vestigate the cause of the tragedy
a enough to indicate | —the coroner, a citizens' committee,
s of life was heavy. | and Armour & Co. Officials of the
firemen and police | company have stated they believe
ned on the single tele- | natural gas caused the explosion,
hich had not been de- | but this has met with a denial from
he explosion. | officials of the gas company.
s Flock to Scene. | Meanwhile, business is going on
spread over South St. | as usual at the plant. The loss of
e many packing house | the one department does not seri-
side. The roads and | ously cripple the operation at pres-
ng to the plant were | ent. The usual number of laborers
with anxious relatives | is being employed.
of the plant, seeking | The corps of workers at the scene
there, brothers and sis- | was this afternoon continuing its
rst body was removed | feverish pace in tearing away the
f hour after the blast. | mass of ruins in the effort to reach
er twenty-four hours | the other persons known to be
r bodies has been car- | buried in the mass of brick and
| timber.
of the building were | Had the explosion occurred only
yield their victims. | a few minutes later it is doubtful
laborers worked fran- | if any lives would have been lost,
ght. some without rest. | as most of the workers in that part
as piled as high as the | of the building were getting ready
Hundreds of tons of | to leave.
d to be moved. Huge | A dull thud and a crashing roar
ns a foot square and | informed those outside of the build-
long had to be moved. | ing of the catastrophe. Volunteers
| rushed to the scene and were met
· Fumes Prevalent. | by ammonia fumes that made res-
pipes, which ran | cue impossible for a short time.
the entire building, | Companies from the South Side
· their deadly vapors. | fire station, in charge of Assistant
· of firemen were balk- | Chief Alex Mason; the Armour fire
| department, and the St. Joseph
| Stock Yards Company used what
| gas masks they had in beginning
| the rescue. A wind soon carried
| the fumes away and the masks
| were abandoned.
| The first body to be taken from
| the wreckage was that of Arthur
| Rogers, 6208 South Ninth street. He

THE CASUALTY LIST

THE DEAD.

Arthur Paul Rogers, twenty-seven, 6208 South Ninth street.
Earl Walter Hansen, thirty-two, 823 Harmon street.
Clement Ray Rickman, thirty-four, 2820 Mary street.
Mrs. Matilda Loar, forty-four, 8410 Renick street.
Mrs. Mary Johnston, thirty-two, 715 Mary street.
Lloyd Fox, twenty-three, 1009 Mitchell avenue.
Charles Theodore Moore, twenty-six, 6418 Carnegie street.
Gerald Munden, twenty-two, 204 West Nebraska avenue.
Miss Margaret Lee Willis, nineteen, 6312 Sherman street.
Miss Verna F. Durkin, twenty, 6538 Carnegie street.
James R. Staples, twenty-five, 6402 King Hill avenue.
Joseph Scott, twenty-seven, 910 East Hyde Park avenue.
Dexter Bowlin, twenty-eight, 220 West Colorado avenue.
L. E. Wiles, forty-five, 403 Michigan street.

THE MISSING.

George R. Roberts, route No. 4, twenty-four years old, married.
Ora Paxson, 8320 Belding street, twenty-two years old, single.
Frank Wieczorek, 1202 South Twenty-sixth street, forty years old.

THE INJURED.

Orville Wise, 816 Rudy street; employed in the smokehouse; badly burned and crushed; condition somewhat improved, but not expected to live.
George Kless, thirty-four years old, 1119 Prospect avenue; employed in the dry salt cellar; burns on hands, face and head; condition not serious.
James Sparks, thirty-four years old, Kirschner's addition; employed in the smokehouse; fractured ribs and burns; condition serious, but will recover.
Gottlieb Weidener, 808 Woodson street; sixty years old; employed in the sweet pickle department; scalp wounds; condition fair.
Mrs. Flora Miller, about sixty years old, 6106 King Hill avenue; employed in the smokehouse; fractured ankle, burns on face, hands and head; condition fair.
Mrs. Louise Webb, twenty-three years old, 1917 South Tenth street; employer in the smokehouse; severe burns on hands, feet and face; condition fair.
Walter Kline, rural route No. 7, employed in the sausage department; badly bruised and burned about face and body; condition fair.
Carl Pape, twenty-four years old, 2001 Mitchell avenue; employed in the operating department of the St. Joseph Gas Company; overcome by ammonia fumes; condition not serious.

---

he ominous ringing of an am-
lance bell replaced the cheery w
tle of the workmen. Scarcel
man left the plant. Rescue w
demanded the attention of ev
person in the entire personnel
more than 2,000.
Thirty minutes later anxi
faces tried to peer through
spaces in the picket fence. H
dreds of women gathered. Line
anxiety were drawn on pale fa
Children, fearful that fathers w
trapped in the ruins, held ha
Some of them were barefoot,
they stayed until late hours of
night.

'Wives Were Frantic.

Supper time came, and hundr
of men failed to come home
their meal. Wives were fran
but how were they to know t
their men were alive and doing
assist in the rescue of their fel
workmen?
By 8 o'clock the front gate of
plant was the scene of a sol
packed mass of humanity. Child
cried. Women's shouts could
heard above the noisy hum.
wrecked building itself was out
sight from the main gate. The
fice of the company was besie
by men and women seeking no
of relatives.
Policemen found it difficult
restrain the crowd whenever
gate was opened to admit a per
Only those who had business ins
the fence were allowed through
gate, although hundreds approac
from the rear and occupied po
tions of vantage on tops of b
cars.

Beg for News.

The gate was opened to admi
newspaper reporter. A woman
a pink gingham dress and ho
slippers begged him to try to f
her husband. A man edged throu

Continued on Page Two.

The Weather T

THE FORECAST.

Friday, May 8, 1936.
St. Joseph and vicinity—Mostly unset
and cooler tonight and Saturday with p
ably showers or
thunder storms.
Missouri—Mostly
unsettled tonight
and Saturday
probably loc
showers or thu
der storms;
tonight in norh-
west portion, cool-
er Saturday except
in extreme south-
east portion
Kansas— Mostly
fair in the west,
possibly showers or
thunder storms to-
night or Saturday
in the east portion; cooler in the east
tion, slightly cooler tonight in the so
west portion.
Nebraska—Mostly unsettled, tonight
Saturday, probably occasional rain; s
snow in the extreme west portion, c
tonight in the west and central por
and in the extreme southeast portion
urday, freezing temperature tonight in
extreme west portion.

The government weather m

The Armour Casualty List

PART SEVEN

The Stories They'll Tell

Some people can be unbelievably creative when a reporter starts nosing around—or after they read what he's written.

Many years ago a man called the *News-Press* office to complain that state hospital patients had painted a private business place in his neighborhood. The office sent me down to get the story.

The place they had painted was a combination restaurant and gasoline station. The state hospital attendant with them turned out to be a former detective I had known when I was police reporter. He and the crew of inmate painters were still at the business place when I arrived.

For that evening's edition I wrote the story about the state patients painting the place and also mentioned that the attendant in charge of them was the father-in-law of the restaurant-gasoline station operator.

The next morning the attendant called me. "The story was all wrong," he said. "See, what happened," he said, "was that the patients had been painting structures out at State Hospital No. 2 and they had done such a good job that I decided to take them on a picnic as a reward."

They had stopped at the restaurant-gasoline station to purchase the food for the picnic, he said, and the painting patients had noticed a number of brushes and cans of paint around the premises. "It happened," he said, "that the men who had been doing the painting had walked off the job."

The attendant's story (unexpurgated) was that while he was inside ordering the food, the patients had picked up the brushes and painted away to their heart's delight.

He said it was the patients' own idea, that he didn't know

177

they were going to do it and was unaware of what had happened until the artists had had their fun.

Maybe some folks believed him. I didn't.

The Interview That Didn't Happen

I missed out on one interview in 1931 that I have always regretted. It was to have been with Al Capone, kingpin of the famed and feared Chicago crime syndicate.

Capone had been able to avoid jail for the murders, robberies and liquor law violations that had been laid at his doorstep—or had *tried*—to be laid there. Officials were certain he was behind wholesale law violations and violence but they couldn't get the evidence on him.

But "Scarface" Al had cheated on his income tax and the government had nailed him. He had been sentenced to eleven years in federal prison as a tax cheat.

On a certain date, according to the wire services, Capone was to be taken from Chicago to Leavenworth, across the Missouri River from St. Joseph and his train was to come through St. Joseph.

David W. Hopkins was our congressman then; more important, he was a member of the House prison affairs committee. I asked his help in lining up an interview with old Al. Dave called the warden and Capone's host-to-be said he would arrange for me to see his new room-and-boarder after he was dressed in. The warden explained it would be up to Capone if he wanted to answer any questions.

The next step was to call Steve Abbott, the highly efficient and genial passenger agent of the Burlington Railroad. Steve arranged for me to ride on the prisoner's car from St. Joseph to Leavenworth.

I didn't sleep much that night as I anxiously looked ahead to being at Union Station at six o'clock in the morning. I got a big jolt when I looked at the *Gazette*. A front page story said there had been a last-minute change in plans—Al Capone was to be sent to Atlanta penitentiary instead of to Leavenworth.

I mentally kicked a few chairs because no reporter likes missing chances at big newsmakers like him. But I could try for a consolation prize. Capone's brother, Ralph "Bottles" Capone, was still coming through on the train. So I went to Union Passenger Station. I got on the train with Steve Abbott's help and the conductor pointed out Ralph Capone to me.

"Bottles" was reading a newspaper when I approached him. I told him I was a reporter and tried to start up a conversation with him.

He told me to get lost, quit bothering him and go to hell. I don't believe, from his manner, that he had read Emily Post.

But the incident has its dividend. I can still tell my grandchildren, "Yep, I knew old "Bottles" Capone. Last time I talked to him was right here in St. Joseph, down at the old Union Passenger Station. I could show you but, too bad, they tore the place down "

April Fool Fools Publisher

In the heyday of journalism, when the daily newspaper almost was a Bible to readers, it was not unusual for reporters to develop elaborate April Fool stories. There was no intent to actually deceive the public, only to produce a tongue-in-cheek article for everyone's pleasure.

Two of the masters of the April Fool story were Harold Slater, who later became city editor of the *News-Press*, and Don Houseworth, former city editor of the *Gazette*.

One of Slater's classics was written nearly fifty years ago, but like a rare wine it is just as savory today as it was then and probably would get some of the same response from those who "skim" rather than read carefully.

Slater's story quoted "nationally known" engineers (in his story he gave them fancy names and even fancier degrees) who had released "an international study" that city streets wore out only on the top side, so the thing to do was to jack them up and turn them over. That way, according to Slater's "brilliant engineer" sources, the other side of the paving would be good as new and streets would last twice as long.

Just to help make it clear to the careful reader that the story was a hoax, Slater gave his "brilliant engineers" an address in an imaginary town which the story described as being located 175 miles east of Boston, Mass.

Several legitimate engineers wrote the paper for more information on this unique concept, but the story-behind-the-story is that Slater's own publisher fell victim to the hoax.

Minutes after the paper came off the presses, he rushed into the newsroom shouting there was an error in Slater's story. "Boston is on the east coast," he exclaimed, "the home of those engineers couldn't be 175 miles east, it must be some other direction!"

There is no record of his comment when it dawned that he had been the first to be hoist on Slater's petard.

A "Royal" Solution
or
The "Siamese" Connection

Harold Slater's classic April Fool "spoof" on jacking up the streets and turning them over so as to get twice as much wear out of them is rivaled only by a Don Houseworth hoax relative to what was then known as the "Free Bridge" connecting St. Joseph and the state of Kansas. Houseworth's ploy required considerable time, effort and planning.

Houseworth at the time was city editor of the *Gazette* and he became increasingly irritated when neither the city nor the state would accept responsibility for giving the bridge a badly needed paint job.

It didn't take long for Houseworth's fertile mind to conceive an idea that would put both the city and the state in an untenable position. Houseworth utilized a local derelict of the day who had been an old Chautauqua performer and bestowed on him the impressive title of Sir Basil Worthington-Worthington. That alone was enough to guarantee that the story would get plenty of attention. But there was more...

"Sir" Basil then showed up on the bridge and claimed it for the Queen of Siam, intimating that he was a close personal friend of the Siamese royal household. Why Siam? Simple. Houseworth knew a missionary lady named Cole who owned a Siamese flag and who was willing to loan it to him to help Sir Basil lay claim to the bridge. The cooperative Ms. Cole also produced a pith helmet, which Sir Basil wore with gusto even though it was February and the pith helmet had no ear flaps.

With Houseworth grinding out the publicity, Sir Basil first set up a pup tent on the bridge to solidify his claim. Subsequently, he moved his tent to the Missouri approach to the bridge because his original location on the bridge interfered with traffic.

Houseworth paid Sir Basil a few dollars a day for his services and also provided his "dignitary" with some impressive looking law books that he had borrowed from a courthouse office. Sir Basil kept them handy in his tent.

Ferd Frankenhoff was police judge at the time and very cooperative with Houseworth's plan. It was arranged to have Sir Basil arrested on a trespassing charge. Several local attorneys offered to defend him, but Sir Basil claimed his personal attorney lived in Cincinnati and could "...get this case thrown out of court in two minutes."

They had a police court trial and Sir Basil was exonerated from the trespass charge but advised he would have to move from the bridge area. Indicating that the Queen of Siam was a very headstrong woman and really wanted that bridge as one of her possessions, Sir Basil declared he would carry his claim all the way to the United State Supreme Court if need be.

Sir Basil's (and Houseworth's) efforts proved most beneficial to the city of St. Joseph. As a result of the publicity, the state finally, albeit reluctantly, paid the city approximately $70,000 to paint and repair the bridge, which incidentally had been built originally with a city bond issue.

Harold Slater played a key role in the hoax and was the individual who located Sir Basil originally. Slater knew Sir Basil as a bum, a round little man standing about five-foot two but weighing in at close to 230 pounds and who slept at the old City Hall when it was opened during the Depression for homeless men. He took his meals at St. Vincent's cafeteria, a "soup kitchen" located on Second Street near Felix, established by Father Charles Buddy to feed the poor during those terrible days.

The story-behind-the-story is that there was a sad note to the conclusion of the affair. The colorful Sir Basil, who played his role so well, turned out to be a pervert and a sex offender and was sentenced to two years in the Missouri State penitentiary.

There's no record of the Queen of Siam making any effort to get him a pardon.

Will The Real Jesse Please Stand Up?

During the 1930's and early 1940's a succession of old men showed up in St. Joseph making the same claim: They actually were Jesse James and the body of another law breaker had been substituted for Jesse and tucked away in a grave as the famed outlaw.

The story of each Jesse followed the same pattern: a great hoax had been played on the unsuspicious citizenry here. In each instance, the doddering old fellow who claimed to be the real Jesse was accompanied by a retinue of several sharp looking young fellows who figured they were going to be rich parading Jesse back and forth across the nation.

One of the first fake Jesses to drop into town took newspaper reporters out to 1328 Lafayette Street where Jesse had been killed April 3, 1882. He had buried a shooting iron at the foot of a tree in the James' front yard just before he supposedly had been murdered, he said.

The old fellow went to a tree a few feet from the house and dug up a rusted revolver. Proudly, he said, "That's the very gun I buried." His story promptly collapsed. Years before, some years after the killing, the James's lot had been graded down and the entire lot and house lowered twenty-five feet. The fake Jesse left town the next day.

Another of the fraudulent claimants induced the management of the Electric Theater to present him on the stage there in lieu of a vaudeville act. "Jesse" discussed his train and bank robberies and other bits of lore, then said, "If I'm not Jesse James, then who am I?"

A smarty out in the audience asked, "Clara Bow?" It broke up the show and ended locally at least old "Jesse's" stage career.

One of the last imposters who showed up here very appropriately was housed at the Jesse James Hotel, then standing at Third and Jule Streets. "I was sent down to interview him the morning after he arrived here." Harold Slater recalled. "He was having breakfast in bed and invited me to share the meal with him. He was having doughnuts and whiskey. I was a sissy and ordered from the regular menu."

That old fellow lost out a few years later when he went to court in southern Missouri in a vain effort to try to collect a $10,000 reward that had been offered by the James descendants for anyone who could prove he was Jesse. He definitely wasn't.

Bad Man Burke Blacks Out Newsmen

The most famous criminal ever arrested by the St. Joseph police department was Fred Burke, the Chicago gangster, who was then a prime suspect in the 1929 Valentine Day massacre in Chicago in which seven of George "Bugs" Moran's mob were gunned down.

That arrest was on March 26, 1931. Harold Slater wasn't in on the main story of his capture. That assignment was handled by *News-Press* reporter Leonard Jordan, but as a "consolation prize" Slater got to interview the man who had been sought by authorities all over the United States for two years.

Slater said later he could sum up in one word what Burke told him in that interview: "Nothing."

Burke had been characterized as the "most dangerous man alive" when four St. Joseph police officers — Captain John Lard, Detectives Melvin Swepston, A.W. Thedinga and Ray Kelly — acting on a tip went to Green City in Sullivan County, Missouri, to arrest Burke in bed at his father-in-law's home. Sheriff Hoover of Sullivan County and two lawmen there backed them up in the action.

Burke was caught before he had time to reach for a .32 caliber automatic pistol in a chair with his clothing near the bed. He offered no resistance, said his arrest was a mistake and gave an alias for his name. The officers didn't buy that.

He was brought to old Central Police Station at Seventh and Messanie Street, where Captain Bert T. Andrews through fingerprints and Bertillon measurements quickly confirmed the identification of the "most wanted man." Burke then meekly agreed they had the right man.

In addition to being sought as a prime suspect in the Valentine Day massacre, Burke also was wanted for questioning about $220,000 in ransom kidnappings in Detroit, the murder of a St. Joseph, Michigan, police officer, a Detroit jewelry store robbery, a mail truck holdup in Toledo, Ohio, bank robberies at Cadillac, Michigan, and Peru, Indiana, the murder of two people in Detroit, a $352,000 bank holdup in Jefferson, Wisconsin, and the wounding of a bank cashier in a holdup at Louisville, Kentucky.

The charges on which he was sought added up to at least a dozen murders and the taking of nearly $1,000,000 in robberies.

The rewards offered for his capture totaled $90,000, but they largely melted away under legal technicalities. The four St. Joseph police officers eventually received only about $1,200 in reward — which went to the police department pension fund and not to them as individuals.

The tip that led to the capture of Burke came from a detective story magazine reader at Green City. He was suspicious of Burke because he did not work, always had money, and refused to get out of his car in the sight of strangers.

There was a rush by Chicago police and Michigan law enforcement men, including those from Detroit, when word of his capture was announced. The Chicago detectives drove here by motor car because train schedules weren't convenient. The carried with them seven murder warrants for the "Massacre" slayings.

Police treated Burke like a celebrity here and in a way he was. He was courteous but admitted nothing other than his name. When a newsman said he knew he had served time in the Missouri state penitentiary, Burke did nod agreement.

He did agree to waive extradition to go to Michigan for a trial on the charge of murdering the policeman. It wasn't that he was trying to cooperate but rather, he told officers here, that he just couldn't go through another session of third degree questioning by the Chicago detective department. That town had a reputation of cruelty in its questioning of criminals.

Burke was taken from here to St. Joseph, Michigan, where he drew a life sentence for killing the police officer, a crime he had committed to avoid payment of $5 to a farmer to repair a fender on his car. He died in prison a few years later.

Calls poured in on Chief of Police Earl M. Mathews as word of the arrest of Burke spread. Mathews permitted an Omaha officer to talk to Burke by phone. When the Omahan asked Burke a question, the prisoner said, "If you want to learn anything about me, you better go see a spiritualist."

Burke, who had had some hard times in police stations along his criminal path, showed his appreciation for the courteous way he was treated here. He gave each of his captors and several police executives top-rank fountain pens before he was taken away.

Now about Slater's interview with Burke:

They had hung blankets around his junky cell at the police station to save him from being seen by the curious. Informed an interview was sought, Burke said, "I don't want to hurt your feelings, but I'm not going to tell anything or say anything." He even declined to chat about the outlook for the Chicago Cubs and the pending mayoral race between Big Bill Thompson and Anton Cermak. "Aren't you ever going to quit asking questions?" he said. "You are just not going to get anything from me."

There was only one consolation for Slater: The top-notch Chicago and Detroit reporters who came here, including nationally famous Bob Casey, couldn't get anything out of Burke either.

The Alcatraz "Caper"

It probably is not the kind of thing to boast about, but the fact remains that to me one of my memorable days as a newsman was when I was kicked out of Alcatraz prison.

I had told United States Marshal F.M. Wilson of my curiosity about Alcatraz where Al Capone and countless other major criminals had been held. I knew that he delivered offenders to prisons all over the nation and asked if he could arrange for me to visit Alcatraz.

F.M. was a man of action. He called me a few days later and said he had a federal prisoner to take to San Francisco and that he would send me along as a guard.

Two days later in Kansas City I met Jack Obink, marshal for the state of Nebraska, who was to be in charge of delivering the convict to San Franscisco. Then I met Charlie, the man we were taking along.

Charlie was about forty-five years old and very talkative. He had been in the rackets, had operated night clubs in New York, had been in several prisons, including Leavenworth, and claimed to have high connections in organized crime. He was trouble from the start.

When they took him out of the Jackson County jail he complained of severe abdominal pains. He was taken to a hospital where a couple of doctors said he was okay and could make the plane trip. So in a speeding car, with a blast siren, we were taken to Kansas City International Airport and ushered onto the San Francisco plane just seconds before it was due to depart.

Marshal Obink put Charlie in a seat next to a window, put me next to Charlie, then took the seat on the aisle himself. I was not armed. Obink was.

Charlie was unhappy. He didn't like lawmen and he particularly didn't like United States marshals. He cursed Obink loudly and at length several times, then tried to shame me by loudly shouting, "You dirty screw, you filthy screw, you rat, you fink." I smiled sweetly at him.

Charlie started anew on how he hated lawmen. "I was in a penitentiary tier where there were five men serving time for having killed or assaulted United States marshals," he said. "You are no better than their victims." he said as he pointed a finger at the very calm Obink.

Two nuns in habits were setting in the plane seats immediately ahead of us. Charlie was very apologetic to them between his blasts at Obink and me. He addressed them as "holy sisters" and said he was sorry for his language. They gave no indication of paying attention.

Upon arriving at Denver, we were met by a very courteous young officer of TWA who notified us that we were barred from continuing further due to Charlie's conduct. Obink thanked him, then started checking to see how we could continue on another airline. He learned their blacklisting of Charlie's party applied to all air lines.

Obink did some pondering. He decided the best thing to do was to take Charlie to the Denver county jail and have him held overnight in the hope we could get a plane out to San

Francisco the following morning. He said if we couldn't get a plane we would have to take Charlie out to California on a train; that it would be a long trip and that we probably would have to stay overnight in Salt Lake City.

So we headed out to the Denver county jail, quite an institution in its own right. It is about ten miles away from downtown Denver and large enough with its surrounding walls to look like a small penitentiary.

The warden was agreeable to holding Charlie overnight. Obink explained to the officials that Charlie claimed numerous medical ailments, and also claimed to need certain medications and told how Charlie had lain down on a runway at the Denver airport and said he was dying. It took some strong urging to get him to rise.

Obink and I spent the night at the Brown Palace Hotel and then went out to the jail the next morning to pick up Charlie. I don't know what they had done to Charlie but he was an entirely different person. He was very affable and said he was going to arrange a mammoth and swank party for us when we reached San Francisco. We didn't know whom he was going to get to attend.

Obink, incidentally, had used strategy to get Charlie on the plane out of Denver. Because Charlie had been barred from air travel the day before, Obink gave him a new name in buying his ticket. It was "F.M. Wilson."

A marshal met us at the San Francisco airport and took us to a federal jail. Obink asked me to escort Charlie back to a cell while he provided the booking information. Charlie claimed illness again. He said he was faint and I practically had to carry him back to a large holding cell where about twenty other men were being held.

After I had lugged Charlie over to a bench I turned around and realized the deputy who had taken us to the cell had disappeared and there was no other officer around. The deputy had assumed I was a prisoner too. I waited in the cell with my "colleagues" about ten minutes before a jailer appeared.

I explained I was not supposed to be a prisoner and he said he would see what he could do. I was locked up for about another ten minutes before a jailer appeared with Obink to let me out. Obink was laughing uproariously. I didn't appreciate his sense of humor.

At the United States marshal's office Obink explained that the two of us wanted to visit Alcatraz. The deputy expressed grave doubts they would allow me to get to Alcatraz.

We weren't giving up. Alcatraz was located on a high rocky island in San Francisco Bay. A small launch operated by a prison guard was used to take people to and from the prison. Obink had an idea. He held me by the arm as if I also was his prisoner, walked up to the guard, gave him his name and showed him his identification, and then marched me on the boat.

The prison structures on Alcatraz were about two hundred feet or more of sheer rock cliffs — above the bay water level. It truly deserves the name given it by convicts many years ago, "The Rock."

Obink and I were put through a metal detector and told to remove anything metallic on our bodies, even to coins and belt buckles and keys. The detector buzzed when I went through and the operator said I apparently had some metallic object in my inside coat pocket. It turned out I had a ballpoint pen in that pocket and that the metal ferrule tube in it had set off the detector.

Straight up to the main prison building is less than two hundred feet from the landing place, but to get there one rode a bus that made numerous hairpin turns along a curving road up the side of the mammoth rock.

Obink and I were taken to the main office and introduced to the warden, O.G. Blackwell. We had been chatting there for about ten minutes about national conditions and the weather, before a prison trusty came into the office and handed Blackwell a note. The warden read it and grew livid.

"You're a reporter," he roared, "and we don't allow reporters on Alcatraz. You didn't give your real occupation when you signed the register. I'm going to get the marshal fired who sent you out here as a guard." He went on berating me, called in a guard and said, "Have this man taken away from Alcatraz immediately."

The guard called for the bus, took me down to the dock, and put me on the launch. As we headed back to the mainland across San Francisco Bay, I made an innocuous remark to the pilot, the only other person on the launch.

"Sir," he said, "I am under instructions not to speak to you."

I should have felt unwanted, but didn't. I had seen quite a bit of Alcatraz, met the warden and, all things considered, it had been a most interesting day.

Incidentally, in signing in at Alcatraz I had put down my occupation as "guard". After all, I had been one for all of two days.

Warden Blackwell asked me to make him a pledge: I would never write or speak of having been on Alcatraz. I told him I would make no such pledge, that I planned to write a news story. That was then he ordered me off the island after first citing to me a federal regulation stating no newspaper reporter or relative of any federal prisoner should ever serve as a guard or be allowed in the prison.

The day was educational. I still don't know whatever became of Charlie.

．　．　．　．　．

Note: Alcatraz was a grim, forbidding place, the drab prison buildings in stark contrast to the sparkling city and beautiful bay surrounding it. It was what many still believe a prison should be. For what it is worth, those who believe that a penitentiary should not be a particularly pleasant place may be vindicated by these words from a former inmate scrawled in large letters across one wall at Alcatraz.

"Nothing is worth coming back to this place for."

．　．　．　．　．

When the federal government decided to close Alcatraz prison it transferred its toughest and most troublesome prisoners to the new penitentiary at Marion, Illinois. Just as at Alcatraz, these new tough and dangerous prisoners were sent to do their time under maximum restrictions.

I was given an opportunity to visit Marion and never saw any prison with controls as tight as those in effect there. Marion is located in a desolate area about ninety miles east of St. Louis. The area largely has been ravished by strip mining over a period of many years.

On a visit there I was impressed by several things. First, the tight surveillance. Then the efforts of the staff to be as humane as possible to men they knew would kill them without regrets if it meant a chance to escape. Somewhat to my surprise, there was an excellent cafeteria. Meals there are served under that system and it is such a fine one that it has won high commendation from national restaurant associations. It is a cafeteria as clean and orderly as you would expect to find in any city.

Excellent food, I found out, is the rule rather than the exception in maximum security penal institutions. The same was true at Alcatraz and officials there said good food is an important element in keeping prisoners from rioting and rebelling. Tourists who visit Alcatraz today are shown the menu for the final but nonetheless typical menu served at the institution. It would delight even the most discriminating connoisseur of fine cuisine.

Among the things I noticed at Marion was that all of the guards carried their cell keys and other keys in their pockets, not dangling from their belts as in other prisons.

A guard explained, "We have some very clever men in these tiers. Some time back one inmate made a key to one area here merely after studying the keys a guard was carrying. The fellow never did have possession of the key. Just by seeing it for a matter of a few seconds at a time he memorized the outline and turned out a duplicate key that worked. All keys have been carried shielded in pockets since then."

Through closed-circuit television, prisoners at Marion are under constant watch by guards and other officials. There are no blind corners and the chance for escape is practically nil. Two men did manage to escape a few years ago, but were speedily apprehended.

"Birdman" Easy to Please

United States Marshal F.M. Wilson dropped by the *News-Press* office and said he had had a very unusual experience the day before. He had escorted Robert Stroud, the famed Birdman of Alcatraz, from the Springfield, Missouri, federal hospital facility to Kansas City for a court hearing. Stroud was the most famous convict in the world at that time. He had become internationally recognized as one of the greatest authorities on bird diseases and cures.

Out in bleak Alcatraz prison in San Francisco Bay, he had studied birds for many years. He even had written books on bird diseases and a major film, "Birdman of Alcatraz," had related his life story.

Stroud had killed a man and been sentenced to a western prison. While there he killed a guard. For that murder he was sentenced to be executed, but President Woodrow Wilson had commuted that punishment to life imprisonment. He had been allowed a double cell at Alcatraz and, in the extra cell section, he had installed cages of birds he was studying to further the world's knowledge about bird diseases.

One time a federal edict had been issued to the effect that Stroud should be treated as any other prisoner, that he should not be allowed to have the birds in his cell. There was an uproar from bird lovers and scientists. They declared Stroud had made a great contribution to society through his bird studies, and that he should be permitted to keep his birds and continue his studies. That public outcry resulted in the order being rescinded. Stroud was permitted to keep his birds.

He had been in prison about half a century the day Marshal Wilson took him to the Kansas City hearing. On the way to Kansas City, Wilson told Stroud that he knew of his long stay in prison and said he knew he didn't get much fancy fare there.

"I'd like to treat you to a good meal," Wilson told him. "You can order anything you want at the restaurant to which I am taking you, and I will pay for it out of my own pocket. What do you prefer?"

Stroud's choice bordered on amazing. Stroud said all he wanted was a pound of raw hamburger and an apple.

And that was all he would take.

Rubbing Shoulders With the KKK

In early 1928 when I was promoted from the South Side run to police reporter one of my new duties was to cover the Ku Klux Klan. At that time the KKK had an office on an upper floor of the old Board of Trade building, a three-story brick structure at the southwest corner of Third and Edmond Streets that was demolished long ago.

The Klan at that time was very active and seeking to become a political power here, an ambition it failed to achieve. There was a secretary on duty at the KKK office most days and there were always some fellows loafing around the office.

The secretary and the others knew I was a Catholic but they couldn't have been nicer to me if I had been the oldest son of the Grand Kleagle. They provided me news and answered my questions.

Being only three years out of Christian Brothers High School, I still was an old blue of my alma mater. I peddled raffle and play tickets from CBHS to the Klan office and enjoyed their good-natured banter as they made their ticket purchases. I don't believe any of them ever won anything in the CBHS raffles though.

The Klan secretary told me I was welcome at their meetings and I attended several of them on my own time, being the only one present who was not masked. I recall particularly attending a night Klan meeting in the bandshell at Lake Contrary Park. By accident, I sat next to a masked man whom I knew. He was a public official and easy to recognize because of his severely-scarred hands I had seen so many times in his office. We had no conversation that night but he was fully aware that I knew who he was.

The next day he called me at work and said he just wanted to set the record straight. He said he was not anti-Catholic, anti-Jewish or anti-Negro, but that he felt as a public official he should be aware of all that was going on and that was why I happened to see him in a Klan mask and robe the night before. I took him at his word. We remained friends for many years after that.

As far as I an aware, the Ku Klux Klan played a definite role in only one political campaign here. That was the mayoralty race in 1924, three years before I became a newspaper reporter, but the story of that election was handed down to me by many people on my courthouse run.

That spring the Klan held a giant rally at the Auditorium. It was closed to the press, in fact, closed to all but card-bearing members of the KKK. Republican Alva F. Linday, distinguished attorney and nominee for mayor, was defeated that April by something like 108 votes. Some oldtimers at the courthouse years later were saying the anti-Lindsay stance taken at that closed meeting of the KKK was what defeated him. No one will ever know.

In the early 1920's when I was in high school, a tragic mixup resulted in fourteen-year-old Nellie Hale being killed by a police-fired bullet. The girl was riding with her brothers at the southeast edge of St. Joseph when officers in a squad car followed the

Hale car in the erroneous belief bootleggers were in it. They fired a warning shot to stop them. The bullet struck and killed the innocent little Nellie.

Public furor was great. Public meetings decrying the incident were held. The chief of police of St. Joseph was forced out of office and other heads at the police station also fell.

The Klan paraded in the cortege of Nellie Hale. Many on horses and some on foot walked up Frederick Avenue and made the turn at Mount Mora Road into the cemetery. I remember standing at the corner of Mount Mora and Frederick and watching that parade. A police edict was that none in the parade could be masked.

I recognized many in the parade, some of them fellows who never had done much in life and some of them businessmen. I know that march was detrimental to many of those businessmen. Their presence in the KKK parade cost them heavily in their business ventures. I knew one fellow who eventually lost his drug store as a result. Many Catholic customers quit him.

Mixed Emotions Covering Armour Explosion

It was a decision that had to be made quickly; the occasion was the explosion at the Armour and Company plant in South St. Joseph that took nineteen lives.

It was a mild May afternoon in 1930. I was twenty-three and courthouse reporter for the *News-Press*. I was supposed to be on duty there that afternoon looking for news and checking on possible wrongs by county officials.

Instead I was asleep in a fireman's bed at Central Fire Station at Seventh and Sylvanie. I had been out late the night before and I lain down to take a nap with the assurance of Roy Regan, fire department secretary, that he would wake me in plenty of time so I could go the the *News-Press* office and check in at ten minutes to five.

The fire explosion alarm came in at 3:20. I followed Fire Chief Leo J. Urbanski down a pole and got into the car with him.

I had no idea of the enormity of the tragedy to which we were riding.

The blast, caused by gas, had leveled a sprawling four-story brick building at Armour's. The first person I talked to there was Opie King, head of the employment office for Armour. "It looks like eighteen people have been killed and are buried in that wreckage," King, a longtime friend, confided. He wasn't exaggerating; the death toll finally reached nineteen.

Here is the problem I faced: I was the first newsman on the scene of the explosion, five miles away from the courthouse where I was supposed to be. The regular *News-Press* fire and police reporter had skipped out early that afternoon and the South Side reporter, who covered the Armour plant regularly, was visiting uptown.

If I called the office with the story, those in charge there would know I had been goofing off on my regular run and there would be repercussions. But it was the biggest news story I had ever encountered, and I was the only one to cover it.

I called the office. Arthur V. Burrowes, the news editor, was at a journalism event at Columbia, Missouri. His assistant, Merrill Chilcote, was in charge. He took my information and the *News-Press* got out an extra late that afternoon.

The office had me stay on the explosion coverage story through the night. It was the most tragic of scenes as bodies of men, some of whom I knew from having been South Side reporter, were removed from the rubble. I still sadly recall standing with Joe Scott, a long-time friend of the family, as his son's broken body was found. It was more than twenty-four hours after the blast before the last body was uncovered.

In due time I got the bawling out from Arthur Burrowes that I knew was coming for my "goofing off." But, typical of him, he raised my salary two weeks later and complimented me on the explosion coverage.

That Made Cents—or Dollars

Checking county financial records as part of my job as courthouse reporter one day in the early 1940's I discovered what to me was an amazing thing.

In the previous month, October, when it had rained on about twenty days, every member of the county bridge painting crew had worked a full day, even Sundays, throughout the month. Most people around the courthouse were fully aware that the bridge painting crew was made up of minor ward politicians noted more for lining up votes than for artistry with the paint brush.

The story had a lead of "Some people sing in the rain but these fellows paint in the rain."

The committeeman who was foreman of the crew offered what he insisted was a complete and honest explanation. "On those days when it was raining we were painting the undersides of the bridges," he said in his business suit between puffs on his cigar.

Why, of course!

That First Byline

A few decades ago, a byline for a reporter was hard to come by. When the co-authors were active journalists, getting his name over a story was a reporter's gold star. No matter how important the story, if it resulted from a reporter's routine coverage of his beat, he remained anonymous. A byline had to be earned for a story "above and beyond," a story that had to be researched or developed on the reporter's own initiative. Or, if he were lucky, he might see his name over a cleverly written feature.

Today bylines sprout like typographical errors, appearing frequently on relatively routine stories. It isn't unusual to see a reporter's name on two or three stories in the same issue. Older journalists tend to think bylines shouldn't be handed out like paper towels at a picnic, but there is a basis for today's more liberal policy.

Jim Sherman, brother of co-author George who worked for the *Gazette* for thirty-six years until he suffered a fatal heart attack in 1988, explained why the more liberal byline philosophy evolved. From his vantage point as city editor, the reason was simple: Television news.

"The names of the television news people have become almost household words," he said. "So we need our reporters to also have a high degree of name recognition."

In many respects that reason makes sense. But many of the journalists of yesteryear have mixed emotions—or still just plain disagree. Because it was hard to come by, most older journalists retain vivid memories of their first byline.

"It was probably 1944," George Sherman recalls his first one. "City Editor Don Houseworth asked for a volunteer to participate in a military exhibition at Rosecrans Field in which an army glider (and passenger) would be yanked off the ground by a plane flying by."

One minute the glider would be on the ground and the next it would be in the air, traveling at 135 miles an hour, at the end of a tow rope hanging from the plane whizzing by. The glider would be be cut loose from the mother plane, would fly around the city for a half hour or so, then the pilot would land back at Rosecrans, stopping with the nose exactly over a handkerchief on the runway.

That's what the news release said.

Sherman had never been in an airplane of any kind, let alone a glider, but he volunteered for the assignment. That's what rookie reporters did in those days, most of them, assuming that a touch of "derring do" was an essential quality in their makeup.

He didn't want a straight news story, Houseworth explained, but rather a feature in which the reporter would emphasize his emotional reactions like excitement or fright. Or both.

"When I arrived at the field," Sherman said, "the pilot was already in the glider. He showed me how the stunt was supposed to work. There was this arrangement for all the world like a football goal post with a rope in between and a metal ring in the middle. Another rope dangled from the plane. That was the one that was to make the 'pickup,' and at the end of that rope was a hook. The object was for the plane to hook the ring and yank the glider off the ground."

Sherman already was beginning to have second thoughts as he climbed into the glider. The glider was a wooden framework covered by canvas and large enough to hold several soldiers.

The *Gazette* reporter shook hands with the pilot—and realized that the flier was bandaged in several places and had numerous cuts and bruises. Sherman, a bit nervously, asked if he had been injured in his glider exploits.

"No, no, not at all," said the pilot. "It's not this glider that's dangerous; it's the automobiles."

It turned out that on the way to the exhibition his car had rolled over several times but the pilot was not seriously injured. Still, for a rookie reporter those wounds were not encouraging. Nor were the flier's words.

The minutes raced by. Soon the mother plane would fly over for the pickup. One final (a horrible word) question Sherman felt compelled to ask: Was this procedure really not dangerous and what should he expect?

No, no danger, the pilot assured him again. And being yanked off the ground was, oh, about the same as the jolt of a trolley car starting up from a standstill. Sherman was about to relax a bit.

"Oh," the pilot had an afterthought. "The mayor of Hartford, Connecticut, did have a little accident doing this stunt. He broke his leg."

Before Sherman could change his mind, the pickup plane made its first pass. And missed. Whether it was an honest miss or one for dramatic effect, Sherman didn't know, but seconds later, on the second attempt, the glider abruptly was airborne.

One minute the glider was on the ground, and the next it was high in the air traveling at the reported 135 miles an hour. The pilot was right; the jolt really wasn't much. Within a minute or two, the glider was cut loose from the mother plane and Sherman's adventure began in earnest.

"Aside from the fact that I was closed in with only a framework and a canvas between me and the outside world, it was a fascinating experience as we sailed gracefully over the city," Sherman recalled, "but the pilot wasn't about to let me off so easily.

"I was crouched looking out the window when the pilot suddenly put the glider into a stall, pulled the nose up and plummeted into a nose dive straight for the ground."

The centrifugal force—and sheer fright—locked Sherman into a paralyzed crouch. Finally, as the pilot was pulling the glider out of the dive, Sherman was able to move. When he saw the pilot laughing at his predicament, the reporter had mixed emotions, equal parts of chagrin and relief. The pilot spent another fifteen or twenty minutes flying gracefully over the city, then landed, as publicized, precisely over the handkerchief.

Sherman poured his feelings and reactions into his story and City Editor Houseworth was satisfied enough to give him a two-column headline on Page One— Sherman's first precious byline story.

Along with the byline, Houseworth, inspired by the heartfelt copy, wrote the following headline for it:

Reporter "Dies" as Pilot Stalls Glider Over City

Several friends called Sherman's mother the next day to express their sympathy. Apparently they had not read the story but someone had told them about it and in the telling Sherman's demise became real. Mother Sherman assured the well-meaning callers that, as Mark Twain had so aptly expressed it years earlier, the reports of her beloved son's death were "greatly exaggerated."

It was a byline justly earned—and long remembered.

That's Reason Enough

When Harold Slater once interviewed a psychiatrist on the staff of the Missouri State Penitentiary at Jefferson City, he received a surprising answer to one particular question.

"I was wondering," Slater said to the psychiatrist, "is there any one category of men who have an easier time adjusting to prison life than others, who cause the least trouble and seem to be more content with prison life than others?"

"That's an easy one," replied the psychiatrist, "Without a doubt the most contented convicts are those here for having killed their wives!"

In the best journalistic tradition, Slater did not elaborate or editorialize on that comment, confining himself to simply reporting the facts.

A Little Matter of Semantics

Police Lieutenant Joe Reynolds, known affectionately as the "Silver Fox" because of his impressive mane of white hair, was an avid reader. Joe in later years was in charge of the booking desk, where alleged law breakers were checked in. Joe would record the necessary information on the arrest report and itemize the prisoner's personal effects which were placed in an envelope and retained until the person either was released or sent to court.

On quiet nights at Central Police Station, Joe had the opportunity to do quite a bit of reading and as a result he acquired an extensive vocabulary which he enjoyed using. Joe's penchant for big words gave everyone a belly laugh one particular evening when officers brought in an especially well dressed drunk, who would be held overnight to "sleep it off" and then released the next morning.

Johnny Mollus was a well-known and popular officer and was the turnkey on duty. It was Johnny's job to take the prisoners to their cells and lock them in. Evidently, Johnny and the prisoner at the bar were not unknown to each other, but for the moment the prisoner was preoccupied with Lieutenant Reynolds.

Lieutenant Reynolds was a tall, somewhat stern looking individual with piercing eyes, but those eyes would reveal a warm twinkle when Joe was among friends.

Prisoners being booked show a variety of reactions. Some are contrite and submissive, some are aggressive and insulting, and some are just plain sheepish and embarrassed.

On this occasion, the prisoner adopted a haughty, patronizing pose.

Straightening up to his full height and brushing off his clothing where the arresting officers had touched him, the prisoner addressed Lieutenant Reynolds rather disdainfully, asking ". . . and with just what am I being charged?"

Lieutenant Reynolds looked the prisoner squarely in the eye and sternly advised the man that ". . . we are charging you with being an inebriate."

The prisoner was crestfallen. His cockiness and his supercilious attitude evaporated like smoke in a strong wind. He almost sagged against the counter and then he turned pleadingly to Officer Mollus and in a hoarse whisper said, ". . .My God, Johnny, can't you get him to change that to just plain drunk?"

If Only He'd Asked Old Charlie

In his fifty-two years as a newsman, Harold Slater missed few opportunities to interview anybody with a potential story but one "if only" still haunts him. He believes he might have been able to resolve a controversy that has swirled around the historic Pony Express since its inception if he had only taken the time to visit a lonely old man.

But Harold was only a boy of ten then, frequently passing by that house on the east side of North Sixth Street in the 1100 block. In good weather an elderly man, wearing a slouch hat and smoking a pipe, was often sitting on the porch, always alone. Everybody knew Charlie Cliff. He was a former Pony Express rider.

"I know now he must have been lonely and would have welcomed the opportunity to talk to someone," says Harold. But the journalist-to-be was a bit too young and timid to make the initial contact, so the mystery and controversy over the first rider continues to this day.

Loathe to leave dangling ends to legends as well as stories, Slater and Sherman offer a reasonable explanation of how the mystery may have come about in the first place. In 1923 a much respected St. Joseph researcher, Mrs. Louise Platt Hauck, was commissioned by the Pony Express Celebration committee to thoroughly investigate the controversy in an attempt to resolve the issue once and for all.

Mrs. Hauck spent long hours researching scrapbooks and library and newspaper files in both Missouri and Kansas. A strong supporting link in her final conclusion that the first rider was Billy Richardson resulted from the discovery of a previously unknown article from the April 7, 1860 issue of the St. Joseph *Weekly West* newspaper. The article specifically named Billy Richardson as the first rider.

Despite what appeared to be overwhelming evidence pointing toward Richardson, the Pony Express Celebration committee did not officially declare Richardson the first rider. Some said the committee was prudent, to avoid a possible backlash from the people who believed Johnny Frye to have been the first. But what some Richardson supporters termed a chicken-hearted response may have been excellent judgment.

In his 1958 book, *Riders of the Pony Express*, Ralph Moody, a western historian and writer, offers a logical and under-standable explanation of the controversy's origin. In his words:

"The mail did go, but less than half the crowd knew who carried it. Just as the mail train pulled in, Bill Richardson, a hostler at the livery stable, rode up on the bay mare that was to make the first Pony Express run. By this time it was growing dark, torches had been lighted and the crowd was in a wild uproar. A newspaper reporter, anxious to be the first out with the news, rushed back to his office and wrote the thrilling story of Bill's grand take off but it was a young man named Johnny Frey who carried the first Pony Mail." (Frey is Mr. Moody's spelling. Frye now is generally accepted as correct but some insist it's Fry.)

The question probably will never be answered to everyone's satisfaction, but Moody's explanation does seem reasonable—that the confusion resulted from the assumption that the man who brought the horse from the stable was the rider who galloped away on it. And Richardson did later become a Pony Express rider.

In a lighter vein, another unverifiable story about the Pony Express is that the doughnut was invented for the convenience of its riders—particularly Johnny Frye who was especially popular with the ladies. In their book, *Saddles and Spurs* Raymond and Mary Settle describe it this way.

"The young women would wait for him (Frye) along the trail with cakes, cookies and other culinary dainties. These he snatched from their hands on the run and ate them as he galloped along. They noticed he had trouble with the cookies for he could hold them with only one hand. The other was required to manage his horse. It occurred to them that if they made them with a hole in the center, he could stick them on his fingers and get along nicely. Thus was born the well-known donut."

If nothing else, it's a charming and romantic story and much more enjoyable to believe than Charles Panati's more mundane version in his book, *Extraordinary Origins of Everyday Things:* The Pennysylvania Dutch and a New England sea captain independently arrived at the donut hole "for the practical reason that the increased surface area allowed for more uniform frying and eliminated the pastry's soggy center."

Amidst the fuzziness surrounding the whole legend, here are some facts:

During the nineteen months, from April 1860 through October 1861, that Russell, Majors and Waddell operated the Pony Express, nearly 35,000 pieces of mail were delivered in relays over an accumulated distance of 650,000 miles—and only one sack of mail was lost!

The average age of the riders was nineteen and they were paid between $100 and $150 a month, plus room and board.

Normal delivery time from St. Joseph to Sacramento, California, a distance of 1,966 miles, was ten days. But the record was set on March 1, 1861 when President Lincoln's inaugural speech was carried through in seven days and seventeen hours.

The original stables, from which the first horse was led, were restored for posterity by the M.K. Goetz family.

And, oh, yes, that horse was a beautiful Kentucky thoroughbred bay mare named Sylph.

George Sherman

Farmer Brown and His Smart Pig

Gust Karras, that lovable, goodhearted promoter, brought many events to St. Joseph, from Spike Jones and his City Slickers to the Harlem Globetrotters, but his first love was wrestling.

With his surefire combination of low prices and good entertainment, Gust had the old City Auditorium buzzing with wrestling fans every Friday night. He'd consistently pack in fifteen hundred to two thousand of them and double that with an "extra special added attraction" like Gorgeous George. With his expensive robes and somewhat feminine antics, George was the wrestling fan's Liberace.

Gust and *Gazette* Sports Editor George Sherman were good friends but Gust was always trying to prove to Sherman that his gladiators were engaging in earnest athletic competition. Sherman always gave Karras's wrestling card good publicity on the sports pages but he salved his conscience by using various alternatives to the word sport. He called Orville Brown or Mildred Burke, for instance, "the best in the business" or "the best in the game." Few readers probably ever recognized the subtle difference. But Gust did, and he was forever trying to find ways to convince Sherman of the events' legitimacy.

In one of his most blatant efforts, he invited Sherman to one of his "extra special" championship matches. Ordinarily, he might have saved Sherman a front row seat or even a seat at the ringside table with the timer and the various and sundry "officials" which clustered around these affairs.

The reason for the special seat quickly became evident when one of the behemoths tossed his quarter-ton opponent over the ropes—right where Sherman was sitting. The sports editor managed to scramble out of the way just in time to see his chair smashed.

Gust was properly apologetic and never admitted that it was a rigged job. Undoubtedly, if Sherman had not scurried out of the way, the wrestler would have grabbed the ropes or somehow avoided committing bodily mayhem. It was a convincing demonstration—but not enough to change Sherman's opinion.

Sherman—with a wary eye on the thousands of diehard wrestling fans in the country and a desire to avoid any tarring and feathering—absolves Slater from any connection with his view. But he suggests that they read the statement adopted in 1989 by the wrestling federation. Rather than be bound by the strict regulations of the New York Athletic Commission, which also governs boxing, the wrestling people adopted a "clarifying" statement. The essence of it is that while wrestlers are athletes in superb condition, they are engaged in a performance for entertaining the public. The statement carefully draws a thin line between a clear-cut sports competiton and a show for entertainment.

But wrestling fans—in St. Joseph and elsewhere—are not to be taken lightly. St. Joseph's own Sonny Myers was nearly fatally slashed across the stomach by an irate fan in Oklahoma. And a fan at City Auditorium once hurled a chair toward ringside from the top balcony. Fortunately, it landed in an unoccupied section and struck a woman a glancing blow but did not seriously injure her.

More humorous—for everyone except the wrestler—was the night when an older lady on the front row got carried away with the desire for revenge when the evening's villain was mauling the local good guy. As the villain leaned back against the ropes after tossing his opponent from the ring, the lady grabbed her husband's lighted cigar, dashed to ringside, pulled back the villain's trunks and dropped the glowing cigar where she thought it would do the most good. Sparks flew as the cigar disappeared into the wrestler's trunks. But the villain and the referee managed to separate the intended victim and the weapon.

Among the weird personalities Karras brought to St. Joseph was a rather mundane wrestler named Farmer Brown. Actually,

Farmer Brown's trained pet pig was the big draw. The 'farmer" always wrestled in overalls with that pig. It was a tiny creature, no bigger than a small poodle, but it acted as intelligent as any dog.

Sherman recalls one interview with Farmer Brown. The weather wasn't too uncomfortable and several people were in Karras's office so the conversation began on the sidewalk at Eighth and Edmond Streets.

Farmer Brown wanted to show all the things his pig could do. "Sit," he commanded the cute little critter.

The pig circled the Farmer, ran back and forth but refused to sit. And repeated, ever sterner "Sits!" brought the same response, much to the Farmer's chagrin.

In Gust's office, now empty of visitors, the interview turned back to wrestling. Farmer Brown was explaining to Gust that the pig apparently had forgotten the correct response.

"See what I mean," he said to Gust. "Sit," he told the pig.

Sit, the pig did. Again and again. Suddenly, a light dawned on the Farmer's face and he roared with laughter.

"I'll be damned," he said. "That pig's smarter than I am."

The floor in Karras's office was warm. And that cement sidewalk outside was cold—even to a pig's *derriere*.

The Farmer probably was right. A smart pig.

The Lady Saves a Scoop

Frances Perkins made history when Franklin Delano Roosevelt appointed her as his secretary of labor, the first woman ever named to a presidential cabinet. But Harold Slater remembers her for another reason.

A year or so after her appointment, either 1933 or 1934, Mrs. Perkins stopped overnight at Hotel Robidoux on her way north to address a college conclave. Slater knew she was stopping in St. Joseph and readily recognized her by her trademark, that flat, tri-cornered black hat. Slater stopped her before she reached the desk clerk to register. He asked if he could interview her, then asked her for a favor.

St. Joseph was a highly competitive newspaper town, he explained, and it was past the day's deadline for the *News-Press*—and if the "competition" saw her name on the hotel register, they'd move in and talk to her and there'd go his "scoop."

Would she do him a favor—register as Frances Wilson, her legal name? The gracious lady would and did—and Slater scooped the *Gazette* with the interview.

Thou shalt be first was one of a newsman's Ten Commandments in those days.

Passion on the Society Page

In earlier days of newspapering, the passion for beating the competition spread even to the society pages. A classic match-up in St. Joseph pitted its two society editors, Ada Lyon of the *News-Press* and Deedie May Austin of the *Gazette*.

They were middle-aged when I knew them, but when it came to competing for stories they went after news with all the vigor and enthusiam of college sophomore. Ada and Deedie May fought tooth and nail to get any story first—and to write the story best.

Appropriately, one of their typical contests involved the Passion Play. Early in 1928 the Frieburg Passion Players announced that they would present the American debut of the centuries-old play in a ten-day run at Krug Bowl in St. Joseph. Deedie May and Ada worked vigorously on the advance publicity. Ada even took some lessons in German so she would be better equipped to converse with the play personnel from Germany.

Finally the announcement was made that the Passion Play cast would arrive at eight o'clock one summer night by train from the East. Ada Lyon was upset: That did not fit her press time. Dismayed she was—but defeated she was not. On the afternoon of the arrival she had a friend take her to Cameron to board the incoming train with the Passion Play cast.

Deedie May was at Union Passenger Station that evening, waiting with her notebook in hand when the Burlington train chugged in with the cast. It was her turn to be dismayed.

Ada, wearing a big smile and a floppy hat, stepped off the train with Christus on one arm and Judas Iscariot on the other. And her interview notes, no doubt, were as full as her smile.

Wild Animals Hit St. Joseph

St. Joseph is far distant from jungle or desert, yet in one year I handled stories about a man being killed here by a tiger and another being fatally bitten by a camel.

The Shrine Circus was playing at the Auditorium here more than forty years ago when H.C. "Cap" Getchell, for years the head of Shrine activities in St. Joseph, moved too close to a tiger's cage in the arena. The animal reached through the bars and practically tore off Getchell's arm. He died the next day.

Getchell, incidentally, had been the director of the census of 1900 that gave this city its highest population total ever—more than 102,000. He had been a classmate and personal friend of President William Howard Taft at Yale.

The same year that Getchell was killed an employee of the St. Joseph Parks Department was severely bitten on the arm and shoulder by a camel that was part of the city's zoo stock. The man died within hours.

Rough Riders Come First

Reporters miss the boat, too.

In 1936 Colonel Frank Knox came to St. Joseph as the Republican nominee for vice president. He spoke from the back platform of a railroad car in the yards of Union Passenger Station at Sixth Street and Mitchell Avenue.

I had a chance to interview him, but I was more interested in the fact that he had been a Rough Rider with Teddy Roosevelt at San Juan Hill than his vice-presidential candidacy. And I found Colonel Knox ready and willing to talk about those days.

Of course, I had to write my story on his campaign speech but my prime interest was that here was truly a God-honest old Rough Rider.

That—nor my story—didn't help him any in the campaign. Along with Governor Alf Landon of Kansas, he was soundly defeated in th6 1936 election.

I may have missed the boat in my interview of him, but Knox didn't. He went on to become Secretary of the Navy in Franklin D. Roosevelt's administration.

Prisoners Can't Kick About This Rule

United States Marshal F.M. Wilson was a man who always looked out for his friends. One day in 1962 he called and asked, "How would you like a trip to Alaska the day after tomorrow? I'm sending a federal prisoner up to Fairbanks and I can send you along as a guard."

I got clearance from the office to take a few days of vacation and bright and early the next day I was in Kansas City. A deputy U.S. marshal was in charge. I carried no weapon. I had convinced them that I wouldn't know how to use one, anyway.

The man being taken to Fairbanks had won a new trial after serving six years of a life sentence in Leavenworth penitentiary before the conviction was reversed. He was a knowledgeable fellow and had used his time in prison to read hundreds of books and to further his education.

We spent the night in Anchorage, then went on to Fairbanks. There the deputy marshal in charge of the prisoner asked me if I would take the fellow to jail while he filled out the necessary papers at the federal building. I agreed. And since both I and the deputy marshal were certain that the fellow would make no effort to escape, he was not handcuffed.

As we started walking along the main street down the six blocks to jail, the prisoner asked a question and a favor. "Do you know anybody here in Fairbanks?"

I shook my head.

"Well, then, I'd appreciate a favor," he said.

He was carrying a shoe box that contained all of the personal effects he had brought with him from prison. On both sides of it were big labels saying, "Leavenworth." He said he knew a lot of people in Fairbanks and he didn't want them to know he was still in custody.

"I'd feel less embarrassed," he told me, "if you would carry this box. People here will think you're the prisoner."

Fine, I said. Anything for a friend.

I escorted him to jail, carrying his box, and stayed there as he was booked. One of the first things they made him do was remove his leather shoes and replace them with rubber-soled Keds.

They had some mean fellows in his jail, the warden explained, and sometimes they would fight and try to stomp another prisoner. If they wore softer shoes, he said, there was less danger of serious injury.

Made sense to me. But, then, I could leave the place. And the guy with the box.

Catching Up With Jones

So you didn't make it to those farewell parties when *News-Press* photographer Dick Jones left for the Navy during World War II? Neither did Dick Jones. None of the three.

His male friends in the news department were disappointed when Dick couldn't make the first party because of a conflicting engagement. But, not to be deprived of a good time, they went ahead with the poker games and drinking and invited Deputy State Auditor Gerald Bliley to fill in for him.

After the second Jones farewell party was planned, Dick again announced he couldn't attend. But a great time still was had by all, including Deputy State Auditor Bliley.

He had never met Jones in his life but Bliley announced that he would host the third farewell party for the elusive Jones. Again, Dick couldn't attend. He did call during the evening's festivities, however, but some losing poker player who answered the phone told him to hang up, that his call was interfering with the progress of the game.

But there's a happy ending. Jones and Bliley finally met months after the war was over and shared a drink down at Harry Herman's watering hole.

Time on His Hands

More than forty years ago a man who had been convicted in a triple murder and sentenced to die spent more than fifteen months in the Death Row of the state penitentiary, and subsequently was returned here for a new trial.

Surprisingly, he had gained about twenty pounds on the fare served death row inmates.

He was tried again; the penalty in the second trial also was death. In one of the many visits I had with him in his jail cell I inquired if there was some small thing I could do to make his Death Row stay more liveable.

He said there was; that he would like to have a watch. "I'm the kind of fellow who looks forward to his meals," he said. "I get anxious to find out how long I have to wait for the next meal and, not having a watch, I keep asking the other fellows what time it is. They are all kind of touchy about the passing time and resent my asking. I'd get along better if I had a watch."

The problem was easily solved. I asked a friendly jeweler if he had any trade-in watches in his stock the fellow could have. He gave me a nice looking one to give the slayer with his compliments. The doomed man was wearing that watch until the day in 1950 when he died in the gas chamber at the Jefferson City penitentiary.

One jokester with a somewhat morbid sense of humor offered the opinion that the St. Joseph jeweler may have given the convict the watch, but the state "gave him the works!"

Prosecuting The Prosecutor

Of the tens of thousands of trials held in St. Joseph and Buchanan County since 1839, one readily stands out as by far the most sensational—the 1916 trial of Prosecuting Attorney Oscar D. McDaniel on a charge of first degree murder in the brutal bludgeoning death of his wife.

McDaniel was acquitted in the case that shook the community with its high drama, suspense, pathos and intrigue. Never solved, the answer lies today in the grave.

I was nine years old when Mrs. McDaniel was found fatally beaten, her head crushed in, the night of July 14, 1916, in her bedroom at the family home at 1806 South 20th Street. It was the event that got me started reading newspapers.

The case has intrigued me for more than seventy years. I was fortunate enough as a young courthouse reporter in the late 1920s to become friends with many of those involved in the trial and I have read everything I was able to find about the arrest of McDaniel and his acquittal.

For sixteen days after his arrest on the murder charge, McDaniel was held a prisoner in the Buchanan County jail. During that period he ran the prosecutor's office from his jail cell. McDaniel was a dramatic man throughout his life. He was young, handsome and debonair while serving as prosecuting attorney. His wife had been a beauty queen at Central High School in 1905.

An outstanding political orator, McDaniel several times was chosen by the Democrats to give the kick-off address for the county political campaign. When he ran for prosecuting attorney the opposition charged he would be lenient with offenders. He turned out to be anything but that, racking up a record that included more convictions and longer sentences than had been the rule previously. He was relentless, according to the gamblers, robbers and burglars who faced his charges.

The son of a wealthy Buchanan County farmer, McDaniel served as an assistant prosecuting attorney before being elected to the office. Working side-by-side with him as an assistant prosecutor was a young man named Bart M. Lockwood. A few years later, he was to file the murder charge against McDaniel and prosecute him.

McDaniel was a man with steel nerves and a granite-like facade that showed no signs of emotion regardless of the intensity of the situation.

St. Joseph was startled when it opened its July 15, 1916, edition of the *Gazette* which carried a two-line, eight-column head "WIFE OF PROSECUTOR DYING FROM ATTACK: ASSASSINS MISS McDANIEL." That morning Mrs. McDaniel died at old Ensworth Hospital, the kiss of her husband on her dying lips.

McDaniel said he had received a phone call at 11:30 the night of July 14 from a man who said a relative of his was drinking and causing a disturbance at the Hart and Blakesley saloon at 604 Messanie Street, and should be taken home. The caller identified himself as Dovey Hart, one of the proprietors, but when McDaniel arrived at the saloon Hart said he had not called him and that no McDaniel relative had been there.

McDaniel bought a drink for the house, then went on to a saloon at Eighth and Messanie Street, stating he thought the troublesome relative might be there. He wasn't. McDaniel bought a drink for the house and headed home. He said that by then he was fearful that something might be wrong at home due to the false call.

McDaniel told police that when he slowed down his car in front of his home a man opened fire on him with a pistol from behind a tree close to the door of the McDaniel garage. Armed, because of threats he had received, McDaniel drew his pistol and fired back. McDaniel said five shots were fired at him and that some of those bullets had hit his car. He told police he rushed into his house to get another pistol and found his wife, her head bashed in. Because he was in a state of collapse, he was taken to the hospital in the ambulance with his dying wife.

Two of the McDaniel children who were in a bedroom next to that of their mother said they had heard nothing. An all-out hunt for the slayer was ordered by Chief of Police James Clouser. The Hartley Detective Agency brought in its bloodhounds. Later the Burns Detective Agency was called in to investigate. The blunt instrument with which Mrs. McDaniel was killed was never found.

Only a few days before, McDaniel had received a letter threatening "death, hell and destruction" if he prosecuted another case against a man already convicted of robbery. Other theories for possible revenge against the prosecutor were discussed. The whole town was talking and just about everybody had their own theory. The Commerce Club adopted a resolution of sympathy stating the city was shocked by "the diabolical murder." The resolution called for action and co-operation. A reward of $1,000 for the arrest and conviction of the murderer was offered by McDaniel and his father. Ironically, had he been found guilty he would have been in the position of paying a reward for his own conviction.

Feisty little Thomas F. Ryan, judge of the criminal court, asked L.A. Vories, later a circuit judge, to serve as a special prosecutor. Vories, who lived only three blocks from McDaniel, declined and Bart M. Lockwood was appointed special prosecutor.

Lockwood proved a hard-working prober. He talked to scores of possible witnesses. He was on duty day and night and during the course of his investigation even ordered the exhumation of the body of Mrs. McDaniel late one night at Mount Mora Cemetery. He was seeking new evidence, but none was found. Hampering the investigation was that, almost immediately after the discovery of the battered Mrs. McDaniel, some friends burned the blood-soaked bedclothes.

Late in September, a full ten weeks after the murder, Lockwood issued a warrant charging McDaniel with the murder of his wife. The order to arrest McDaniel was a sensation, but the manner in which the arrest was made was almost casual. Just about everybody in town had been talking about the possibility of McDaniel being charged, but now, at last, there was official action.

Detectives Robert Maney and Bill Henley took a Messanie Street and Hansen Heights streetcar out to Twenty-second and Duncan Street and walked the three blocks to the McDaniel home. McDaniel, in shirt sleeves, answered the door, and the detectives told them they were there to pick him up on a murder charge. McDaniel asked them if they had a warrant. They told him they did. He didn't bother to read it. He submitted to a search and the officers took his revolver, which, he said, he had been carrying because of threats to his life.

He told his housekeeper he was going to Central Police Station and he made a single request to the detectives. "I'd like to walk to the police station because I have been in the house all day and would like to get some fresh air." The detectives were agreeable; it was a two-mile walk.

McDaniel asked if he could stop at a drug store at Eighth and Locust Streets to purchase medicine and cigars. He shook hands with the proprietor, J.A. Schelhemmer, and told him he wouldn't be seeing him for awhile. Schelhemmer told him to stop his kidding, but McDaniel told him, "This is on the square."

A wagon guard at old Central Police Station, Seventh and

Messanie Streets, thought a joke was being played on him when they told him to put McDaniel in a cell. But he quickly learned it wasn't a prank. McDaniel emptied his own pockets on the booking sergeant's desk.

A *Gazette* reporter talked to McDaniel at the police station. McDaniel told him, "I feel sorry for my mother and Mrs. Moss (his wife's mother), and further wish to say that I will vote for Woodrow Wilson for president, Frederick Gardner for governor, and Charles Booher for congressman." He repeated that statement when asked if he had anything more to say.

After a brief stay at the police station, he was taken to the county jail where he was held for sixteen days as a prisoner before the special grand jury on October 10 returned a murder indictment against him. That same day he was released on a $50,000 bond signed by some of the best known citizens of the county.

He had carried on his official duties as prosecutor from the jail, even ordering that certain gambling case trials be held up until he was released because he particularly wanted to prosecute those cases personally. Even his jail stay was highly controversial. Some people complained when they learned he had been permitted to go to Mike Hilgert's cafe and saloon for lunch one day, that he had been let out of jail to have dinner with friends on North Fourth Street, and that he had been permitted to go outside to watch an aviator on an acrobatics show over St. Joseph.

Sheriff C.H. "Bose" Jones defended his actions in those cases. He said a deputy sheriff had been with McDaniel at all times. Some who went to the jail were surprised when McDaniel unlocked the door to let them in and closed it when they left. He was a trustee and that was part of his duties.

Following the indictment, Governor Elliott W. Major ordered the attorney general of Missouri, John T. Barker, to take over the prosecution. The trial was set for October 18, but Barker charged there had been "jobbing" with the selection of potential jurors, that the body was not truly representative of Buchanan County.

Judge Ryan quashed the jury panel and named a committee of three lawyers to investigate the possibility that there was anything wrong with the selection method. The three reported there was nothing wrong and the trial was reset for November 18.

McDaniel had been renominated for prosecuting attorney

without opposition in August. Some Democratic leaders called upon him to withdraw as the nominee in the general election, but McDaniel rejected the idea. On the night of November 1 — five days before the election — McDaniel made the most unique and most dramatic campaign gesture in the history of the county. He rented the Lyceum Theater for that night to state his case and make his plea for votes to the electorate. The theater was jammed and newspaper reports stated that 2,000 people who were turned away waited outside the theater. McDaniel was the only speaker. On the stage with him were his father, his children and a brother.

Using only notes he had written on the back of an envelope, McDaniel spoke for an hour and a half. A newspaper reporter described his oratory as spell binding. He told of his early life, his struggle to become a lawyer, outlined his hopes and aims, declared his innocence, and sharply criticized those who had spread rumors about him and his family.

Dramatically, he told about how he and his wife had gone on a picnic the afternoon of the day of the murder, and how that night he had kissed her as he left the house "to carry out my fraternal duties." He said that one of the most vicious rumors was that his wife had been with him in his car and that it struck and killed an eighteen-month-old girl.

The rumor, he said, was that he had killed his wife because he was fearful she would testify against him. That was the vilest kind of lie, he declared. (Lorine Tye, eighteen months old, had been missing for several days that summer before her broken body was found near a brickyard.)

The plea was dramatic but not vote-productive. The Republican nominee for prosecuting attorney, Lawrence Bothwell, was the only member of his party to carry Buchanan County in the November election. But he defeated McDaniel by a whopping 3,400 votes.

The McDaniel trial starting November 18 was even more of a sensation than expected. The courtroom was jammed every day; hundreds were turned away, and some gathered as early as six o'clock in the morning to get a seat for proceedings. The trial lasted seventeen days.

Charles F. Strop was chief counsel for McDaniel. Assisting him were Lewis C. Gabbert, a former prosecuting attorney, and Kay Porter. Barker and Lockwood were prosecutors. McDaniel's defense was the expected alibi — that he had been called from his home to a saloon to pick up a troublesome relative, that the call was false, and that he returned home to find his wife brutally beaten. Barker and Lockwood set out to discredit that alibi. They sought to prove that the McDaniels had been having domestic trouble and that she had accused him of carrying on a clandestine affair.

The time element relating to the fatal beating was the crux of the case. The state contended that McDaniel had left home that night after telling his wife he was going to a lodge meeting, that she had called the lodge hall and found that McDaniel had stopped there only briefly. McDaniel had admitted that was true, saying he had left the lodge session to check on alleged illegal activities, including the operation of a bawdy house near 17th and Buchanan Avenue.

The state tried to prove that McDaniel became enraged when his wife charged him with acts of infidelity when he returned home. The state alleged that he had fatally beaten her, then set out to establish an alibi by his saloon visits, making his stops there particularly noticeable by buying drinks for the house. Here the time element entered. McDaniel said he received the alleged call from the saloon at 11:30 that night. The state contended the fatal beating actually occurred between 10:15 and 10:30 and that McDaniel then left home and developed his alibi.

The state offered testimony that screams by Mrs. McDaniel had been heard between 10:15 and 10:30 that night. One of the state witnesses was an elderly German woman who lived next door to the McDaniel home. She came near to collapse on the witness stand, but held to her story she had heard the woman's screams between 10:15 and 10:30.

The defense countered with a young woman in the neighborhood who said she was the one who had been screaming. She testified she was in a tree swing and screamed when the swing was pushed high and she was fearful a tree limb might cause her to fall to the ground. The state contended it had witnesses who would prove the girl had not been screaming.

Prosecution and defense both played tough at the trial. The state was not asking for a prison term for McDaniel. It wanted him hanged. The state did not even ask for a manslaughter instruction, nor did Judge Ryan give one. The only choice left to the jury was a conviction of murder with death by hanging or acquittal.

A prominent St. Joseph educator, a neighbor of the McDaniels, testified that he went by the McDaniel home late that night and that he had seen Mrs. McDaniel at the window of the second floor bedroom. The state came back with a witness who testified he had been to a political meeting with that educator the same night and that when the educator went home he couldn't hit the ground with his hat because of his degree of intoxication. The witness said the educator certainly wouldn't have been able to see anyone in the room across the street.

McDaniel retained his composure during long and intense cross-examination. He changed not a bit of his story. The McDaniel children, barely old enough to be in school, were called as witnesses. They testified they knew of no disagreements between their parents. The two girls, who had been in the bedroom next to the one in which their mother had been attacked, said they had heard nothing. They did not learn of the horror for more than an hour after McDaniel said he found his diabolically battered wife.

Strop gave a six-hour summation of the evidence for the defense as the lengthy trial neared its conclusion. Attorney General Barker gave one of the greatest and most dramatic courtroom pleas in the county's history as he asked the jury to send his fellow lawyer McDaniel to the gallows.

Barker called upon the spirit of Harriet Moss McDaniel to give some sign showing her husband was guilty. As Barker concluded his call for death by hanging for McDaniel, defendant McDaniel stepped up to him and said, "General Barker, that was the finest speech I have ever heard." Truly the McDaniel nerves were of steel.

McDaniel's mother approached Barker in the courtroom and said, "I still believe my boy is innocent." Barker brushed a tear from his cheek and told her he admired her faith.

The jury was out two hours deliberating; on the fourth ballot it acquitted McDaniel. The first vote had been 10 to 2 for acquittal, as was the second; then 11 to 1 for acquittal, and then, of course, unanimous for acquittal.

An elated McDaniel announced that he had a lead on two men who might be the murderers and that he was following through on it. McDaniel was back in his office the next morning carrying out his duties as prosecuting attorney with no sign of the ordeal he had been through. His term in office had twenty-six days to run.

Leaving the prosecutor's office January 1, 1917, he rented an office suite on the second floor of Donnell Court, just across the hall from the law office of Bart Lockwood, his former colleague who had filed the murder charge and told the jury he should be hanged.

A little more than a year later McDaniel married Zora Lee Cook, daughter of a St. Joseph telephone executive. Drama stayed in the life of McDaniel. About a year after his second marriage, McDaniel was cast in a hero role when fire destroyed their home. Using a rope, he lowered his wife and two daughters to safety from the second floor of the blazing house. Since then another commodious house has been erected at that 1806 South Twentieth Street address.

Less than three years after his acquittal, McDaniel mysteriously disappeared along with his wife and three children. He was known to be in debt, the story being that the Credit Bureau alone was seeking to collect $4,000 from him. That seemed to be the most valid reason for the vanishing act. The only notice he gave was provided by a note on the door of his law office that requested callers to turn their legal business over to the firm of William H. Sherman and Merrill E. Otis.

All through his life McDaniel had inspired loyalty. His disappearance gave further proof of that. Many here undoubtedly knew where McDaniel had gone, but they weren't talking about it. His secret was safe with them. Word did trickle back some years later that his second wife had been killed in a mountain accident out west. Then all was silent.

The men who had staffed his office while he was prosecutor were tight-lipped when asked about Oscar. They included Duval Smith and Homer C. King, both of whom later were elected prosecuting attorney, and Ace Porter, who became municipal judge. By a quirk of fate, Duval Smith was to serve as circuit judge in the same courtroom where McDaniel had been tried and acquitted.

One day while sitting in the editorial offices of the *News-Press* veteran reporter Charles J.L. May told me, "That man who just left the office of Mr. Sprague (Hugh A. Sprague, then publisher of the *News-Press* and *Gazette*) is Oscar McDaniel. McDaniel was gray-haired, trim and neatly dressed. It was the only time I ever saw him."

Arthur V. Burrowes, editor of the *News-Press* and *Gazette,* in the late 1930s was tipped off by a cab driver that there had been a secret burial the night before and that it might have been McDaniel. Mr. Burrowes assigned Norman H. Steward, then police reporter for the *News-Press,* and me to check into the matter. I was then courthouse reporter.

The undertaker would provide no help, so Steward and I made

Mount Mora cemetery our next stop. We were told there had been no recent McDaniel burial there, but we went ahead and checked the McDaniel burial plot. In that plot we found a fresh grave.

After more checking, Steward and I found that a man had been buried there under the name of Oscar Mack. That was the name under which McDaniel had been working in Washington, D.C., for a number of years. It was learned that his dying request was that he be buried at the side of his wife of whose murder he had been acquitted. To some it would seem like a strange reunion.

High drama had followed Oscar McDaniel to the grave.

It Was A Perfectly Logical Observation

Although it has been more than thirty years, one of the sports anecdotes Sherman remembers concerned a hole-in-one made by local golfer Bill Schreiber.

If there is any truth in the saying, "...No man is a hero with his own wife," golfer Schreiber certainly understood how the adage may have come about.

The St. Joseph businessman was understandably proud of his achievement and mentioned it numerous times around the house and to friends.

Then in one brief matter-of-fact comment, Mrs. Schreiber punctured the ego balloon on which her husband had been floating rapturously...

"As much as you play, I don't see why you haven't done it a long time ago," Bill's ever-loving wife observed sweetly.

Bill's reply was never reported.

A Good Place to Raise a Family

The one thing that frequently comes as a surprise to strangers who visit St. Joseph for the first time, especially if they are from cities in the northeastern part of the United States, is the friendliness of the people here.

Time and again, visitors have expressed how unusual it is to them to have strangers on the street smile and say, "Hello."

St. Joseph's proximity to Kansas City is a major asset today. For one thing, the outstanding Kansas City airport is more convenient for St. Joseph residents than for many Kansas Citians.

For another, St. Joseph's location only fifty miles away gives her citizens easy access to all the cultural and professional sports and entertainment offerings of a major city while at the same time not being subjected to the traffic and crime problems of a big city. (There are some who might question the traffic statement considering the congestion on the Belt Highway, which grows worse every month.)

Almost universally today when St. Joseph citizens are asked about their city, they respond....

"It's a good place to raise a family."

A Crusader Gets His Chance

Nearly every newspaperman has a secret desire to run his own newspaper with no editor to say "yes" or "no" to a story and without fear that a major advertiser will cancel if he doesn't like what is printed.

Co-author George Sherman had that rare opportunity in 1954 when he was the editor of a St. Joseph weekly newspaper which he named the *Times Review*.

Many people thought the *Times Review* was owned and controlled by St. Joseph industrialist J.P. Barclay, Sr., but that was not the case. Mr. Barclay made the newspaper possible, but he neither owned nor controlled it.

Sherman describes the founder of the multi-million dollar Wire Rope Corporation as a "...very rare human being, one who had the intelligence, the desire and the financial resources to make the world better for the ordinary working man.

"Mr. Barclay was convinced," Sherman said, "that the working people of St. Joseph bore a disproportionate share of the tax burden and he was determined to correct this perceived injustice.

"I was doing radio news for a local station at the time," Sherman recalls, "when Mr. Barclay came to me with an offer I couldn't refuse."

According to Sherman, the St. Joseph industrialist had crews of clerks who were on the Wire Rope payroll but who spent their days gathering information from the tax records at the city hall and the courthouse. Mr. Barclay was a sensitive man, Sherman explained, and he realized the information he was obtaining would be highly aggravating to some of the major advertisers in other publications in town.

Consequently, he approached Sherman with the following idea:

If Sherman wanted to become editor of a weekly newspaper, Barclay would guarantee one to two full pages of advertising every week. This income would cover the bare essentials and an advertising director could then sell enough additional advertising to insure the paper's success. Fortunately, Burton Dunbar of St. Joseph, an experienced advertising salesman, was available and that key position was quickly filled.

Technically, Max Dawson was publisher but it was understood from the beginning that Sherman would have the sole say over what was printed in the news columns of the *Times Review*. Dawson was in the picture because the new weekly was to be printed in a building in South St. Joseph which he leased and where he was editor and publisher of the *Stock Yards Journal*, a weekly paper serving St. Joseph's large livestock industry.

Sherman remembers Barclay telling him, "You will be in sole charge as editor, you can disagree with me, you can call me an S.O.B. if you like, the ads Dunbar sells will soon make the paper completely independent." Barclay went on to explain that in turn no one but he would have any control over what he said in his paid one or two pages of advertising. He did assure Sherman that he would have his ad copy checked by Wire Rope attorneys to avoid any possible libel suits.

"And that," said Sherman, "is exactly how it worked. I had a free hand."

The paper was controversial from the beginning. Certain

members of the local "establishment" deeply resented the publication because of the "Barclay Bootstrap," as he called the weekly advertisements. Others resented the aggressive stance the paper took in its news columns.

"We had to be aggressive," Sherman emphasized, "there would have been no readership or following for a bland publication or for one that would simply echo the establishment view."

The paper broke many important stories and editorially fought for several important causes.

One of Sherman's most successful crusades involved a policy that was being applied in local high school sports whereby black athletes could not compete against white athletes in school competition in St. Joseph.

The most assinine aspect of this ridiculous policy was that it did not apply, of course, when Missouri teams crossed the river to compete in Kansas.

For instance, when the Central High School basketball team travelled to Atchison, Kan., the Kansas school's black players competed against the Central players. When Atchison came to Missouri to return the game, however, the black Atchison players were forbidden to participate and were forced to sit on the bench.

One can only imagine but never fully appreciate how those young Kansas black athletes must have felt.

At first, the impression was given that this was a Missouri State High School Athletic Association ruling. However, when contacted by Editor Sherman, the executive director of the state association, Jake Noel, said no state high school regulation existed and that it was purely a local matter. He pointed out that black players on Catholic high school teams in St. Louis had regularly been competing with white athletes. (In St. Joseph at that time, there were no black players in the Catholic schools and there was a separate local high school for black students.)

When this was brought to the attention of the then superintendent of schools, George Blackwell, the *Times Review* was told that it was a local regulation but was based on a provision in the Missouri State Constitution. Mr. Blackwell said he had done nothing about the policy since the constitutional question was being reviewed.

The St. Joseph superintendent made no comment when advised that black athletes already were competing with and against their white counterparts in St. Louis. Shortly thereafter, whether based on a constitutional interpretation or otherwise, the despicable practice was stopped.

Editorially, the paper campaigned against the mistreatment of rape victims by defense lawyers—an issue still very much in the headlines today.

Another issue where the paper was ahead of its time was in supporting Dr. Jacob Kulowski, a pioneer in advocating seat safety belts for automobiles. Dr. Kulowski was joined by another St. Joseph doctor, H. Ewing Wachter, in his crusade, which eventually was successful after meeting considerable early resistance.

Other campaigns involved a hospital policy in which a badly burned man was refused treatment and ended up in jail; opposition to a grossly unfair annexation proposal which took in acres of farmland and intentionally avoided businesses that were using city services without having to pay city taxes; private meetings of the city council; a sewer law that was "lawful but awful," lenient fines for traffic offenders who had influence and inadequate water pressure in the city.

Sherman also said that at the time his newspaper was summarily closed down he was working on two stories that would have had ramifications all over the state in the event the leads he was following proved out.

One involved a claim from the sister of an inmate in the state penitentiary that paroles were available at a price tag of $5,000 each.

The other concerned serious misuse of federal subsidies and expense account privileges in a tax-supported institution.

Both investigations ended with the untimely end of the newspaper and no proof ever was submitted.

Both Barclay and the *Times Review* were enormously popular with the ordinary citizens and Barclay was elected by a wide margin to the state legislature, where he had planned to carry on his tax crusade.

Just when everything looked most promising, with certain individuals talking of making the *Times Review* a daily, the roof fell in. Sherman tells the story:

"In mid-October of 1954, death claimed Mr. Barclay. The Wire Rope executive had been healthy all his life and the end came unexpectedly.

"Three months later, after one full year of operation," the establishment forces ruthlessly and with malice aforethought closed down the *Times Review*.

"On Friday I was editor of a thriving weekly newspaper and on the following Monday I was unemployed." Here for the first time in print is Sherman's first hand account of what took place:

"I showed up at the usual time on Monday morning," he said, "and a badly shaken Max Dawson was waiting for me.

"Max wasted no time. He told me powerful and influential individuals had given him an ultimatum. 'Either the *Times Review* stopped immediately or the lease would not be renewed on the building which housed the printing press and influence would be used to see that the $20,000 a year subsidy for Max's paper, the *Stock Yards Journal,* would be cut off.'

"We were not even allowed the privilege of a final farewell issue," Sherman said. "Obviously, they were afraid of what we might say and even more afraid of how the public would react.

"The city lost a great champion with Mr. Barclay's untimely death," Sherman observed, adding, "…and I have no regrets over my role."

Sherman said one of the things he most appreciates relative to those years was the opportunity to at least meet Barclay.

"I wish I had gotten to know him better," the newsman said. "He was a wonderful person."

Sherman said the industrialist was not particularly tall, had white hair and wore glasses but the most striking thing was his smile and eyes that took in everything but still sparkled with friendliness and good cheer.

"I think in many ways he was a lonely man," Sherman said. "Certain of his peers didn't like the idea that his crusade most likely would lead to their paying higher taxes.

"After his death, there were those who referred to him as 'uncontrollable,'" Sherman said. "And while they didn't mean it as a compliment, to my way of thinking, it was a fitting tribute to a really great man."

The Sports Editor Has a Close Call

Nearly every newsman who has worked at his craft for any length of time has been threatened with everything from bodily harm to outright extermination.

George Sherman's closest call in this respect was over an item which he didn't write. The old *Gazette* used to have a daily column on the editorial page which carried the same byline but which was written by a variety of different news people during the course of a week.

One column dealt with the Green Tree Tavern, a notorious watering hole on South Sixth Street, and it made some reference to the establishment's crude, toothless owner. The owner was Virgil Townsend, a stocky and well-muscled character whose missing teeth had nothing to do with age or gum disease. Virgil had quite a reputation as a barroom brawler and that was how he'd lost several teeth, which he hadn't bothered to replace.

Virgil took exception to some of the derogatory remarks in the column. He showed up in the newsroom that night, shaking a copy of the newspaper in one massive fist and demanding to know who had written it. He moved from desk to desk, loudly demanding to know if that individual was the writer.

No one admitted responsibility and Townsend finally made his way to Sherman's desk. Sherman was sports editor at the time and had not written the offending column but, perhaps somewhat foolishly, didn't say so.

"Did you write this?" Townsend demanded, shaking the newspaper in Sherman's face.

Outweighed by a hundred pounds or more, certainly out muscled and certainly lacking the burly Townsend's experience in back alley brawls, Sherman came up with the immature and rather ridiculous reply of, "So what if I did?"

"If you did, then you've got a beatin' coming," was Townsend's response as he made a menacing move toward Sherman.

Sherman was saved from the quite likely prospect of having his features rearranged by the intervention of copy boy Bill Bennett, now the nature and wildlife editor of the newspaper.

"He didn't write it," said Bennett, "He's the sports editor!"

With one last glowering look at Sherman, Townsend turned and stormed out of the newsroom.

Sherman said later he didn't know what prompted him to say what he did. "I guess I was just in a bad mood," he told City Editor Houseworth.

As it turned out, Townsend was a bully and like all bullies, when someone called his bluff, he had no stomach to continue his rampage through the newsroom.

Also in typical bully boy tradition, from that night on, Townsend had the upmost respect for Sherman. Whenever he would see Sherman on the street, Townsend would treat him like a long lost brother. Even if he were on the other side of the street, Townsend would bellow out the same greeting:

"Hi, ol' buddy, how ya doing,"

Even so, Sherman didn't see fit to spend his spare time at the Green Tree Tavern.

Discretion Is The Better Part of Valor

Perhaps everyone at one time or another has been caught up in the excitement of an event without thinking of the consequences.

George Sherman has vivid memories of one such incident. In Sherman's police reporter days, it was common practice for the newsman to ride along in a patrol car. In some ways, it was a practical arrangement. Any emergency would come in over the squad car's radio and the reporter could immediately be taken to the scene.

On one occasion, the radio flashed that a burglar alarm had gone off at Einbender's Department Store, then located on South 8th Street. Sherman was rushed to the scene and arrived at the same time as two other squad cars and the ADT representative, who unlocked the front door. Sherman and the police officers quickly fanned out into the rather large store and began searching for an intruder or intruders.

Several minutes later as he was searching behind racks of women's dresses and opening dressing room doors, Sherman suddenly realized he was alone in that section of the store and the officers were off searching elsewhere.

"It dawned on me," Sherman said later, "that, unlike the police officers, I had no weapon. What would I do if I opened a dressing room door and standing there would be some vicious character holding a gun or a knife?"

Sherman's enthusiasm for the hunt abruptly evaporated and he quietly and meekly joined one of the police officers for the remainder of the search.

No one was found in the store but an open window in the back indicated that an intruder had been frightened off by the alarm.

Needless to say, prudence was Sherman's watchword in such future events.

Underhanded, Yes, But Effective

Even seemingly trivial things were big news when it came to the Greenlease kidnapping story.

One incident concerned the time of the funeral services for Bonnie Heady after she had been executed in the Missouri State Penitentiary.

Fearing that curiosity seekers would overrun the cemetery if the time of burial services were made public, the mortuary refused to disclose the time to any except authorized individuals.

As a further control, Maryville Attorney Harold M. Hull issued passes approved for the services. (Harold Slater got one.)

Those with passes, of course, were expected not to disclose the pertinent information. Sherman had not requested such a pass and consequently was not privy to the time of the service.

Subsequently, he was contacted by International News Service, the wire service to which he had been supplying information on the story. For some unaccountable reason, INS decided it just had to have the burial information.

It became almost a challenge to Sherman and he formulated a scheme to get the information. He simply put in a long distance call to the people in charge of the service. He posed as a St. Joseph florist who was commissioned to send a large floral display to the funeral.

Informed that the time wasn't supposed to be disclosed, he made an impassioned plea to what sounded like a little old lady on the other end of the line. He explained the problem of delivering the spray too late. Fortunately, he had called at lunch time. The "little old lady" on the other end of the line said, "Well, they're all out to lunch but under the circumstances I guess it won't do any harm," and she proceeded to provide the "precious" information.

Sherman later admitted to a twinge of conscience over the ploy he had used, but not severe enough to keep him from passing the information along to INS. Friends claimed newspapermen had no conscience and said the twinge Sherman felt probably was nothing more than a touch of indigestion!

As it turned out, it really didn't matter. Neither the secrecy nor the cemetery passes were necessary. By this time, people were fed up with the whole sordid mess and only a handful showed up for Mrs. Heady's last rites.

There was no weeping.

It Was Just Another Story

Young journalists frequently do things to get a story that their older, wiser brethren prefer to avoid. It isn't that younger journalists are more courageous, just more foolish.

Recalling the success of the glider flight episode which earned him his first byline, Sherman, now a sports writer, volunteered to ride along when a local hotrod race car driver announced that, as an added attraction at the races, he would crash a hotrod through a flaming wood wall.

A sturdy wooden wall was built and placed across the track. The wall was saturated with gasoline and then set afire as the hotrod built up speed on the oval track. The timing was just right and the blaze was at its height when the driver crashed through the barricade.

"Actually, it was all over in an instant," Sherman said, adding, "I'm sure it was much more spectacular from the grandstands than it was in the car.

"I'm not sure 30 years later who the driver was," Sherman stated, "but I think it may have been Hy Fasching." (Fasching was a local hotrod and race car driver and something of a daredevil himself.)

The only scary part, said Sherman, was that the car had no windshield, but he didn't realize until it was all over that pieces of flaming board had literally been hurled into the car and were burning themselves out in the area where a rear seat normally would have been.

"Actually," Sherman admitted years later, "I didn't consider either the glider or the flaming wall episodes as requiring any particular excess of courage.

"It was simple logic," he explained, "if the pilot, in the case of the glider and the driver in the case of the flaming wall, were willing to do it, then I figured it wasn't that much of a risk for me.

"Most important," he concluded, "it gave me material for an interesting feature that was fun to write."

A Recalcitrant Postmaster Cooperates

After the local esablishment had summarily shutdown his *Times Review* weekly newspaper, Sherman's next job was a city editor of the Independence *Daily News,* a small paper struggling to compete with the entrenched Independence *Examiner.*

It was a very brief stint because, a short time later, Sherman, based on the recommendation of former *Gazette* Sports Editor Norman Coder, was offered a job as sports desk copy editor for the prestigious Omaha *World-Herald.*

Sherman recalls one (to him anyway) humorous incident in particular while editor of the Independence paper.

He had assigned his photographer to go to the post office and get a photo of the usual Christmas rush. A short time later, the photographer returned and told Sherman that the postmaster had refused him permission to take pictures. It wasn't clear whether the postmaster was trying to favor the other newspaper or just had quarreled with his wife that morning and was in a bad mood.

Sherman immediately picked up the telephone and placed a long distance call to the postmaster-general of the United States. He asked if the department had a policy to forbid Christmas photos. Sherman was advised there was no such policy and the editor then explained how his photographer had been rejected by the Independence postmaster. He was advised the matter would be taken care of.

Fifteen minutes later, Sherman received a phone call. It was a very subdued Independence postmaster. "You can send your photographer over anytime," he said, and then added, "For ____ ' __, sake, I didn't know you would go that far?"

"Why do you suppose he cooperated so quickly?" the photographer asked and Sherman replied, "I haven't the slightest idea — unless, of course, it's because he is a Republican postmaster and this happens to be a Democratic regime!"

Living Down a Bad Reputation

St. Joseph once was the third largest city in the state, but went through a period of stagnation which resulted in both Springfield and Independence moving up to third and fourth, respectively.

Many people believed St. Joseph's lack of growth and failure to attract new industry was intentional, that certain business people in key positions did not want competition, either for people or in pay and benefits.

Former U.S. Congressman Phil J. Welch of St. Joseph was one of those who had the courage to speak out on what appeared to be concerted efforts to discourage new industry. Considering his status in local and national politics, the influential Democratic politician was surprisingly blunt when he was quoted on July 8, 1954 as follows:

"This city has too long been in the control of a small, select group which passes on the reins from generation to generation."

Welch referred to the controlling hierarchy as "...either too selfish or too conservative" to aggressively go after new business and industry.

Mr. Welch was not the only one to speak out on this question. W.R. Toler, district manager of the Prudential Insurance Company of America, in a speech at Kansas City, asserted that "...Leavenworth and St. Joseph were giants compared to early day Kansas City but they have been bypassed because they were too timid to gamble with destiny."

Dick Hankin, manager of the Zale Jewelry Company, stated that Kansas City had "...more dynamic leadership."

There are two other incidents which support the contention that St. Jopseph at one point discouraged competition, one involving a former Lafayette High School football coach and the other a personal experience of co-author George Sherman.

Former Lafayette Coach Bob Matheson met two strangers on a golf course in Kansas City. When he introduced himself as being from St. Joseph, their comment was "That's the city that doesn't want new industry!"

Sherman had a similar experience at Fairview golf club. He was getting ready to tee off alone when a man requested to join him. During the course of the round, the man said he wanted to open a "...shirt factory" in St. Joseph but got the cold shoulder from the city fathers. He said he was particularly interested in St. Joseph because he had friends and relatives here, in addition to the excellent central location.

Snubbed by St. Joseph, he located his factory in Iowa where the community offered him a facility rent-free with the understanding that the city would receive a percentage of the profits once it was a going business.

While that may have been the situation thirty years ago, it has not been true in the last fifteen or twenty years. The city has had a very aggressive Chamber of Commerce effort in recent times and has fared surprisingly well against fierce competition from all fifty states.

While the city lost more than 5,000 jobs when the packing houses closed, the Chamber of Commerce has replaced these with a great many smaller enterprises of twenty-five to two or three hundred employees. This diversification has protected the city against the vagaries of layoffs that can plague a large employer.

Still Worth Checking Out!

During an interrogation session by police after his capture, Carl Austin Hall, the kidnapper and murderer of six-year-old Bobby Greenlease, revealed that he had planned his horrible crime while a prisoner awaiting parole at the Missouri State Penitentiary.

For sometime prior to the Greenlease case, George Sherman had been doing personal research into the various uses of the polygraph (lie detector) machine.

Sherman's interest in the polygraph resulted from numerous conversations at the St. Joseph police station with Ed Burke. Burke, a detective on the St. Joseph force, took time out to serve in the Secret Service and later became chief of detectives and then chief of police of St. Joseph. Burke also was an expert in using the polygraph.

Burke was assigned to guard the Franklin Delano Roosevelt family and was extremely close to President Truman. It was once claimed he had to "...put Walter Winchell in his place" over a protocol matter during a Truman press conference. Winchell's rather large ego was bruised and he later is reported to have referred to Burke in one of his books as "...a smart alec FBI agent." (Burke was Secret Service, not FBI.)

With his interest in the polygraph stimulated by his conversations with Burke, Sherman went on to do considerable research on the instrument. He discovered that the leading expert in the country on the polygraph was Cleve Baxter, who ran a school in Chicago on using the polygraph, not only in police work but also as a crime deterrent in industry.

For example, one of Chicago's largest department stores was experiencing inventory losses of over a million dollars a year, the result of petty thievery by the store's employees. Clerks and other employees, almost without a second thought, would help themselves to small items such as shaving cream, hosiery, hardware items, etc.

The company decided to bring in the polygraph. All employees were advised they would be tested but no past transgressions would be held against them. In the future, however, the company would pull in employees at random to be tested on the polygraph as to whether they had stolen anything since the original test. The idea worked and reduced the company's inventory losses by more than ninety percent. Employees were not about to jeopardize their jobs and their reputations for a two dollar item.

With this knowledge and other details on the successful application of the polygraph filed away in his memory banks, Sherman went on to other pursuits. Kidnapper Hall's casual and callous remark about having planned the whole terrible crime while awaiting parole triggered what Sherman thought was an inspiration.

Why not use the polygraph as a tool in the parole interviewing procedure? A question could be posed along with others relative to whether a parole applicant had any criminal intent if released. Burke said there was no reason why it wouldn't work. It could even be voluntary on the part of the prisoner whether he would take this test.

A well-known New York syndicated columnist and broadcaster, Irene Corbally Kuhn, heard about the idea, liked it and gave it wide distribution in the East, giving Sherman appropriate credit as the originator of the concept.

Unfortunately, from Sherman's viewpoint, at least, that was the end of it. Missouri parole officials gave the excuse that it "...would be too expensive and too time consuming."

Sherman thought the reasons given lacked substance. He pointed out that Highway Patrol units all around the state were using the polygraph and that the examination did not necessarily have to take place at the same time as the parole hearing.

Sherman's point was simple. If using the polygraph would prevent even one crime as horrendous as the Greenlease atrocity, it would be worth whatever time and expense it would take.

Undoubtedly, Mr. and Mrs. Greenlease would agree.

It Paid to Stay Sober

An important asset to a newsman in the days of highly competitive journalism in St. Joseph was the ability to stay sober while a potential news source over-indulged.

Such was the case for *Gazette* Sports Editor George Sherman at a time when his arch-rival was *News-Press* Sports Editor Gene Sullivan.

Although fierce competitors to be the first to break an important sports story, Sherman and Sullivan remained on speaking terms outside the news room. In fact, thanks to a strong endorsement from Sullivan, University of Missouri Basketball Coach Sparky Stalcup offered Sherman a free ride at the school—room, board, books and tuition. Sherman was grateful but in the back of his mind couldn't help but wonder if his rival was trying to get rid of him.

Sullivan had one big advantage in this rivalry. The *News-Press* was the dominant paper in those days, had the greater circulation and, most important, Sullivan was responsible for the Sunday paper, which not only had ample room for sports coverage but also had the combined circulation of the two daily papers. It was easy for Sullivan to convince a news source to capitalize on these important advantages of the Sunday paper to get the most out of their news items.

That was the situation confronting Sherman one day when he learned that a prominent former major league star had been named as the new manager of the St. Joseph Cardinals' minor league baseball team. It may not have been a big story elsewhere, but it was the biggest sports story of the year in St. Joseph.

Sherman learned that Sullivan, using the Sunday circulation

ploy, had obtained an "exclusive" on the story from St. Louis Cardinal management. Apparently Sullivan had a story written and a photo layout all prepared for Sunday release.

The tip started Sherman's adrenalin pumping and his competitive juices flowing but he ran into a stone wall from top Cardinal management on down, and even though it was only mid-week, prospects of cracking the story looked dismal. Sullivan had done his homework well and had effectively shut down all possible leaks.

Sherman was aware that the local business manager of the St. Joseph Cardinals had the precious name locked away in his mind but the Cardinal official wasn't about to tell, even though he and the *Gazette* sports editor were on very friendly terms. Since it wasn't unusual to have a few drinks with the business manager from time to time, Sherman casually issued an invitation the next evening. As usual, it was accepted.

In the wee hours of the morning — after who knows how many beers — the Cardinal business manager indvertently let the name slip out. It was former St. Louis Cardinal great, Harry "The Hot" Walker.

When he realized what he had done, the team's business manager was appalled. "Good Lord," he said, "if you use that, I'll get fired!"

It's a Cardinal rule in journalism that a newsman never reveals his source of confidential information. Reporters have gone to jail on contempt of court charges rather than reveal a news source. Sherman assured his stricken companion, who was sobering up rather rapidly, that he would be protected at all cost.

Here, for the first time in print anywhere, is how it was done:

Sherman at some time in his reporter days had been a "stringer" for International News Service. A "stringer" is a local individual who from time to time supplies information to a wire service or newspaper in some other part of the country.

The *Gazette* sports editor recalled the name of one of his former contacts with International News Service in Chicago, where Harry Walker lived. He informed his Chicago contact that he had the story, was convinced of its accuracy but, in order to protect a source, couldn't break the news locally. He asked the Chicago newsman to put the story on the INS news wire with a Chicago dateline and to never, ever reveal that the original tip had come from St. Joseph.

The item came out on the INS news wire. Sherman spiced

it up with the local angle and broke it in the Saturday morning paper.

Word came back that Sullivan was furious, that he had the telephone lines humming between the *New-Press* office, the local Cardinal team office, St. Louis and Chicago but he was never able to identify who had leaked the story. The local business manager was never connected with the leak.

An unfortunate aftermath is that Sullivan exerted his considerable influence to prevail upon the St. Louis Cardinal management not to send Walker to the St. Joseph team. It deprived the city of having a noted baseball figure at the helm of the local team but Sullivan's Irish temper had been triggered and in this case he wasn't about to accept the setback gracefully.

That was newspapering in those "good old days" of competitive reporting.

After a Half Million Questions

These have been a few random—and some of my fondest and most vivid—recollections from fifty-two years as a newspaperman in St. Joseph. I once figured that during those years I asked more than half a million questions to all kinds of people—from bishops to bums, from robbers to wrestlers, and hundreds of just average citizens.

I'm amazed, in thinking of all those questions I have asked, about how few people ever were impolite to me. I have relatively few memories of vicious reactions from people who may have been offended by the questions I put to them.

I do remember one official who was very upset when the boss sent me out and told me to bluntly ask the man (after he had been convicted of embezzlement), "What did you do with the money you stole?"

Two of the man's friends threw me bodily out of the house.

But, all in all, this has to be the friendliest city and the most delightful beat that ever existed for a newsman.

HAROLD SLATER

This picture was taken Jan. 27, 1953, a week after Mr. Truman had completed his service as president. The location is his office in the Federal Reserve Bank Building in Kansas City. At right is Harold Slater and at left is his son, Robert, then a student at St. Benedict's College in Atchison, Kansas.

EPILOGUE

The State
of the
Fourth Estate

THE STATE OF THE FOURTH ESTATE

The Spirit of Competition

by Harold Slater

One of the things that is sort of surprising to any oldtime newsman, especially locally, is how the spirit of competition has vanished.

There was a time when getting it first ranked second only to getting it right, but today many newmen don't seem to mind if the opposition comes out with the story first.

In the old days city editors roared at a reporter when the opposition scooped him on a story on his run even if it wasn't too important. There were instances 60 years ago when a newsman got bawled out for missing a story of only a paragraph or so.

That was when reporters were taught the opposition was the enemy, when any fraternizing with a reporter on your run was taboo. Also there was pride in getting the story first, and that was true even before bylines appeared on local stories here.

Also back in those days reporters apparently did more to cultivate the deputies and clerks at such places as the courthouse and city hall. The theory was that such underlings, if treated decently, often could give valuable news tips and they did.

News personnel work hard these days but much of their own personalities has been destroyed by the advent of press releases, and press conferences. In the old days, the reporter got his political stories first hand from the celebrity and both he and the news personage came across more clearly and more personally.

One ex-newsman here says he never saw a news release or went to a press conference until after he had been a reporter twenty years. It had all been one-on-one with news contacts.

Evolution and Revolution in Journalism

by George Sherman

Popularity is one of life's luxuries that a dedicated, conscientious journalist must learn to live without. About all he (and, more and more, she) can expect from his readers—and often even from his friends—is respect.

A good newsman should be the conscience of his community. Often that means being a nagger. Friends, relatives, dignitaries and even big advertisers are all the same as the man on the street when it comes to exercising journalistic responsibility.

From the time I was a wide-eyed cub reporter writing weather and obituaries, I've thought Rudyard Kipling surely must have had reporters in mind when he wrote his oft-quoted classic poem, "If:"

"If you can keep your head when all about you
Are losing theirs and blaming it on you;
 If you can trust yourself when all men doubt you,
But make allowance for their doubting you;
If you can wait and not be tired by waiting,
Or being lied about, don't deal in lies,
Or, being hated, don't give way to hating,
And don't look too good, nor talk too wise;
If you can dream—and not make dreams your master,
If you can think—and not make thoughts your aim;
If you can meet with triumph and disaster
And treat those two imposters just the same . . ."

And, finally, the four lines in the last stanza which reflect everything that a newsman ought to be . . .

"If you can talk with crowds and keep your virtue,
Or walk with kings—nor lose the common touch;
If neither foes nor loving friends can hurt you;
If all men count with you, but none too much . . ."

While Kipling's immortal lines paint a word picture of the ideal newspaperman and while the need for those qualities hasn't changed, the profession itself has undergone a dramatic philosophical transformation. Whether your inclination is to call it an evolution or a revolution, the fact remains that the profession will never be the same.

"Objective" journalism was the philosophy which governed Harold Slater and me and most newsmen of our time. Our aim was to keep our personal thoughts and ideas out of the story, to print the facts as selflessly as possible and to save our opinions for the editorial page. We were idealists of sorts, I guess, operating under what we believed to be rather lofty principles.

Those we considered the kooks and crazies and the lunatic fringe (who seem to have ready access to the news columns and television screen today) were not welcome in our news rooms. They didn't fit into our concept of objectivity. Neither did what we call the "yellow journalists" who specialized in the sensational. We believed that these scandalmongers sacrificed integrity for income and responsibility for readership.

Actually, there was perhaps a much more practical reason for our objectivity than we realized. The era of objective journalism coincided with the emergence of the wire services, which in turn were an outgrowth of the telegraph. Since the wire services provided news stories for a wide variety of newspapers, many with sharply conflicting political and social viewpoints, totally objective reporting was essential.

The wire services, whether by accident or on purpose, did a great service for the profession. The almost religious fervor to maintain objectivity helped establish a reputation for reliability and credibility in journalists that few professions enjoyed. In the heyday of objective journalism, the comment ". . .I read it in the paper," was tantamount to saying ". . . I heard it from my minister."

I firmly believe that Harold Slater and I were fortunate to have been a part of journalism during its most influential period. I also am convinced that the next step was necessary and inevitable.

That stage has been described as the period of "interpretive journalism." Under this concept the reporter was expected to give the facts objectively and, at the same time, explain and interpret them to make the story more meaningful to the reader. Obviously, the reporter had to do a bit of editorializing and expressing of his personal opinions.

This has been both a strength and a weakness of interpretive journalism. The reader gets more than "bare bones" facts but also detects the reporter's personal judgments. And that creates doubt and suspicion in his mind, especially if his evaluation of the facts differs from the journalist's. Consequently, there has been a diminishing of the trust and credibility readers once had for newspapers and journalists. But this stage probably was inevitable. The sanitized sterility of strictly objective reporting would not be as interesting to today's more sophisticated reader.

A major factor in the evolution to interpretive reporting has been the considerably higher level of education possessed by today's journalists. The news today is far more complex than ever before. A journalist who has the education and knowledge to report on a complex congressional bill or a scientific breakthrough would not be satisfied with just presenting the essentials. Of course, the advent of television news and its accompanying saturation of analytical overkill has had its influence on the print media, too.

Now "activist" or adversial journalism is upon us. And it is more revolution than evolution. The activist journalist becomes personally and emotionally involved in a story. He tends to think his position and training qualify him—and, more and more, her—in some cases even to create the news to conform to his or her own intellectual commitment.

These journalists have paid a price for their intellectual freedom and independence in reporting the news. Now pollsters report that people put the media representatives near the bottom of their list of most respected professions.

Interpretation is a good thing as long as the reporter does not try to alter the context or omit essential facts to manipulate the reader. But activist journalism is blatantly manipulative, dangerous and destructive. The pure activist journalist believes that he knows what is best for the reader and attempts to manage the news accordingly. He attempts to mold public opinion in his own image. Two good examples are the media's reporting of the Vietnam War and the Nicaraguan Sandinista-Contra situation.

Along with the activist groups in this country which have their own agenda, the activist journalists saturated the American public with all the rotten aspects of the war where the United States was responsible and omitted most of the more odious transgressions of the enemy.

In the past eight years I have traveled widely all over the world on behalf of Moral Re-Armament, an organization which attempts to build bridges between nations through honesty, dialogue and basing actions on a philosophy of what's right, not who's right. On several trips to Central and South America, I have met and discussed problems with bankers and businessmen, trade union leaders, politicians of various parties and with the very poor from what we used to call "shanty towns." On numerous occasions, I've been shocked on returning to the U.S. to find that our media have been painting a totally different picture from the one I encountered. The facts were twisted and distorted beyond belief.

The ultimate tragedy of this journalism is that it provides the fodder for partisan in-fighting which, in turn, generates bewilderment and confusion throughout our society. Equally devastating is the reaction it triggers among our Central and South American neighbors. Domestically, this journalism has helped to aggravate the racial misunderstandings which permeate much of our society.

These are serious allegations. And I think the seriousness is magnified by the fact that control of the most influential newspapers in this country and of television rests in the hands of a comparatively few individuals. For example, ten newspaper chains control more than one-third of the newspaper circulation in the United States. To make matters worse, wire services competition is diminished. International News Service (INS) expired years ago. United Press International (UPI) has lost ground and no longer is a major voice, leaving the Associated Press (AP) clearly dominant.

One final thought. The lack of trust and confidence in the media today is aggravated by the fact that most media representatives in the influential areas of the country are of a liberal persuasion. Recent elections and poll after poll, on the other hand, signal clearly that rank and file Americans are basically conservative. The would-be opinion molders are out of touch with reality—at work diligently on their own agenda.

Their heady excursions into the power centers of Washington and New York have found them failing to measure up to one of Kipling's most important yardsticks "...or walk with kings—nor lose the common touch."

The once respectable and respected profession of journalism continues to get bad reviews from its constituency.

Grassroots America has said "NO" to the revolution!

This picture of the Slater family was taken about twenty-five years ago in Mr. Truman's office in his Independence library. From the left are Mrs. Marguerite Slater, wife of Harold; the former president; Harold Slater; Mrs. Charlene Slater, wife of Robert L. Slater, with their children, David, Charles, Jim and John, in front. Their father took the picture.

EPILOGUE

As We Used to Say . . . That's Thirty

Most of the stories in this book are Harold Slater's personal recollections of his experiences. I've added a few and, in some cases, re-written material to emphasize a point.

We've made no effort to put these stories and memories in any specific time frame. And we've jumped back and forth from first to third person, as exigencies other than good grammar might require.

We hoped merely to entertain readers in the St. Josephs everywhere with true stories of items either never published or long since forgotten, and to re-create a bit of the colorful life of our city that never will be found in any historical document.

If we've achieved this modest objective with you, two old typewriters will happily go silent.

George Sherman